PRAISE FOR *COMPETING FOR TALENT*

"In this pragmatic, comprehensive book, Nancy Ahlrichs guides the reader to the promised land of 21st-century enterprise—the Employer of Choice organization. Money, methods, and products alone won't get you to the top. That requires certain kinds of employees. This book will help you find them and keep them."

PHILIP SUTTON CHARD, PRESIDENT & CEO,
NATIONAL EMPLOYEE ASSISTANCE SERVICES, INC.

"EMMIS Communications has become an Employer of Choice and a 'destination' organization for talented employees by branding its culture and embracing other principles outlined by Nancy Ahlrichs. Her insights into the 21st-century workplace will serve as a valuable resource for any company or professional interested in attracting and keeping talented workers."

JEFF SMULYAN, CHAIRMAN AND CEO,
EMMIS COMMUNICATIONS

"Ahlrichs presents a comprehensive, compelling, and accessible framework to understand the economic and psychological realities and the hard work involved in winning the war for talent. Human resource leaders and their business partners will use this book to clarify their current position, and to chart a course to ensure that the best talent will work for them, not for their competition."

NANCY ARNOSTI, PRINCIPAL, ARNOSTI CONSULTING

"An important read for corporate America. The statistics Ahlrichs presents clearly depict the advantages of becoming an Employer of Choice, including direct improvement of bottom-line financial performance. I picked up two ideas in the very first chapter that will be of significant value to my company."

JACK FARNAN, VICE PRESIDENT, HUMAN RESOURCES,
MITCHELL INTERNATIONAL

"A must-read for employers trying to hire and retain 'Gen X'ers' and/or employees with specific skills for which demand exceeds supply. A catalyst for creative thinking about how to both distinguish your organization in the mind of the recruit and create a culture that reduces the rate of costly and disruptive turnover."

> MARTIN KLAPER, PARTNER,
> LABOR AND EMPLOYMENT SECTION,
> ICE MILLER DONADIO & RYAN

"The innovative recruitment and retention strategies presented in this book help connect employees to each other and to the organization. Employers of Choice know how to build a committed and productive working community."

> PATRICIA K. FELKINS, AUTHOR OF *COMMUNITY AT WORK:*
> *CREATING AND CELEBRATING COMMUNITY IN*
> *ORGANIZATIONAL LIFE*

COMPETING
FOR
TALENT

▼

COMPETING
FOR
TALENT

KEY RECRUITMENT AND RETENTION STRATEGIES FOR
BECOMING AN
EMPLOYER OF CHOICE

NANCY S. AHLRICHS

DAVIES-BLACK PUBLISHING
PALO ALTO, CALIFORNIA

Published by Davies-Black Publishing, a division of CPP, Inc., 3803 East Bayshore Road, Palo Alto, CA 94303; 800-624-1765.

Special discounts on bulk quantities of Davies-Black books are available to corporations, professional associations, and other organizations. For details, contact the Director of Marketing and Sales at Davies-Black Publishing; 650-691-9123; fax 650-623-9271.

Visit the Davies-Black Publishing web site at www.daviesblack.com.

08 07 06 05 04   10 9 8 7 6 5 4 3
Printed in the United States of America

Library of Congress Cataloging-in-Publication Data

Ahlrichs, Nancy S.
   Competing for talent : Key recruitment and retention strategies for becoming an employer of choice /
Nancy S. Ahlrichs—1st ed.
      p. cm.
Includes bibliographical references and index.
ISBN 0-89106-148-7 (hardcover)
   1. Employee retention. 2. Employees—Recruiting. I. Title.

HF5549.5.R58 A37 2000
658.3'111—dc21
                                                                                                00-056122

FIRST EDITION
First printing 2000

CONTENTS

CONTENTS

PREFACE

Today, a senior management team is meeting to discuss the issues that have been keeping them awake at night: delayed new-product development, missed sales opportunities, and lower profits. Woven into the discussion are the high costs of recruiting and training new hires, managers who can't manage, the exodus of mid-career employees, the rapid turnover of new hires, and the long job-fill times resulting from poor-quality candidates. They are also discussing their collective "gut feeling" that some of their organizational contemporaries are conquering these issues in spite of the same tight hiring market, the same demanding customers, and the same overall business issues.

It is true. And what's more, these other employers are turning greater profits because they understand that *people* (not technology or products) are the key to organizational success, innovation, and profitability. They have learned that customer turnover is directly related to employee turnover. They also know that competing for market share begins with competing for quality employees—*and winning.* To achieve faster product development, thoughtful service delivery, real customer intimacy, and targeted profitability goals, these employers first achieved their hiring and retention goals. By doing so, they have become Employers of Choice!

All across America, in companies and not-for-profit organizations alike, in all vertical markets, in both urban and rural settings, the senior management teams of Employers of Choice (EOCs) are charting new strategic directions that put *people* in the profit equation.

While some EOCs are known for being preferred employers in their fields, others are in the process of reversing years of being known as "toxic" cultures with revolving employment doors that make it as easy to be fired as hired. They know that toxic organizations, with their "lean and mean" structures and policies, are not positioned for success in the 21st century. The new business environment—heavily impacted by globalization, changing technology, knowledge management, and the growth of the service industry—requires new approaches to recruiting and retention in order to meet marketplace demands. EOCs know that their "choice" status is a significant achievement attained through consistent application of comprehensive strategies and tactics, as well as top-to-bottom organizational responsibility for retention.

The demographics of America's present workforce are known, and since the next few generations of employees will come from the existing population, its makeup in the near future can be foreseen as well. The current shortage of candidates for available jobs is expected to continue—and even grow—because of the declining numbers of graduates at both the high school and college levels. A 1999 survey conducted by the META Group (**www.metagroup.com**) revealed 400,000 open jobs for systems analysts and computer scientists in the information technology (IT) field alone. In many other fields, too, there are overwhelming numbers of job openings—and not nearly enough applicants to fill them. This trend sounds a clear message: If employers are to meet their staffing needs, they must learn to retain and develop their current employees. Using traditional recruiting and retention tactics will actually result in fewer successful hires and more turnover!

EOCs cannot change demographics—but they can change their response to today's recruiting and retention realities. They note the trends in requirements among job applicants, listen to the needs of their longtime employees, and ally themselves with other employers to develop solutions. The same can be true for your organization. Only by rethinking your recruiting and retention strategies and becoming an Employer of Choice will your organization have the one *true* strategic advantage over its competitors: the right people with the right skills in the right jobs.

This book is the culmination of years of research, and it includes valuable input from clients, audiences, and a wide range of EOCs. Certainly, there is no single cookie-cutter approach to becoming an Employer of Choice. Each organization must face its own specific recruiting and retention issues, address them, and commit to the ongoing challenge of becoming an EOC. But there are lessons to be learned from organizations that have successfully met the challenges and become Employers of Choice. This book contains the strategies, tactics, worksheets, forms, and anecdotes that have worked for others and may be implemented immediately by your organization to retain the quality and quantity of employees you need to achieve your growth and profit goals.

The book's Introduction will be of particular interest to organizations committed to improving profitability. It examines profitability where it begins: in the current tight hiring marketplace, where turnover rates have a significant impact on the bottom line. In the Introduction, you will find ways to document the costs of your organization's turnover, formulas to calculate three types of turnover, and ways to uncover the causes of turnover in your organization.

Part One of this book explores the successful strategies of employers who refuse to be "Toxic Corps" and concentrate instead on winning the talent wars. Chapter One describes the characteristics of an Employer of Choice, and the power of formal and informal designation as an EOC, as well as Maslow's Hierarchy and how it affects the approaches used by EOCs. Chapter Two uncovers six interlocking EOC Foundation Strategies and shows how EOCs turn strategies into reality. Chapter Three offers 15 ways to raise your organization's positive profile with customers and potential employees, as well as tips on how to prevent a media crisis and how to react if one does occur.

Part Two takes on the challenge of successful recruiting. Chapter Four explores the processes, tactics, and technology that enable an EOC to hire well and minimize hiring failures. Chapter Five instructs EOCs-to-be on how to woo candidates and stand out among potential employers. Chapter Six teaches employers to "webify" their recruiting processes by outlining how to build a career-focused Web site, how to attract "eyeballs" to the site, and how to e-cruit the best of the best candidates. Chapter Seven explores 40 underutilized sources of high-quality candidates.

Part Three zeroes in on the means to achieving growth goals: retention strategies. Chapter Eight asks and answers the question "Why do your employees leave?" Employers will learn tactics that take action against turnover—before and after an employee gives notice. This chapter also discusses the larger goal of translating the EOC Foundation Strategies into processes, programs, and actions that minimize the need for reactive tactics. Chapter Nine discusses the new psychological contract and five changes necessary to manage and lead employees who arrive with a variety of expectations. This chapter offers four ways to ignite employee discretionary effort through organizational culture. Chapter Ten looks at how employers can develop the dominant competitive weapon of the 21st century—the quality of their employees—by continually retraining and motivating their people to be capable, competitive, and content! Chapter Eleven examines the last retention strategy—compensation and benefits—in the light of market competitiveness. It explores compensation and benefits planning, emphasizing the need for organizations to develop guiding philosophies. It also reviews resources for employers who need help in assembling competitive programs.

The concluding bonus chapter, "Retaining Information Technology Brainpower," takes a look at the special challenges of recruiting and retaining technical staff. Guided by the results of several surveys of IT professionals, the Special Resource Section augments strategies and tactics discussed throughout this book, including approaches tailored to recruiting, developing, and retaining IT specialists.

Every day, Employers of Choice demonstrate that *people* are their greatest asset. In return, EOCs receive the loyalty, creativity, discretionary effort, candidate and sales referrals, attention to detail, service to customers, and *profits* that make all their efforts worthwhile. Every day, EOCs ask, "How will this new policy, procedure, announcement, or addition to staff enhance recruiting and retention?" If the result will be neutral to negative, the proposal is withdrawn, reconsidered, reshaped, and only then announced. The cost of turnover is so great that it must be balanced against the benefits of any new initiative.

This book is intended to provide the research, strategies, tactics, and results demonstrated by a wide range of Employers of Choice. The organizations that focus on becoming EOCs know that their past employment practices were not profitable. They know that becoming an EOC is a continuous process of evolution. The title "Employer of Choice" is not an accolade that, once achieved, can be taken for granted. Employers of Choice earn that designation every day—and they do it uniquely in every company.

ACKNOWLEDGMENTS

This book was made possible because of ongoing support from a small group of people. My husband, Karl, who cheered me on daily, read every word, and then reread every word, deserves special thanks. Joe Huffine, Sally Breen, Steve Kellam, and all of the employees of ONEX^{SM}, Inc., energized me with their telephone calls and e-mails. Thank you!

ABOUT THE AUTHOR

Nancy Ahlrichs understands how to win the war for talent. She has more than 20 years' experience in various aspects of human resources, management consulting, training and development, change management, and organization development, as well as 5 years' experience in managing public relations firms. Her knowledge of a wide variety of businesses—from entrepreneurial start-ups to Fortune 500 companies—gives her keen insight into the needs and concerns of organizations of all sizes. An Indianapolis native whose career includes business experience in Chicago, Orlando, and San Diego, Ahlrichs returned in 1990 to the Midwest, where she has been active in civic and professional organizations.

She is a frequent speaker on the topics of recruiting and retention. Company presidents, CFOs, hospital management teams, senior human resources managers, and even plant managers have found her approach to be both strategic and tactical. She manages her own speaking and consulting business, EOC Strategies, LLC. Alrichs was the Director of Organizational Evolution for ONEX^{SM}, Inc., a high-tech consulting and recruiting firm based in Indianapolis. Earlier in her career, she was a partner in a full-service human resources consulting and outsourcing firm.

Ahlrichs serves on the board of directors of Interactive Information Service, Inc., a Cleveland-based high-tech software development firm and service bureau that uses telephony, the Internet, and interactive technology to leverage human resources processes. She is also a board member of the Kiwanis Club of Indianapolis and president

of her church council. She is an active member of the Venture
Club of Indiana, the Society for Human Resource Management
(SHRM), the Technology Partnership, the Indiana Personnel
Association (IPA), the Human Resource Association of Central
Indiana (HRACI), the Indiana Society of Healthcare Human
Resource Administrators (ISHHRA), and the Association for
Psychological Type (APT).

Ahlrichs received both her B.A. and M.S. degrees in anthro-
pology from Purdue University, where she graduated with Phi Kappa
Phi and other honors. The Human Resource Certification Institute
has certified her as a Senior Professional in Human Resources (SPHR).

THE COMPETITION FOR TALENT IS HERE TO STAY

Every organization with any history at all—no matter how short—has developed a reputation. Every company is in the process of becoming either an Employer of Choice (EOC) or a "toxic" organization that undervalues employees. One way to uncover the direction of your organization is to play a game at the next gathering of your peers. Ask them to finish the following sentences:

• Lean and _____ .

• We don't have time to train people. We want to hire people who can hit the _____ .

• Career development is up to the _____ .

• If you don't like it here, _____ .

• You should be grateful just to have _____ .

• Anyone off the street could do _____ .

• It's not personal; it's just _____ .

• Upon receiving notice from an employee, the spoken and unspoken message from the company is, "Don't let the door _____ you on _____ ."

You will probably hear, in unison, "Lean and *mean*." "We don't have time to train people. We want to hire people who can *hit the ground running.*" "Career development is up to the *employee.*" "If you don't like it here, *leave.*" "You should be grateful just to have *a job.*" "Anyone off the street could do *your job.*" "It's not personal, it's just *business.*" And upon receiving notice from an employee, the company's spoken and unspoken message is, "Don't let the door *hit* you on *the way out.*"

These "mental tapes" still guide the daily management style of the majority of America's supervisors and senior executives. These stereotyped replies form the basis of our communication approaches, problem-solving methods, and assumptions about employees. These negative statements are the foundation for most of our existing organizational policies, procedures, and cultures. Management that undervalues employees creates a negative, or "toxic," culture.

It's so easy for employees to find new positions these days that they need not tolerate toxic Theory X–style management as defined by Jim Stoner and R. Edward Freeman in their book *Management.* Characterized by coercion, control, detailed directions, and threats of punishment, this management style results in an overall negative culture in the workplace. Today's employees want a Theory Y–style organization that encourages them to think like owners, seek responsibility, and participate in management decisions. Participative management is a key characteristic of Employers of Choice.

This Introduction explores the skyrocketing cost of turnover to a company and offers formulas you can use to track it in your organization. The startling costs of turnover revealed by these formulas set the stage for the remainder of this book: motivating business leaders to develop retention strategies that allow their organizations to thrive and be profitable as EOCs in the current business environment of global competition, Internet-based businesses, and new employee expectations.

The Turnover Crisis: Why Recruiting and Retention Will Remain Top Priorities

Simply put, an Employer of Choice is an organization that is able to meet growth and profitability goals because it attracts and retains the quality and quantity of employees it needs. EOCs work hard every day to meet this standard. They can be of any size and in any industry, and they are found throughout every state in America.

The big difference between an EOC and other companies lies in what it does to attract and retain employees. This difference is also what enhances an EOC's bottom-line profitability.

In the mid-1990s, American employers hit an unexpected obstacle to hiring and growth: the number of entry-level employees dropped dramatically. According to *Work Force 2020,* a study by Richard W. Judy and Carol D'Amico, part of the reason for this drop was that the population grew more slowly during the 1970s and 1980s than at any time since the Depression. In the engineering field alone, this drop translated into 33 percent fewer graduates between 1990 and 1996 than prior to 1990, as William T. Archey, president and CEO of the American Electronics Association, stated in testimony before the Senate Judiciary Committee in October 1999.

The number of engineering graduates has not increased since 1996. Advertisements for engineers fresh out of school or with a few years' experience can be expected to bring few responses throughout the foreseeable future. Other fields are experiencing this same dwindling supply of new talent. Employers hoping to hire entry-level employees in almost any field will continue to experience frustration. Fill times have grown longer. Desperate managers make the demand to their human resources (HR) managers: "Just get me *somebody!*"

This chasm in the employment-age population will continue to be a barrier to easy, successful recruiting well into the 21st century. Richard Judy of the Hudson Institute, speaking at the state-level Society for Human Resource Management (SHRM) conference in Indianapolis in August 1999, made the shocking prediction that the pool of potential new hires in America's workplaces will continue to shrink until 2006! In fact, according to research in *Work Force 2020,* the annual population growth rate will remain at 1980s levels until 2020.

Even filling the amorphous request "Just get me *somebody (anybody)!*" will be tough because the low Generation X birthrate cannot supply enough first-time and early-career employees to the market. Entry-level employees—Gen X'ers born between 1960 and 1980—are only 44 million strong. They follow on the heels of 76 million Baby Boomers.

America's surging economic growth may eventually be limited by the extreme shortage of qualified workers. According to a study by the Computer Technology Industry Association, the shortage of information technology (IT) professionals alone is costing the U.S. economy $105 billion per year. Even if future total economic growth remains as low as 2.2 percent, organizations will continue to have difficulty finding qualified workers because the number of job seekers is expected to grow by only 1 percent per year.

The low birthrate problem is exacerbated in many areas of the country by the continued severe brain drain when high school and college graduates migrate to the coasts to start their careers. California, Florida, and Texas are the beneficiaries of the exodus of entry-level employees from Midwest and Northeast states.

A second type of brain drain is also occurring at the opposite end of the hiring continuum as experienced workers leave the employment pool. This drain is caused by companies that encourage early retirement and provide generous retirement benefits starting at age 62—or even 55! In addition, after two decades of downsizing, many displaced executives have started consulting firms, purchased franchises, or established their own businesses. They now compete for employees along with larger enterprises. Even employers who receive unsolicited résumés complain of the disparity between candidates' skills and the skills required in our customer-focused, technology-heavy world of business.

In the past, employees competed for positions. In today's seller's market, employers compete for employees. The new business challenge is to manage successfully in a low-unemployment or full employment market.

As if *finding* employees is not enough of a challenge for America's businesses, *keeping* them is proving to be an even tougher problem. While most senior managers agree that some turnover is desirable, they also agree that unplanned turnover is a strategic managerial concern.

Turnover does have its positive side. It can create opportunities for advancement, act as a catalyst for restructuring and reorganizing, infuse new ideas and experiences into an organization, and reveal new resources for needed skills. Turnover provides opportunities to shed low performers and hire stars.

Too often, however, employee turnover also results in customer turnover, missed deadlines, late shipments, lost marketing windows, low morale, and difficulties in recruiting top-quality new hires. Successful EOCs walk the tightrope between positive and negative turnover. In particular, they must

- Attract qualified candidates to enhance existing departments

- Balance desirable turnover

- Minimize unwanted departures

Opportunities to change jobs abound for almost any employee in today's market. Rare is the employee who has not been invited "just to talk" about another position, or even to interview formally. From the receptionist to the CEO, your employees are being recruited on a regular basis by their friends, neighbors, ex-bosses, and ex-peers who have moved on to new companies, as well as by professional recruiters. Your vendors and your customers are also calling your employees "just to talk."

On a recent shopping trip, I was startled by a hand reaching past me toward the sales clerk. The clerk accepted the proffered business card, compliments, and invitation to an interview from the person behind me. "I like your style. You give great customer service. If you ever decide to leave [Store X], please call me. We have competitive benefits and a great work environment," the voice said over my shoulder. The clerk smiled, quickly pocketed the business card—and no doubt later called for an interview.

Among Generation X employees who make up the majority of entry-level and early-career employees, retention is an issue for a variety of reasons. Most Gen X'ers do not see themselves building a career with a single employer. "Three jobs by 30" is their rallying cry. They have surprised their supervisors by declining promotions, regularly demanding to leave work on time or early, and giving up their jobs entirely to stay home to raise their families. Clashes over work style—combined with the ease of finding alternative employment with competitive compensation—ensure a higher-than-desired rate of turnover in this age group.

Turnover is not limited to lower-level positions. Organizations eager to reinvent themselves often realize that a new image and culture require new leadership. With so many organizations undergoing this process, the competition for top talent has also been fierce. High-tech and dot-com companies are actively recruiting attorneys, investment bankers, management consultants, and senior management from a variety of businesses. The unplanned loss of even one senior executive can result in an exodus of upper-level direct reports—both to follow the preferred senior executive and to avoid his or her replacement. This next-level change results in a cascade of turnovers in a downward progression throughout the organization.

At the other end of the hiring spectrum, many companies initiate merger discussions as a strategy, to acquire—overnight—the number of highly trained employees they need to remain competitive. More radical—and even more risky—than hiring one by one, this option is nevertheless regularly discussed and acted upon in executive meetings and boardrooms around the country.

Employers have not ignored the hiring and retention crisis, but their choice of responses has been inadequate at best and off-target at worst. Misled by memories of applicants lined up outside the door, they have focused on the recruiting portion of the problem and largely ignored retention. They have regarded employees as mere lists of hard skills, as plug-in parts who are interchangeable as long as the résumé matches the job description. They continue to hound their HR departments for more and better candidates while ignoring the cost of turnover and HR's strategies to bond with, develop, and retain existing employees. Too few hiring managers can answer the question "Why work for GreatBiz, Inc.?" when it is asked by potential new hires or current employees. Without a compelling reason, candidates and existing employees are easily lured elsewhere. "Because we have an opening" and "Because you have a job" are not answers that help to attract or retain employees!

Many employers have gone the quick-fix route and raised entry-level pay to attract employees. Some employers have increased their recruiting and new-hire training budgets. Others have added recruiting staff or engaged external recruiters. Too many employers are raiding specific competitors or nearby companies. Even if there were enough qualified candidates available, such tactics would not be sufficient to resolve such a complex situation in the face of these formidable demographics.

To address the specific recruiting and retention issues in your company, a comprehensive approach is needed. The answer lies in creating an organization that attracts the appropriate caliber of job seeker—and retains the employee for three or more years. The answer lies in becoming an Employer of Choice. The first step in this process is to understand the costs and causes of turnover; you can then use that knowledge to stimulate new approaches to both recruiting and retention.

Reducing Turnover to Increase Profitability

Current economic trends are expected to continue. Increased supply of nearly any component needed for any product, declining costs, and low inflation have been positive for consumers, but such an environment has made it very tough for many businesses to achieve their profit goals. Global competition has resulted in a loss of pricing power. In times of low inflation, organizations have few opportunities to pass on increased operating costs to their consumers. As if this were not enough, many suppliers now provide products directly to customers through the Internet, putting their distributors at a disadvantage. Even banks have cannibalized themselves by offering free services for Internet customers. Businesses of all types need to examine all of their costs in order to implement processes that will keep them competitive.

Until now, the HR function has not been valued as a profit center or even a source of sustainable cost savings. While the focus on profits will not diminish, traditional cost-cutting options are no longer an effective means of increasing profits. Downsizing has forced many organizations to scrutinize their business processes, cut the fat from their budgets, outsource non-core functions, integrate technology throughout their operations, and put in place controls and quality assurance procedures to minimize waste of all types. Unfortunately, the cost savings from these practices have been too quickly outpaced by other business costs.

In keeping with the axiom "Measurement is the key to proving value," organizations have begun to measure HR's impact on the bottom line. As a partner with senior management, HR can provide strategies and tactics to improve recruiting and retention, thereby improving the bottom line. An as yet unmined source of profits is turnover reduction.

Turnover is a strategic issue when it affects growth, profitability, and value creation. In too many toxic organizations, senior executives believe turnover is just part of doing business. They repeatedly use individual layoffs, department downsizings, and other short-term means of cost cutting. Planned turnover begets unplanned turnover, and unplanned turnover is very expensive. A history of downsizing creates a revolving-door reputation that scares off not only the best employees whom the organization hoped to keep but the top-quality candidates to replace them as well. EOCs, however, reduce turnover and redirect dollars into programs that increase retention so that unplanned turnover does not interfere with the organization's business strategy.

The Payoff for Reducing Turnover

Unplanned turnover is a strategic managerial concern because it is so costly—and avoidable. According to the Corporate Leadership Council's report "Workforce Turnover and Firm Performance, 1998," only 16 percent of U.S. companies track turnover costs at all. Of the organizations that do, very few calculate the cost of lost productivity associated with the departure of experienced staff at any level.

Various research and consulting organizations have produced estimates of turnover costs that vary widely, but none are low. The Saratoga Institute estimates turnover costs for exempt staff range from one to two years' pay and benefits. Development Dimensions International (DDI) estimates it costs $78,000, to replace an employee in a $46,000/year job, or approximately 170 percent of annual pay. Kwasha Lipton reports that turnover costs range from 150 percent to 175 percent of annual pay. According to the Corporate

Leadership Council's report, "As lost productivity costs can account for upwards of 75 percent of total turnover costs, traditional tracking methods significantly underestimate the total cost of turnover, which can be as high as 200 percent of annual salaries in certain industries."

Without a doubt, turnover is expensive and should be tracked. Most organizations estimate their turnover costs at a modest 150 percent of annual salary and benefits. What is the financial advantage of reducing turnover? SAS, an international software development company with 5,400 employees, reported that it saved more than $65 million in one year—money that was then put into EOC benefits such as training programs, an employee gym, and two on-site daycare centers. Unlike other software firms the size of SAS, which typically lose 1,000 employees per year, SAS lost only 130. Assuming the replacement costs for each of those employees is 1.5 times an average salary of $50,000, SAS saved $65.25 million on the 870 replacement employees they did not have to recruit, train, and get up to speed. Further, SAS encourages employees to go home at 5:00 P.M.—and still meets project deadlines for clients (see Fishman, 1999).

Reducing the turnover rate of even one position can save an organization hundreds of thousands—if not millions—of dollars. According to the turnover costs researched at six hospitals and featured in "Nursing Watch," replacing a specialty nurse at a hospital costs 156 percent of that nurse's salary (approximately $41,000 per year). If a hospital succeeded in reducing its annual turnover rate from 13 percent to 10 percent, the savings would be $575,640 (see Table 1, on page 10). Imagine if the turnover rate could be reduced just 3 percent across the board for *all* positions at the hospital. It is hard to find ways to cut costs in a hospital—and in any other organization. Reducing turnover would appear to be one of the best methods of maintaining levels of service and quality while keeping costs low—and simultaneously building the type of organization that attracts and retains employees.

Clearly, lower turnover and increased retention is a profitable strategy, yet we are all averse to change. We want different results, but we continue doing the same things. Until turnover costs are tracked and the costs proven, senior management is unlikely to make the changes necessary to improve recruiting and retention. EOCs calculate the

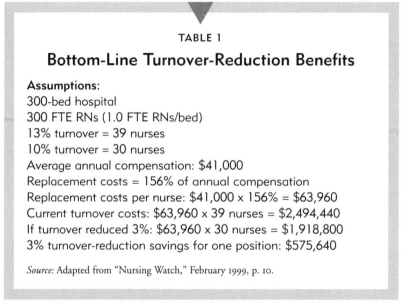

TABLE 1

Bottom-Line Turnover-Reduction Benefits

Assumptions:
300-bed hospital
300 FTE RNs (1.0 FTE RNs/bed)
13% turnover = 39 nurses
10% turnover = 30 nurses
Average annual compensation: $41,000
Replacement costs = 156% of annual compensation
Replacement costs per nurse: $41,000 x 156% = $63,960
Current turnover costs: $63,960 x 39 nurses = $2,494,440
If turnover reduced 3%: $63,960 x 30 nurses = $1,918,800
3% turnover-reduction savings for one position: $575,640

Source: Adapted from "Nursing Watch," February 1999, p. 10.

true cost of turnover at their organization as a means of providing information to drive management decisions. Once tracked, turnover costs will become a regular line item on profit-and-loss reports because these costs can be measured and controlled. EOCs realize that activities on the employee recruiting/retention continuum can be monitored for savings opportunities.

The Total Turnover Iceberg = "Green Money" + "Blue Money" Costs

Think of turnover costs as an iceberg that blocks the way between your organization and project completion or profitability. Icebergs are a well-known hazard to oceangoing ships because only one-fifth of their mass can be seen and four-fifths lurks beneath the water-line, where it can do irreparable damage. Small fishing boats, luxury cruise ships, oil tankers, and other vessels must plan their routes to avoid icebergs. The bigger the iceberg, the more time and effort must be put into charting a course around it. In an organization with more than 20 percent turnover, this turnover iceberg is made up of lost time, lower productivity, and unnecessary costs. It results in product roll-out delays, slow paperwork processing, aggravated clients, and delayed achievement of departmental and organizational goals. As seen in Figure 1, on the following page, an organization's turnover iceberg has visible and invisible parts just like a real iceberg.

Tracked turnover costs are usually "above the waterline"—these are the visible, or "green money," costs. Individual green money expenses are planned expenditures found in budgets. Green money expenses are usually found in the form of invoices for services rendered (employment advertising, recruiter fees, criminal checks or drug screens, etc.) or supplies purchased (to produce and print recruiting materials). The green money portions of many organizations' recruiting budgets have been increasing annually since the mid-1990s.

The invisible, or "blue money," costs of replacing employees are below the waterline on the turnover iceberg. Tougher to track than green money costs, blue money is invisible because it is paid out in lost productivity—but it adds up more quickly and more insidiously to reduce the bottom line. The activities necessary to accomplish successful hiring take time and productivity away from other management, non-management, and even HR-related activities during three time periods: notice, vacancy, and hiring/orientation. Blue money is spent for the salaries of those involved in the entire hiring process—hiring managers and HR staff, as well as co-workers and subordinates whose productivity is reduced throughout the three phases of the turnover/rehiring process. A calculation of lost productivity requires determining the per-hour earnings of salaried and non-salaried employees involved in the three time periods and using those figures as multipliers for the amount of time needed to perform specific activities in the hiring process.

Recognizing the True Costs of Turnover

As shown in Table 2, on pages 14 and 15, all three of the transition time periods—notice, vacancy, and hiring/orientation—involve both blue money and green money costs.

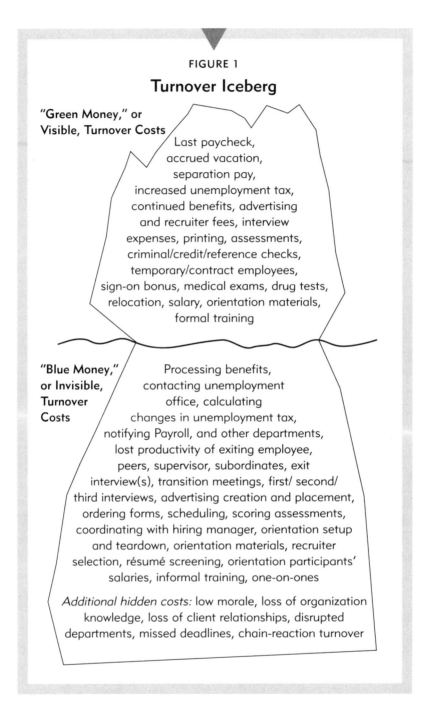

FIGURE 1

Turnover Iceberg

"Green Money," or
Visible, Turnover Costs

Last paycheck,
accrued vacation,
separation pay,
increased unemployment tax,
continued benefits, advertising
and recruiter fees, interview
expenses, printing, assessments,
criminal/credit/reference checks,
temporary/contract employees,
sign-on bonus, medical exams, drug tests,
relocation, salary, orientation materials,
formal training

"Blue Money,"
or Invisible,
Turnover
Costs

Processing benefits,
contacting unemployment
office, calculating
changes in unemployment tax,
notifying Payroll, and other departments,
lost productivity of exiting employee,
peers, supervisor, subordinates, exit
interview(s), transition meetings, first/ second/
third interviews, advertising creation and placement,
ordering forms, scheduling, scoring assessments,
coordinating with hiring manager, orientation setup
and teardown, orientation materials, recruiter
selection, résumé screening, orientation participants'
salaries, informal training, one-on-ones

Additional hidden costs: low morale, loss of organization
knowledge, loss of client relationships, disrupted
departments, missed deadlines, chain-reaction turnover

The *notice period* costs the organization blue money in the form of time spent on transition meetings and knowledge transfer by the departing employee's peers, supervisor, and subordinates. Productivity often plummets, as distracted peers and subordinates focus on their own feelings of loss, the political implications for their own careers, and other work-slowing activities. Additionally, the HR staff spend blue money in the form of their own salaries as their activities are redirected to process benefits; contact the unemployment office; calculate any changes in unemployment tax; notify Payroll, Information Services (IS), and other departments of the expected end date; and schedule and conduct an exit interview. Green money costs include the employee's last paycheck, accrued vacation payout, plus any continued benefits.

During the *vacancy period,* considerable blue money is spent (though these costs may be initiated during the notice period), but typically only green money costs are tracked. HR staff, often in conjunction with the hiring manager, spend blue money while they update the job description and write and place ads in newspapers and trade journals and on the Internet. Blue money may also be spent to locate, select, and contract with recruiters. Blue money is spent to review the résumés, coordinate with the hiring manager to review the shorter stack of qualified résumés, and respond to HR with questions, candidate preferences, and available times for interviews. It costs blue money to pay the salaries of the supervisor, co-workers, and subordinates who cover the open position while their own tasks remain uncompleted. Overtime is frequently required (and sometimes becomes a significant cost factor) in order to meet deadlines and customer expectations during the vacancy period. Blue money is spent to cover the salaries of everyone involved in the first, second, third, and subsequent interviews and salary negotiations. It costs blue money for the salaries of those who must order yet more reprints of the annual report, make copies of application forms, schedule and score assessments, and coordinate internal communication about the results. Concurrent with blue money costs are green money costs that typically are budgeted items: advertising and recruiter fees, costs of printing company marketing materials, assessment or other examination

TABLE 2

Blue Money and Green Money Turnover Cost Calculations

NOTICE PERIOD

Green Money (actual) Costs:

1. Last paycheck, accrued vacation, separation pay $_____
2. Increased unemployment tax $_____
3. Continued benefits $_____

Blue Money Costs (appropriate salary/hour × time spent on each activity):

1. Administrative costs for processing the separation: process benefits; contact unemployment office, Payroll, IS departments; schedule exit interview; etc. $_____
2. Lower productivity: employee, peers, supervisor, subordinates $_____
3. Exit interview, transition meetings $_____

VACANCY PERIOD

Green Money (actual) Costs:

1. Advertising and recruiter fees $_____
2. Interview expenses (meals, mileage, or other) $_____
3. Printing costs for company marketing materials $_____
4. Assessments $_____
5. Criminal checks, reference checks, credit checks, etc. $_____
6. Medical exams and drug tests $_____
7. Temporary/contract employee costs $_____
8. Overtime costs $_____
9. Relocation expenses and salary $_____

Blue Money Costs (appropriate salary/hour × time spent on each activity):

1. Lost productivity: peers, supervisor, subordinates $_____
2. Advertising creation and placement $_____
3. Recruiter selection $_____
4. Administrative costs: ordering forms and copies of annual reports, scheduling and scoring assessments, coordinating with hiring manager and others, etc. $_____
5. Résumé screening $_____
6. Interviews: first, second, third $_____

TABLE 2 (CONT'D)

Blue Money and Green Money Turnover Cost Calculations

HIRING/ORIENTATION PERIOD

Green Money (actual) Costs:

1. Orientation materials (handbook, video, handouts, etc.)	$_____
2. Formal training programs (materials, course fees)	$_____
3. Informal one-on-one training (materials, if any)	$_____

Blue Money Costs (appropriate salary/hour × time spent on each activity):

1. Orientation participants' salaries	$_____
2. Lost productivity: peers, supervisor, subordinates	$_____
3. Administrative costs: orientation setup, ordering materials, etc.	$_____
4. Informal training and one-on-ones	$_____

HIDDEN COSTS

1. Missed deadlines and shipments	$_____
2. Loss of organization knowledge	$_____
3. Lower morale due to overwork	$_____
4. Learning curve	$_____
5. Client issues due to turnover	$_____
6. Loss of client relationships	$_____
7. Disrupted department operations	$_____
8. Chain reaction turnover	$_____

TOTAL REPLACEMENT COST	$_____

costs, medical examination costs, criminal/reference/credit check fees, and relocation expenses. Additional green money costs include the selected candidate's salary and may include a referral bonus and sign-on bonus—as well as the salary paid to one or more temporary employees brought in to assist during the vacancy period.

The "turnover cash register" continues to ring up costs during the *hiring/orientation period* once the best candidate joins the organization. Blue money pays for the overhead and salary costs of informal orientation processes, including the many one-on-one mini-meetings and mini–training sessions needed to bring any new hire up to speed. Formal orientation typically costs both blue money for the salaries of the individuals involved (officers, managers, and others) as well as green money for orientation materials such as handbooks, videotapes, and handouts. The supervisor, peers, and subordinates of the new hire will continue to experience lower productivity until the learning curve is completed.

Hidden costs (including loss of organization knowledge, disruption or loss of client relationships, disruption of the department's operation, lower morale, missed deadlines, late shipments, and more turnover) vary depending upon the position vacated and the individual situation. Hidden costs may be very easy to track in some cases (dollar loss of a specific client) but difficult to track throughout the organization.

Calculating Blue Money and Green Money Costs

Hiring to fill new positions is a visible sign of growth. Turnover is the opposite of growth. Any time an existing position is refilled from outside the organization, the process exacts all possible blue money and green money costs for that position. Hiring from within, however, allows for considerable cost reductions in both green money and blue money areas due to the candidate's familiarity with the organization and the omission of out-of-pocket expenses such as recruiting costs and sign-on bonuses. Dollars spent on filling *new* positions (growth) are dollars well spent—while dollars spent on unplanned turnover are dollars that could be going to the bottom line. High turnover is the organizational equivalent of setting money on fire. EOCs calculate the true cost of turnover for their organizations and reallocate dollars historically lost to turnover for retention strategies that will enhance the bottom line.

To be valued as a lever for increasing profit margins, the blue money and green money costs of replacing staff must be calculated. As an initial exercise, select the position in your organization with the highest turnover and use the turnover cost guide provided in Table 2.

Calculate the per-hour salary costs of individuals involved in the notice, vacancy, and hiring/orientation periods using actual salary data. Ask each participant to track or estimate time spent on each activity. Get input to ensure that all hiring activities are documented and costs are tracked. Cross-check the expense categories and add expenses that may be unique to your organization; delete those that are irrelevant. Even if the first analyzed position is for an hourly assembly worker or the company receptionist, the final turnover cost will prove enlightening.

Next, do the calculations for a senior management position that was filled from outside in the past year. The final tally—especially when viewed against the average two-year turnover rates for typical executive positions—should drive home the high cost of turnover.

To analyze your true total turnover costs from last year, give serious consideration to hiring an intern or engaging a business class from a nearby university to handle the research and calculations. The figures that will emerge will give credence to the frequently quoted turnover cost of 1.5 to 2.5 times the annual salary levels of replaced employees. In your organization, the costs may be more, particularly for certain positions. These are wasted dollars that could be used for the proven retention programs discussed later in this book.

Turnover costs vary from organization to organization, department to department—and manager to manager. While the calculation of total organization-wide turnover costs is an excellent motivator for changing organization strategies, the calculation of turnover by department and even by manager will help to pinpoint the need for specific retention tactics. Use these figures—either the figures from individual positions or the total costs from the previous year—to drive home the need to uncover the true causes of turnover in your organization and to implement the strategies of an Employer of Choice.

EOCs Measure Turnover Rates: Standard, Avoidable, and New Hire

The purpose of measuring turnover rates is to provide information for management decisions. The cost of turnover is reason enough to track its impact on the bottom line. The devastating effects of turnover on morale, productivity, and client relationships have the additional potential to damage recruiting fill times, production quality, customer confidence, and repeat sales.

There are several ways to measure turnover rates. The standard formula measures monthly turnover by dividing the number of employee separations in a month by the total number of employees at mid-month:

$$\frac{\text{Employee Separations}}{\text{Total Employees at Mid-Month}}$$

Multiply the resulting number by 100 for a figure that can be compared with the figures released by the U.S. Bureau of Labor Statistics or the BNA *Quarterly Report of Job Absence and Turnover.* These figures may be analyzed to discern seasonal or even departmental turnover trends.

Although a portion of turnover is unavoidable, the persuasive power of these figures provides the basis for developing solutions to avoidable turnover. "Unavoidable turnover" is easily defined. If an employee leaves to follow a spouse who has been relocated, returns to school full-time, develops an incapacitating disease, or dies, the employer does not have a reasonable chance of reversing the employee's decision. By subtracting unavoidable turnovers from all others, the employer then knows the percentage of avoidable turnovers, or those that could be reversed. It is important to include terminations as avoidable. Terminations are the result of either bad hires (if within six months of hiring) or bad management (if after six months of hiring).

The formula for determining the rate of avoidable turnover is

$$\frac{\text{Total Turnover} - \text{Unavoidable Turnover}}{\text{Total Number of Employees at Mid-Month}}$$

Again, multiply the resulting figure by 100 to obtain a number that can be compared with your industry's turnover rates or typical turnover rates for that position.

The turnover of new hires is often regarded as the worst waste of dollars in any organization. These are individuals who do not show up on their first day, do not come back after their first day, take another job during training, finish training but decide that "this is not for me," or otherwise leave before the expenses of hiring and training can be recouped. When this happens, employers must initiate the hiring cycle once again.

To calculate new-hire turnover, you must track the names of the individuals hired each month and then track their retention after three months, and again after six months. The formula for new-hire turnover is

$$\frac{\text{New Hires This Month}}{\text{New Hires on Staff After Three Months (After Six Months)}}$$

Multiply the resulting number by 100. Because the cost of new-hire turnover is so high, it is important to know which positions and departments are showing the highest rates so that a targeted effort can be made to uncover causes and implement solutions.

It is easy to console a manager with statements such as "Call centers have high turnover" or "IT specialists are being recruited so much these days that we can't do anything to stop the turnover." Turnover can be reduced, and dollars can be saved for use elsewhere in the organization—but only if the causes of turnover are uncovered and addressed. In Part Three of this book, we will look at processes that uncover the reasons behind turnover in your organization so that you can make the changes necessary to increase retention, increase the quality of new-hire candidates, and redirect dollars currently wasted on turnover-focused activities.

Turnover Information: Use It—or Lose Them!

The cost of turnover—trackable, avoidable, and critical to the profitability of any organization—cannot be ignored. EOCs seek not only the true costs of turnover but also the true causes. Information gathered through a variety of means provides the best picture of your organization's strengths and the areas in need of improvement. Results from exit interviews, surveys, and focus groups may be analyzed to determine the differences in turnover causes for men and women, long- and short-term employees, departments, branch offices, and managers. If at all possible, involve employees in the development of solutions. Management must act on the gathered information if employees are to have faith in the process and respond to future surveys.

Turnover reduction enables organizations to focus on their business, lowers stress and increases morale, frees dollars for better long-term use, and contributes to a workplace where employees are happier. EOCs know the bottom-line value of turnover reduction, and they know the value of other recruiting and retention practices. Successful organizations of today and tomorrow are charting a new course based on understanding their own organizations and learning from other organizations.

PART ONE

HOW EMPLOYERS OF CHOICE ARE WINNING THE TALENT WARS

▼

CHAPTER ONE

LEARNING FROM
EMPLOYERS OF CHOICE

Most employers know that sustainable business growth does not come from a strategy of cutting costs through layoffs, significant use of part-time or contract employees, salary and promotion freezes, or reductions in training and development. Employers have lived in that bleak world, and it has produced disappointing (if any) profitability—followed by a lengthy slump in morale, lower productivity, increased unplanned turnover, increased recruiting costs, longer fill times, and, sometimes, the fire sale of the company. This was true in the early 1990s when job candidates were plentiful, and it is especially true today when they are scarce. Today's low unemployment and readily available job opportunities ensure that employees will seek work elsewhere if the going gets tough and they are not strongly bonded to the organization. We know what *doesn't* work to keep turnover low and profits high—but what does work? The answer: becoming an Employer of Choice.

Looking for a silver bullet, executives often ask me, "Who are the Employers of Choice—and what qualifies them for that title?" Fortunately, there is considerable research available about EOCs, as well as lists, articles, and even books about them. These organizations did not attain EOC status overnight—but achieving the designation of "preferred employer" is a deliberate business strategy. These employers continue to refine their tactics because they know there is a strong connection between how firms manage their people and the economic results.

In the Introduction, we identified an Employer of Choice as an organization that meets its growth and profitability goals because it is able to attract and retain the quality and quantity of employees it needs. This chapter will discuss research about the characteristics of EOCs, the ways in which organizations are selected as EOCs, the benefits of being an EOC, where to look for lists of EOCs, and the names of many EOCs. These are the organizations that not only say, "People are our greatest asset," but demonstrate this commitment through their processes, cultures, management styles—and profitability. In this and all others chapters, "company," "corporation," and "organization" are used interchangeably to refer to both for-profit and not-for-profit groups.

Characteristics of an Employer of Choice

The term "Employer of Choice" first appeared in the business press in 1984 as part of an announcement of the building of a childcare center by the Howard Johnson restaurant chain. Its chairman was quoted as saying, "We are anxious to be more of an employer of choice than we were in the past." He knew that the company could expect to benefit from employee preference and positive image.

An era of cost cutting, downsizing, and restructuring ensued in the years following 1984. These activities turned corporate management's attention away from growth strategies. Yet even now, as then, if companies are to gain a competitive advantage, they must attract and retain the best talent. And since the best talent is attracted to the best workplaces, surveys of employers and employees have been conducted to determine the most desirable workplace characteristics. Six studies bring into focus the characteristics of an Employer of Choice.

"CORPORATE CHARACTER"

In 1994, changes in the hiring marketplace were dramatic enough to get the attention of several employers. Walker Research (now Walker Information, a 60-year-old, Indianapolis-based, multinational research organization serving more than 75 countries) conducted a comprehensive study to measure the impact of corporate social responsibility on potential consumer, employee, and investor behaviors. "Corporate Character," the published research report of this national study, offers an insight into the minds of workers as they evaluate specific organizations as potential employers.

The overwhelming message from this research is that an organization's viability in its consumer and investor marketplace is the same as in its employee marketplace: success depends upon the public's perception of the organization as a good corporate citizen. The findings indicate that employee treatment is by far the most important consideration among prospective employees. Business practices rank second. Also, a socially responsible organization nurtures more satisfied employees. "As quality, service and price become less differentiated among companies in competitive industries, investment in social responsibility (especially employee treatment and business practices) will have a greater payoff," according to the report.

Certainly the previous decades of downsizing and staff reductions had not left many employers famous for positive employee treatment. This survey was the first of many to look at the critical subject of attracting employees.

THE 100 BEST COMPANIES TO WORK FOR IN AMERICA

In 1994, 10 years after the publication of their groundbreaking bestseller *The 100 Best Companies to Work for in America*, Robert Levering and Milton Moskowitz published an updated study under the same title, profiling organizations where the "work experience is life-enhancing rather than life-deadening." Employers gladly allowed on-site visits from the authors and also submitted thousands of handbooks, annual reports, videos, magazine and newspaper articles, and scrapbooks in hopes of being included in their book. In foundries, hospitals, and high-tech companies alike, the authors asked employees, "Do you like working here?" "Why?" "How does it compare to other places you have worked?"

Companies received ratings of up to five stars on six criteria:

1. PAY/BENEFITS. The company's pay/benefits are at or near the top of the industry range and include unusual or unique benefits. Health and retirement benefits are among the best in this company's industry, and there is sensitivity to work, family, and health needs.

2. OPPORTUNITIES. Numerous training opportunities give employees the chance to advance up the ranks. The company promotes from within, and there are specific mechanisms for advancement, such as annual reviews and job postings.

3. JOB SECURITY. There is a written or implicit no-layoff policy, and alternatives to layoffs have been used. Rare or well-handled layoffs were also considered.

4. PRIDE IN WORK/COMPANY. Employees feel connected to the company's product or service. They are recognized for their accomplishments. They feel good about working for a company that is known as a good corporate citizen.

5. OPENNESS/FAIRNESS. Top executives are accessible to all employees. The company has multiple methods of two-way communication, including a specific grievance process. Employees can offer input and criticism without fear of retribution. Special perks for executives are held to a minimum.

6. CAMARADERIE/FRIENDLINESS. Employees talk about being part of a team, family, or community. They enjoy working and socializing together. Laughter can be heard in the halls.

"COMPETING AS AN EMPLOYER OF CHOICE"

When the recruiting tide turned against employers, the Conference Board—a not-for-profit, non-advocacy organization with membership of more than 2,800 companies worldwide—conducted a survey of its members in the United States and Europe.

Of the 101 companies in the Conference Board's bellwether survey, "Competing as an Employer of Choice," 68 percent responded that an organization's ability to provide career opportunities and development is the attribute highly qualified workers value most. More than two-thirds of the respondents believed that career development had a "great deal" of impact on a worker's choice of employer. Other top characteristics included compensation (the overall level and/or plan design itself), the company's reputation in the community, its management style and leadership, the corporate culture, and the company's profitability. These data are shown graphically in Figure 2.

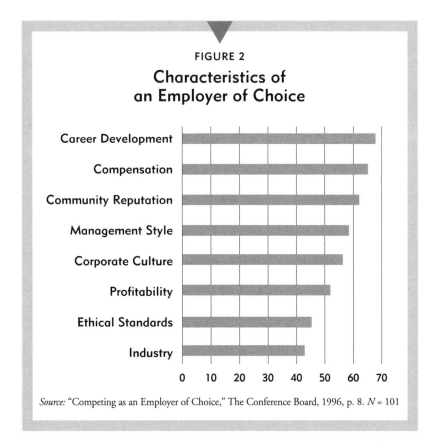

FIGURE 2
Characteristics of an Employer of Choice

Source: "Competing as an Employer of Choice," The Conference Board, 1996, p. 8. N = 101

Of the 21 characteristics of an EOC reviewed by the Conference Board, these first 6 were listed by more than half of the respondents as most important in a worker's choice of employer and were also the ones mentioned in later surveys.

THE HUMAN EQUATION: BUILDING PROFITS BY PUTTING PEOPLE FIRST

In his book *The Human Equation: Building Profits by Putting People First,* Jeffrey Pfeffer states that "Substantial gains . . . 40 percent or so in most of the studies reviewed, can be obtained by implementing high-performance management practices." He notes that too few organizations, however, are heeding the "research, experience and common sense" that point to the relationship between a company's financial success and its commitment to treating people as assets—not as costs or liabilities.

To uncover high-performance practices, Pfeffer reviewed the five-year survival rates of initial public offerings, studies of profitability, and stock prices of companies from multiple industries and conducted detailed research on the automobile, semiconductor, apparel, oil refining, steel manufacturing, and service industries. While there is no single "best" management style or culture for all organizations to emulate, Pfeffer concludes that seven high-performance management practices are effective and applicable across all industries. These practices echo and amplify the earlier research about the characteristics of an Employer of Choice:

1. SELECTIVE HIRING of new personnel

2. EXTENSIVE TRAINING

3. COMPARATIVELY HIGH COMPENSATION contingent on performance

4. EMPLOYMENT SECURITY

5. REDUCED STATUS DISTINCTIONS AND BARRIERS, including dress, language, office arrangements, and wage differences across levels

6. SELF-MANAGED TEAMS AND DECENTRALIZATION OF DECISION MAKING as the basic principles of organizational design

7. EXTENSIVE SHARING OF FINANCIAL AND PERFORMANCE INFORMATION throughout the organization

"THE WAR FOR TALENT"

In 1998, McKinsey & Company conducted its study "The War for Talent" with 77 large U.S.-based companies from a variety of industries. The companies selected were at the top- or mid-quartile level within their industries (as defined by two-digit SIC codes), based on 10-year total returns to shareholders. Additionally, 20 companies from the larger sample were selected for in-depth study because of their reputations for superior talent and meteoric growth and performance, or because they have perfected an approach such as building talent through acquisitions.

"The War for Talent" focused on the characteristics of companies that attract high performers and found that organizations "must offer a compelling reason for these people to not only join but choose to stay . . . a powerful value proposition that is a magnet." The responses from nearly 6,000 executives revealed that to attract employees, companies do not have to be in a "sexy industry" or "pay the big bucks that other companies offer." Rather, they must "be a great company and offer a great job." How is this defined? See Figure 3, on the following page.

Great companies attract great talent. Companies known for strong performance and growth and for being industry leaders have an advantage. The pride generated by being a part of a great company fuels workers through the tough times: proposals that flop, strategies that fail, reorganizations, and petty infighting. Second, great jobs—defined as those that offer opportunities to stretch—are equally important as magnets for top talent. A well-structured job is critical to executive development. The third part of the equation—compensation—must also be present. While competitive pay alone will not attract top talent, its lack may cause a company's efforts in the war for talent to founder. These results echo the findings of the earlier Conference Board and Walker Research studies.

"NATIONAL EMPLOYEE RELATIONSHIP REPORT"

The "National Employee Relationship Report," a 1999 nationwide survey co-sponsored by Walker Information and the Hudson Institute, looked at loyalty and its impact on retention as reported by 2,300 full-time and part-time workers. Again, "employee treatment" was cited as the reason that one-third of workers surveyed do not plan to stay with their current employers for more than two years. The study suggests that organizations interested in improving retention should focus on six factors:

1. FAIRNESS AT WORK: fair pay, performance evaluations, and corporate policies

2. CARE AND CONCERN: career development opportunities and family-friendly benefits

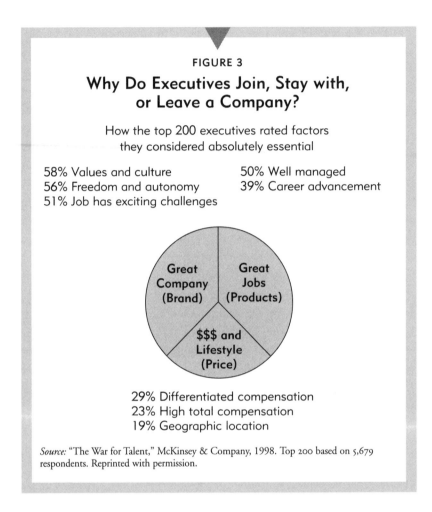

FIGURE 3

Why Do Executives Join, Stay with, or Leave a Company?

How the top 200 executives rated factors
they considered absolutely essential

58% Values and culture   50% Well managed
56% Freedom and autonomy   39% Career advancement
51% Job has exciting challenges

Great Company (Brand)
Great Jobs (Products)
$$$ and Lifestyle (Price)

29% Differentiated compensation
23% High total compensation
19% Geographic location

Source: "The War for Talent," McKinsey & Company, 1998. Top 200 based on 5,679 respondents. Reprinted with permission.

3. SATISFACTION WITH DAY-TO-DAY ACTIVITIES

4. REPUTATION: employer has a strong, capable management team, is financially sound, and produces high-quality work

5. TRUST IN EMPLOYEES: employees have the freedom to make decisions, manage their own time, control resources, and try new things

6. WORK AND JOB RESOURCES: employer has the right number of people and the right equipment to do the job

To more easily understand these EOC characteristics in the different surveys cited, see Table 3, on page 32. Note that the specific descriptors become more detailed through time as both employees and employers refine their understanding of reasons to apply for a job and stay with a specific employer. As the unemployment rate has declined over time, employees have become more selective and specific.

THE IMMEDIATE BENEFITS OF BEING AN EOC

EOCs are known in their client and hiring communities, so they receive unsolicited résumés and have an easier time developing a candidate pool from which to select new employees. Twenty years ago, most employers had more résumés in their mailboxes than they could process or use. Today, unsolicited, high-quality résumés come only to Employers of Choice—and only after a multifaceted effort.

Many EOCs charge their marketing or corporate communications departments with the tasks of seeking out and securing a mention in "best places to work" lists, articles, and books; winning industry accolades; and competing for local and regional "entrepreneur of the year" awards. So great is the positive effect of these awards on recruiting and retention—as well as on client, banker, and vendor relations—that companies gladly fill out pages of essay questions and allow their employees to be interviewed in depth.

The "winning" organizations soon learn that job hunters tend to research companies and not-for-profit organizations by networking, combing through "best places to work" lists in magazines and books, and surfing the Internet. They also go to libraries to read business articles, and they contact organizations directly to ask that information be sent to their homes. EOCs make information readily available through as many media as possible.

Upon the publication of award winners or "best places to work" lists, many job seekers devise a strategy of how to get their résumés noticed by the EOCs they've selected. Many are willing to make a lateral or even downward move in order to work for an EOC. They know that if they are hired, the odds are excellent that career development is in their future! Existing employees of listed companies

TABLE 3

Characteristics of an EOC: Research Findings

Categories	Corporate Character	The 100 Best Companies to Work for in America	Competing as an Employer of Choice
Career Opportunities		Opportunities	Career development/advancement
Compensation/ Benefits		Pay/benefits	Compensation plan/level
Reputation	Good corporate citizen		Reputation in the community
Culture	Employee treatment	Job security Camaraderie/ friendliness Pride in work/ company	Corporate culture
Management and Leadership Style	Employee treatment Business practices	Openness/ fairness	Management/ leadership style
Other Factors			Profitability

TABLE 3 (CONT'D)

Characteristics of an EOC: Research Findings

Categories	The Human Equation	The War for Talent	National Employee Relationship Report
Career Opportunities	Extensive training	Great jobs (product)	Career development opportunities
Compensation/ Benefits	Comparatively high compensation	Money and lifestyle (price) including total compensation	Fair play Family-friendly benefits
Reputation		Great company (brand) including values, culture, challenges	Strong management team Financially sound High-quality work
Culture	Employment security Reduced status distinctions	Great company (brand) including values and culture	Trust in employees Employee freedom to make decisions, manage time, etc.
Management and Leadership Style	Self-managed teams Sharing of financial information	Great jobs (product) including freedom and autonomy	(Fair) performance evaluations (Fair) corporate policies Right number of employees and equipment
Other Factors	Selective hiring	Money and lifestyle (price) including location	Satisfaction with day-to-day activities

receive congratulations and other positive attention that reinforces their bonds to their employers. They are often asked to verify information in the articles or books, and they play an important role in disseminating validating statements that in turn increase the number of unsolicited résumés received by the organization. Pride in company membership fuels the drive toward multiple organizational goals—including profits, quality standards, recruiting, and retention.

Formal and Informal EOC Status

Formal designation as an EOC is based on meeting specific criteria set forth by research entities (such as the Conference Board, Walker Information, the Hudson Institute, and McKinsey & Company), business writers, and business and industry publications (such as *Fortune, Working Mother,* and *Computerworld*). In addition to in-depth interviews with employees, extensive surveys and questionnaires are used to verify employer claims. Once listed as an EOC, employers must continue the policies and procedures that won them EOC status, and they must be alert to emerging employee needs. Just as powerful, however, is the informal designation as an Employer of Choice.

Employer of Choice status is often communicated and reinforced through word of mouth because employees describe their experience of the corporate culture and its benefits on a daily basis to their families, friends, fellow hobbyists, vendors, and colleagues. The sentiments and information in these conversations are passed on and become the organization's buzz, or its vibes, in the community of potential employees and clients. The vibes either support or refute the organization's official public relations efforts. In other words, "What goes around, comes around."

One way to understand the power of the informal designation of Employer of Choice is to ask yourself, "When my son or daughter graduates, where do I want him or her to apply for a job?" Chances are that you will name organizations where your happily employed friends and relatives work—and/or organizations that have publicized their excellent career opportunities, compensation programs, management and leadership style, and culture. An employer is rarely named as an EOC if it does not have a strong communication plan within its client and hiring communities.

When I ask my seminar audiences around the country to name EOCs, they respond immediately with the names of organizations that they hope their children will contact after graduation. They often cite IBM, Southwest Airlines, Microsoft, Eli Lilly and Company, Nordstrom, 3M, and Deloitte & Touche as EOCs. Usually there are also names of locally owned businesses that have risen to the forefront of their communities and cultivated Employer of Choice reputations.

Asked why they named specific organizations, the audience often replies with a mix of formal public relations messages and personal or secondhand information that echoes the company's public relations message. "I hear they have more women in management-level positions than any other pharmaceutical company . . . and they really believe in promoting from within." "I hear that they are the fastest-growing information technology consulting firm in the Midwest . . . and my friends there say it is because the culture makes it easy to recruit top talent." Organizations can aim for EOC status through their community relations and public relations efforts, but the official message must match the buzz generated by their employees. When it does not, doubts arise in the minds of potential candidates and clients, and instead you might hear, "They say they are a great place to work, and they are one of the biggest employers, but their tough work environment makes it impossible for them to hold on to their employees." This refutation of the corporate line about being a great place to work hinders the achievement of recruiting goals, which, in turn, affects the achievement of growth and profit goals—all of which leave the organization off preferred-employer lists.

Sources for Lists of Employers of Choice

Preferred employers—EOCs—are listed throughout the year by a variety of magazines, books, and Web sites. Each list uses different (but usually overlapping) language to describe criteria used in their selection process. These lists include

- "100 Best Places to Work in America" is published every January by *Fortune* magazine (**www.fortune.com**). It ranks employers with 500 or more U.S. employees.

- "Best Places to Work in Information Systems" is published each May in *Computerworld,* a weekly newspaper. The list surveys the 1,000 biggest public companies and 40 biggest consulting firms.

- "100 Best Companies for Working Mothers" is published each fall by *Working Mother* magazine (**www.workingmother.com/ 100best/**). This list covers small employers.

- *Students Shopping 4 a Better World,* published by the Council on Economic Priorities. The 166 listed companies are evaluated on their policies on issues such as advancement of women and minorities, childcare, pollution, charitable giving, and community outreach. Working for a good corporate citizen matters to potential employees.

- *The 100 Best Companies to Work for in America,* by Robert Levering and Milton Moskowitz, contains detailed information on listed companies as well as shorter lists of "Most Beautiful Headquarters," "Companies Where You Can Get a Free Lunch," and more.

These and other similar lists provide insights into the range of opportunities, pay and benefits, and company cultures. Validated through additional in-depth interviews of employees, "best employers" lists are often used by job seekers to determine their next employment destination. Depending upon the life stage or special interests of the job seeker, some EOC lists may be of more value than others.

One of the challenges facing organizations that are selected as Employers of Choice is that employees, once hired, may not give the same weight to various job characteristics as would a potential new hire. Certain attributes, such as image and reputation, may be the foundation of a candidate's initial interest, but that interest may shift to issues such as the job itself or compensation once the employee has been hired. The focus of newly hired employees often turns to career development opportunities, work environment, specific policies, benefits, and services that affect life at work. The challenge for the company is to cover all bases at each stage of employment.

Employees at various levels within an organization also have different priorities, possibly due to their differing income levels and the amount of organizational information available to them. In the Conference Board survey results discussed earlier, 70 percent of the executives believe that such differences do exist. As one respondent put it, "Management-level workers look more at the company as a whole, rather than just the site where the job is." Other respondents expressed similar points of view, suggesting that employees higher up in the organization give greater weight to business issues—profitability, culture, management structure and style—in addition to their own career opportunities, while those in lower ranks focus on pay and benefits, job security, and working conditions that have a direct impact on their lives. Demographic and life stage differences are also likely to influence employee preferences. To better understand differing employee motivations as they relate to being an Employer of Choice, we need look no further than Maslow's Hierarchy of Needs.

Maslow's Hierarchy of Needs

Abraham Maslow theorized that people are motivated to meet five types of needs, which can be ranked as a hierarchy. The individual's current situation dictates which level of need is most powerful at a specific point in time. Maslow believed—as do many managers today—that before incentives designed to provide a sense of belonging, self-esteem, or opportunities for growth can be effective, employees must feel that their physiological and security needs are met.

Depending upon the employee's situation, he or she could be at the bottom of the hierarchy, at a survival level where physiological needs such as food, air, water, shelter, rest, and clothing may be motivators. Entry-level employees who earn a minimum wage—or even $8 to $10 per hour—are motivated by a difference of 50 cents an hour more because, as a percentage of their total pay, 50 cents is significant. To an $8-an-hour employee, a raise of 50 cents an hour equals a 6.25

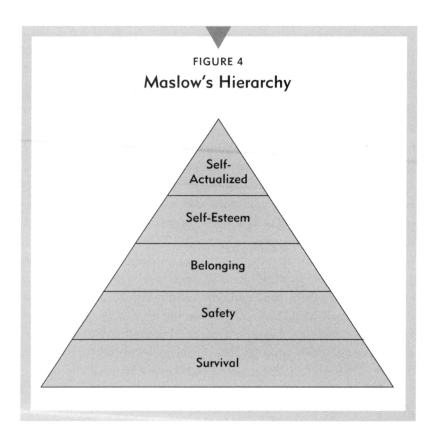

FIGURE 4

Maslow's Hierarchy

percent pay increase! At this level, many employees are just "one flat tire away from bankruptcy." Money must be so tightly controlled and carefully spent that almost any position with an increase in pay is seen as the wise career choice.

Maslow's theory tells us that as survival needs are met, employees are motivated differently. At the next level, they focus on safety and security needs. Job security may fill this need—but for some employees, bulletproof glass, silent alarms, safety training, or a firm's zero-tolerance policy toward violence may also be needed. In addition to jobs that are literally unsafe, other factors can keep employees at this level of focus. Stressful environments that induce fear keep employees at a very unproductive level. The psychological sword of

Damocles felt by employees during a merger or under authoritarian management robs them and the organization of energy and productivity that could otherwise benefit all parties. Until the needs at the first two levels of Maslow's Hierarchy are satisfied, the employee remains self-focused and unable to do more than the minimum to keep his or her job.

The third level—social needs—moves employee motivators outward to relationships and a sense of belonging. At this stage, being accepted as part of a group or team is a major motivator. Since the approval of management is important, recognition programs, different work structures, and different supervisor and peer interactions are all key motivators. Being part of a team enhances an employee's performance.

Recognizing the tremendous competitive pressure for entry-level employees, many McDonald's franchise owners made the strategic decision to win the competition, minimize new-hire training costs, and increase retention. (In as little as two months, significant dollars can be saved in high-turnover positions.) At a time when the minimum wage was $5.25 per hour but no one was responding to ads, McDonald's took a lesson from Maslow and offered $8 to $10 per hour, free lunch/dinner, flex scheduling, immediate benefits, training, career paths, and uniforms. Workers in factories, mail rooms, distribution centers, and other fast-food restaurants flocked to join the McDonald's "team." McDonald's enabled its employees to leapfrog up Maslow's Hierarchy to the third level.

With social needs satisfied, esteem needs rise as a motivator. High self-regard and valuing the respect of others characterize this level. Managers require a high level of self-esteem if they are to readily build it within their staffs. A supervisor builds self-esteem in others when he or she expresses respect and/or confidence in their capabilities and offers other demonstrations of support. Organizations responding to this level of motivation often encourage employee participation in quality improvement and public recognition programs that feature awards and certificates. With confidence and high self-esteem, employees more readily "think outside the box" or "think like owners" and make the effort to improve their own performance for the betterment of the organization.

In a very few organizations, employees are encouraged to achieve the highest level and to meet their own self-actualizing needs. At this level, the employee focuses on greater realization of personal potential. Organizations with employees at this level may offer sabbaticals and encourage the employees to pursue graduate degrees, engage in public speaking, and author articles. These employees are the self-starters and independent thinkers who will help move the organization beyond its current boundaries.

Employers of Choice understand that employees must be at least at the third level in order to focus on the organization's betterment as well as their own. It is the feedback between the employee and employer at this point that enhances both the work experience and the work outcome for both parties.

As your organization focuses on addressing its own retention issues, look first at the individuals involved. Different solutions will work for different levels of employees within your organization. Are your employees at a survival level economically? If so, they will not be able to make decisions that will result in the greater good of their peers or the company. Are your employees paid competitively but thwarted in their desire for recognition and self-esteem? Exit interview data, employee survey results, and other information at your disposal will help you begin to plan for improved retention.

Can Organizations Become EOCs for All Employees?

The challenge for many organizations is to be an Employer of Choice for all people in the organization while acknowledging that there are somewhat different priorities for management and non-management employees, high-tech and other employees, and employees of different ages. Can an organization be all things to all people, or must the priorities of certain critical or core employees be given precedence over others? Would addressing the EOC preferences of core employees subsequently benefit all employees—who might then respond with greater job longevity? There is no one perfect answer. For many years, organizations have recognized a certain degree of variation in the needs of their employees. Cafeteria-style benefit plans and flextime are great examples of the acceptance of variation. Because the demographics of the current and near-future workforce are so diverse, even more flexibility will be required of employers. Each organization will need to take a slightly different approach based on its particular population, goals, product/service, and market.

The new business environment of fewer potential employees has so changed the expected success rate for hiring that organizations of all types—even current EOCs—must regularly review how their business practices affect recruiting and retention. Organizations must determine what is needed to move them from here (an organization that is not attracting and retaining its top talent) to there (an organization that is continually honing its practices in order to maintain its competitive edge of excellent employees).

The bar is being raised. *Business as usual won't do!* The forecast for more early retirements and fewer potential new hires in the 20- to 35-year-old age bracket between now and 2020 ensures that continuing current recruiting and retention practices will actually result in *less* satisfactory results! The days of treating every employee exactly like every other employee (and if some did not like it, they could leave!) are over. More individual, as well as group-specific, approaches will be needed to attract and retain employees.

A "lean and mean" culture has become synonymous with a revolving door for employees—the opposite of an Employer of Choice! Refilling the same positions is like using a treadmill to run a cross-country race: all of the energy is expended, but no ground is covered. For organizations, running in place in terms of hiring and rehiring actually means falling behind because it drains the bottom line of dollars that could be used for raises, capital investments, expansions, research and development, training, and employee-relations development activities, etc. Additions to staff are evidence of growth—*and EOCs grow!*

To break the costly turnover-rehiring cycle so that staff additions and company growth can become the focus, the organization needs to shift to recruiting *well.* Qualified hires stay and can be developed. As we will see in the next chapter, recruiting well is a fundamental step to becoming an Employer of Choice.

CHAPTER TWO

EMPLOYER OF CHOICE
FOUNDATION STRATEGIES

Employers of Choice share certain fundamental approaches to doing business. There are "antecedent traits and beliefs that drive the formulation[s] . . . [of] the best human asset management practices," according to Jac Fitz-Enz, founder-president of the Saratoga Institute, a research firm that focuses on performance measurement and improvement. After studying more than 1,000 companies over four years, his firm's research "buried the idea that the best management practice is any specific process, project, or program."

Too often, "best practices" research consists of telephone calls or brief visits to companies. While the reporter or other investigator endeavors to document business practices, time and other pressures inevitably influence the resulting report. True research requires time—that elusive, scarce resource. Further, specific processes, projects, or programs may not be transferable in their entirety and so may be dismissed by an organization desperate for the same outcomes. As Fitz-Enz says in his book *The 8 Practices of Exceptional Companies,* "A better method is to find the basic truths of organizational health and effectiveness and commit ourselves to a consistent and persistent regimen."

This chapter will look at the Employer of Choice Foundation Strategies that can apply to any organization, in any industry, at any time. The Foundation Strategies, when combined with appropriate, measurable tactics framed as objectives, enable an organization to attract and retain the quality and quantity of employees it needs to achieve organizational growth and profit goals.

EOCs know that recruiting and retention of intellectual capital is very difficult in today's low-unemployment marketplace. EOCs want to hire the best of the best, and they know that the HR department cannot do it alone. Success requires the ongoing effort of every manager and every employee working to support six basic strategies. Plans change annually and tactics can change more frequently, but Foundation Strategies endure business ups and downs, changes of leadership, and changes in markets. EOCs in all industries and all sizes have put in place their own versions of six interlocking strategies that work:

1. ADD IMPROVED RECRUITING AND RETENTION to the strategic plan of the organization; set measurable objectives for each supervisor, manager, director, and vice president.

2. BUILD AND COMMUNICATE A TOP-EMPLOYER REPUTATION.

3. HIRE WELL—or not at all.

4. TREAT EMPLOYEES AS IF THEY WERE CUSTOMERS.

5. RETRAIN AND DEVELOP current employees for tomorrow's needs.

6. BUILD SUPPORT PROCESSES to ensure ongoing success of the Foundation Strategies.

Add Improved Recruiting and Retention to the Strategic Plan of the Organization

EOCs have learned the cost of missed goals caused by poor hires and turnover—and they have vowed not to repeat that lesson. They know that without the right people in the right jobs, no strategy can be fully implemented, no goals met, and no significant profits made. To ensure that other strategic goals are met, Employers of Choice have elevated improved recruiting and retention goals into their written strategic plans. To ensure that this and other strategic goals are not just words on a page, EOCs also link achievement of these goals to the performance plans and compensation of all supervisors, managers, directors, and vice presidents. By focusing on the specific outcomes of certain activities, EOCs transform the quality (and quantity) of their workforce.

Through their daily activities, hiring managers at all levels have a critical impact on successes and failures in recruiting and retention. They drive the quality of hires that come into the organization. Hiring managers are the living culture of the organization as experienced by their direct reports. They must be ready to move swiftly to hire mission-critical candidates and to take action at the first whiff of potential employee turnover. It is critical for employers to understand that the common approach of "just get some bodies in here to do the work" is fundamentally and expensively flawed. "Bodies" don't stay, and, as pointed out in the Introduction, turnover is too expensive to tolerate. Instead, the organization—from hiring managers to all employees—must be uniformly focused on improving recruiting and retention in order to achieve other strategic goals.

The partnership between hiring managers and the HR department must be strengthened so that the needs of the organization are met. Most EOCs have a closed-loop, 360-degree feedback process that enables them to gather information about the performance of specific activities for use at review time. Measurable hiring and retention activities include the following:

- TURNAROUND TIME for hiring managers to respond to either external recruiters or HR regarding agreements to interview candidates and times available for interviews. Successful hiring requires lightning speed to catch sought-after candidates, but these two activities have proved to be bottlenecks in the recruiting processes of many organizations. Some EOCs require hiring managers to respond favorably or unfavorably within 24 hours of résumé receipt and schedule an interview if appropriate. Other EOCs bypass this step altogether and do not require managers to respond to HR about qualified candidates. Instead, HR or the external recruiter has access to the manager's calendars and sets up interviews as needed. At the manager's performance review, HR provides input regarding the hiring manager's cooperation and turnaround time. Speed and responsiveness have a direct impact on compensation.

- TIMELY PERFORMANCE REVIEWS that include development plans for direct reports are built into the performance objectives of managers in many organizations. Performance reviews (with development plans) are critical retention tools. Many organizations so value timely performance reviews that they send their managers lists of employees and dates of hire two months before the expected reviews. Copies of dated performance reviews are filed with HR and tracked for timeliness. Complaints from employees regarding late reviews can also be tracked.

- ATTENDANCE AT ANNUAL MANAGEMENT TRAINING is a retention double bonus—and can be measured. Just as ongoing development is a retention motivator for non-managers, annual training is a tool for keeping managers. As the manager's skills improve, so does his or her comfort level with—and performance of—the job. There is evidence that direct reports of trained managers are less likely to leave due to mismanagement. Training received by each employee should be tracked and noted in the accomplishments section of the development plan goals during an annual review.

- TRACK TURNOVER RATES BY BUSINESS UNIT, DEPARTMENT, AND MANAGER. Each manager can provide input on setting reasonable goals for reducing turnover. Clearly, a department with a 35 percent turnover cannot reasonably be expected to reduce turnover to less than 20 percent in one year—but a sliding scale of incentives for the manager could result in surprisingly lowered turnover.

Build and Communicate a Top-Employer Reputation

When potential and current employees know that your organization is an Employer of Choice, they flock to apply, refer their colleagues, and feel confirmed in their decision to remain as employees. This strategy becomes the foundation for achieving your organization's bottom-line objectives! EOCs plan the work of recruiting and retaining employees, implement the plan—and communicate the plan. Organization-wide communication and accountability ensure that every employee takes pride in being part of an EOC and understands his or her role in attaining and *maintaining* that status. External communication about your organization and its employees, as well as internal communication to and about employees and the culture, is the framework on which to build the achievement of other goals. Building and maintaining a positive reputation among potential and current clients and employees is so important that Chapter Three is devoted to the subject.

Hire Well—or Not at All

EOCs are not using every trick in the book—they are writing a new book about recruiting top talent. Instead of wringing their hands about the lack of response from qualified candidates, EOCs are busy recruiting in the colleges—at the sophomore level—or reaching out to much-missed ex-employees in their "would rehire" files, forming alumni clubs and rehiring as many as possible! EOCs use technology in new ways to drive candidates to their doors, or they fish in entirely new candidate pools. They are definitely not letting demographics prevent them from achieving growth goals. Nearly half of this book is devoted to the successful recruiting approaches, resources, and processes of Employers of Choice.

EOC hiring managers focus on retention from the beginning of the recruiting process, as opposed to hiring a body to fill the job opening. EOC managers not only hire to fit organizational needs; they hire with the idea of keeping the employee beyond the average length of employment. They know that it is tough (or impossible) to replace high-quality, longtime employees one-for-one in terms of soft and hard skills, company knowledge, customer relationships, and overall competencies. EOCs focus on hiring well from the start.

Longer fill times are preferable to hiring mistakes. Organizations that do not hire to fit the positions and the culture do not have the raw material with which to develop a long-term employee. Indiscriminate hiring is costly in five ways:

1. THE INDIVIDUAL IS UNLIKELY TO STAY. Hiring an unqualified individual who does not have relevant experience or transferable

skills, or who does not exhibit the competencies needed for the job (in sales, for example, these might include persistence, resilience, organizational and communication skills, and follow-up) significantly reduces the likelihood that the individual will stay. Either by quitting in frustration or by being terminated for non-performance, this individual will leave. Poor performers who cannot or do not respond to training, coaching, and management are not motivated to stay where, despite their efforts, their lack of success prevents them from bonding with other employees. Without positive work results and/or relationships, they have no reason to stay. Besides, in the low-unemployment business environment, they can easily find other jobs.

2. THE INDIVIDUAL IS LIKELY TO HARM CUSTOMER RELATIONSHIPS. "Warm bodies" deliver poor-quality workmanship, cannot answer questions or solve customer problems, and miss deadlines and shipments. Even an overworked *qualified* employee will make an effort (and have the knowledge!) to deliver quality work and meet customer needs.

3. THE INDIVIDUAL IS LIKELY TO SPEED THE TURNOVER OF HIS OR HER PEERS. Unqualified, apparently untrainable individuals lower the morale of their qualified peers, who ask themselves whether their own efforts are even noticed. These qualified peers have no problem finding a new employer who appreciates quality output.

4. THE INDIVIDUAL WILL DRAIN THE ORGANIZATION. Mismatches and unqualified employees require extra training and hand-holding, have high rates of absenteeism, must repeat their work, and otherwise drain the organization of resources and salary dollars.

5. IN A SUPERVISORY POSITION, THE INDIVIDUAL MAY CAUSE LEGAL PROBLEMS. Unqualified, untrained supervisors often create harassment, sexual harassment, and other employee relations issues.

Clearly, hiring managers and HR personnel create significant problems for the company overall if they do not define the open position, recruit and hire to fit the need, and provide additional training and guidance. For the fiscal and cultural health of the organization, hiring managers and HR must agree to make only *qualified* hires.

Treat Employees as if They Were Customers

We know that dissatisfied customers vote with their feet and take their business to competitors. Dissatisfied employees do the same thing. Just as customers and clients have choices, so do employees. They either choose us as their employer or choose the competition— any other employer. In many toxic organizations, only senior managers are treated as well as external customers, but in an Employer of Choice, everyone is considered a value-adding employee.

For too long, companies have focused exclusively on the needs of the external customer. Our employees are our *internal* customers. Data from "Corporate Character," a national survey conducted by Walker Research in 1994, suggest that companies "may be trading the satisfaction of workers in order to provide better quality and service to the customer. This strategy could backfire if dissatisfied employees are unable to meet the demands of the customer." Employees are unable to deliver better service than they themselves receive.

The "Corporate Character" study stated, "The importance of employees as a stakeholder group can be expected to grow in the future." The future is now: today's low unemployment level means that all hires are critical hires. Retention of each employee is key to a company's ability to meet goals and keep costs down. EOCs have reviewed the cost of turnover and determined that replacement of qualified employees is so costly and so undermines the achievement of other strategic goals that it must be minimized.

A decade ago, a critical hire might have been the president, the vice president of marketing, or a middle manager in a strategic business unit. Critical hires were perceived as qualified management-level employees. Today, EOCs know that the definition of "critical hire" must be expanded to include those employees who have customer contact—sales representatives, accounting clerks, call center employees, service representatives and technicians, and the receptionist. Further, EOCs recognize that crackerjack administrative support staff are the glue that holds a department together so it can function smoothly. They can even make specific managers look good. Keeping good people throughout the organization depends upon treating them at least as well as customers are treated. Part Three of this book is devoted to retention.

Retrain and Develop Current Employees for Tomorrow's Needs

We no longer work in a world populated with pre-trained job seekers. Thanks to the speed of technological change and its impact on literally every position in every organization, even the best-qualified new hires will probably need technology or other hard skills training and will most certainly need additional soft skills training. Current employees are struggling to keep up with their peers in competing organizations. We know (and they know) that job requirements will continue to evolve. Our customers, employees, and new organizational initiatives require that we regularly "raise the bar" of skills and competencies needed to do jobs well. Additionally, we must develop current employees so that they can be promoted. Organizations today must budget for considerable training, not only to remain competitive, but to satisfy employees' hunger for learning and development. Development opportunities and alternatives are discussed in Chapter Ten.

Build Support Processes to Ensure Ongoing Success of the Foundation Strategies

In many organizations, strategic goals are set at annual executive meetings—and are then forgotten until the next annual meeting. EOCs do not waste the effort that goes into those meetings: they translate goals into objectives that cascade down through the organization. Business unit objectives support the organization's strategic goals. Department objectives support business unit objectives. Department objectives are met by achieving individual employee performance objectives.

Senior management must provide continuous, visible support to ensure that the entire organization follows through to meet overall organizational objectives. Further, EOCs set up cross-functional teams, committees, and/or review boards that ensure that milestones are met throughout the year. Performance recognition programs that focus on individual as well as team contributions are powerful factors in achieving organization-wide endeavors.

For many organizations, nothing short of new values, new strategies, and a new culture are required to reverse the ultimately fatal process of becoming a toxic organization. This is a journey, not a leap—and it requires heading in a new direction altogether. The journey to becoming an Employer of Choice starts with a new vision of the future, a vision of job seekers beating down the door to apply because current employees are excited about their career direction and the future of the organization. In tight hiring times, this is a radical vision. Organizations of all types can make this growth-oriented vision a reality by committing to EOC Foundation Strategies and by using the best tactics to implement them.

CHAPTER THREE

BUILDING AND COMMUNICATING A TOP-EMPLOYER REPUTATION

Think about your last high school reunion. Wasn't it hard to forget the various reputations of your classmates? Even with dramatic turnaround stories and clear evidence that the adults in the room were no longer the nerds and bad boys or bad girls of the past, did conversations still include verbal jabs and snickers about past faux pas? Did many classmates still stand back and stare—instead of shaking hands and catching up with the *new* news?

Remember when Mom said that your reputation and your name were more valuable than gold? Mom was right—and her comparison is also true for organizations. Americans identify so strongly with their jobs that their employers' reputations matter very much. If it is hard to live down mistakes made in high school, it is even harder to live down mistakes made in business that result in negative headlines. An elephant's memory is nothing compared to the public's collective memory—because the public's memory is aided by the news media.

A negative reputation results in high turnover and lower profits for a company. This chapter will focus on a company's need for a positive community reputation among potential customers and potential employees, as well as ways to develop and maintain a positive reputation and respond to a crisis.

Name recognition enables an Employer of Choice to attract unsolicited, high-quality applications and résumés. It eases the entire recruiting process because applicants receive positive reinforcement from friends, colleagues, and families for even applying! That same name recognition either reinforces retention by instilling pride in existing employees or loosens the employment bonds by making them want to cringe when friends ask for their comments on negative rumors or news items. The "National Employee Relationship Report," a study of 2,300 full-time and part-time workers conducted by Walker Information and the Hudson Institute in 1999, found that "companies interested in improving retention should do all they can to maintain a good reputation." EOCs know how to trumpet their victories and act appropriately in response to threats to their reputations.

When I ask my audiences around the country to name their local EOCs, I frequently recognize the names of the organizations. This is no surprise since EOCs *seek* positive publicity and try to avoid the negative variety. EOCs use their ethical policies, procedures, and community involvement to ensure that the public—buyers of their products and services, as well as potential employees—know who they are, what they do, and that they are "good" organizations.

When Bad Things Happen: Negative Headlines

Negative headlines about an organization's safety or environmental standards practices, ethics, harassment suits, layoffs, board of health violations, violence in the workplace, Medicare or other certification problems, or EEOC violations drive off potential new hires, clients, bankers, vendors, strategic partners, and investors. Worse, negative headlines and the resulting negative reputation can *end relationships* with current employees, clients, bankers, vendors, strategic partners, and investors!

Negative headlines and/or rumors about an organization remain in reporters' files for years and resurface in future articles and broadcasts. Locally and nationally, negative stories like these can prevent an organization from attaining its growth goals:

- Senior management of a national retail chain watched their stock plummet after the corporation received back-to-back negative headlines about unethical treatment of bankrupt cardholders and rip-off auto repair practices.

- For five years, every article printed about one prominent Midwest CEO mentioned her very public, very nasty divorce from the organization's co-founder. Repeated awards for entrepreneurial excellence, prominent board positions, and generous donations to a variety of worthy causes did not overcome the old reporters' files *for five years!*

- Two prominent automobile manufacturers have had many lengthy articles written about their class-action sexual harassment suits and EEOC violations.

- One government agency has had so many incidents of shooting sprees and violence in the workplace that bizarre behavior and bad temper are now characterized as someone "going _____." Can you fill in the blank?

- Prominent sports figures—who are themselves "organizations" in many ways due to the number of employees and the revenues they generate—have lost millions of dollars in promotional deals because of a return to gambling, drugs, and/or alcohol abuse.

- Numerous high-profile restaurants and bakery chains have closed due to the negative cash-flow impact of an article about board of health violations.

- A television manufacturer that moved jobs to Mexico but did not retrain or redeploy thousands of employees experienced bad publicity followed by lawsuits and more bad publicity.

- Numerous organizations have been hounded on the Internet by current and past employees dissatisfied with their handling of a variety of issues from changes in retirement health benefits to unsafe procedures. Fake Web sites created to draw attention to unpopular corporate policies resulted in confusion and damaged the reputations of the employers.

Depending upon the nature of the bad press, an organization can suffer recoverable damage, wither slowly due to the impact of negative publicity on critical relationships, or die immediately due to the loss of multiple income sources.

Americans *are* their jobs. One of the first questions we ask after meeting someone is "What do you do?" Who wants to work for an organization whose name alone either stops conversation or invites rude comments? Negative headlines are like bait for sharks: they tell recruiters where to fish for candidates. Only those who feel they have no choice are likely to resist when the recruiters come calling.

Negative headlines harm more than just an organization's recruiting efforts. What company would team up to sponsor an event with an organization that has a negative reputation? Who would refer business to such an organization? What bank or venture company would extend credit or invest money? The long-term financial impact of negative headlines is incalculable. Reputations *are* more valuable than gold.

No Reputation = Difficult Recruiting

"Why are you going to take the job with GreatBiz, Inc., when you could work for Mega Corp? No one's ever heard of GreatBiz." We are all influenced by the comments of others and by our own knowledge of the marketplace.

- If a recruiter calls with an interesting job description, but we have never heard of the recruiter's firm, we may not be willing to take the time to learn more about the job.

- If a recruiter or a friend tells us about a job opening, but we have never heard of the company, we might not bother to interview.

- If a blind ad and an ad for a well-known company contain the same basic opportunity, we would most likely respond to which one?

- If we have two offers to consider but only one is with a well-known organization, how much more positive reinforcement are we likely to receive from friends and family about the offer from the known entity?

- If a recruiter called you on behalf of an EOC in town, would you listen?

A neutral reputation ("I've heard of them—what do they do?") or a positive reputation ("Gee, who *wouldn't* want to work for GreatBiz, Inc.? They have a great culture.") is better than no reputation ("Who?") or a negative reputation ("Are you sure you want to apply there? Did you know that last year they were investigated for...?").

How can the management of an organization of any size raise its profile so that it receives unsolicited résumés, wins in a showdown for a new hire, and makes its employees feel proud to work there? It can be done—and it can be done on a budget!

The Payoff for a Positive Reputation

"Corporate Character," the mid-1990s Walker Research study of the effects of corporate responsibility, makes the following prediction: "As quality, service and price become less differentiated among companies in competitive industries, investment in corporate responsibility (especially employee treatment and business practices) will have greater payoff."

The 1999 Cone/Roper "Cause-Related Trends Report" finds that American employees and consumers strongly support cause-related activities and that organizations see benefits to image, reputation, and bottom line when they implement these efforts. The research, based on a nationwide cross section of nearly 2,000 men and women, shows that "Americans expect companies to address issues that are important to them and to their community," according to Carol Cone, chief executive officer of Cone, Inc. The top three concerns of the survey were education, crime, and the environment.

For Delphi Automotive Systems, a commitment to environmental management is a critical business strategy—so Delphi is in the process of certifying its 168 manufacturing sites worldwide under ISO 14001, a global standard that recognizes proactive management and reduction of environmental impact. Delphi is not alone with its strategy and positive results.

In the past, the management of many organizations thought that social responsibility came at the expense of financial performance, but today there is persuasive evidence that the opposite is true. In fact, ignoring social responsibility may give your competitors an advantage. To measure an organization's reputation in specific marketplaces, a variety of tools and information are available through "Big Five" management firms as well as organizations such as Walker Information (**www.info@walkerinfo.com**) and the webzine *Responsibility.com*.

Organizations that have successfully linked their employees to the community have

- Set clear goals and targets
- Effectively communicated their values
- Aligned corporate behavior with goals
- Monitored achievements and continuous improvement against goals
- Spotlighted corporate and employee efforts in the media, in advertising, and on their Web sites

15 Ways to Create Good Vibes

Your employees are "walking billboards" who take their affiliation with your organization with them wherever they go. We all talk about work. Home is where we sleep, but work is where we live! We also live in our communities and have a tremendous responsibility to make them better places. A desire to support the community cuts across age, race, sex, department, and other barriers. Community involvement connects your employees to a variety of positive causes that can be tailored to their individual interests. It is a cost-effective way to build relationships among your organization's employees, as well as between your employees and the community. The more GreatBiz, Inc., employees are involved in the community, the more potential hires and clients will hear the GreatBiz name!

1. CONNECT CURRENTLY INVOLVED EMPLOYEES WITH WANNA-BES. Ask your employees about their community activities. Chances are good that you have active Eagle Scouts, blood donors, workers for Habitat for Humanity, drivers for Meals on Wheels, and employees with other volunteer activities to share. Give these employees company shirts to wear when they do their volunteer work. Create a bulletin board in the workplace or on your intranet where they can encourage other employees to join them for fun runs and other volunteer activities.

2. SPONSOR A TEAM FOR A FUND-RAISING WALK OR RUN. Supply the team with T-shirts or running shorts bearing your organization's logo to wear during the event. Take photos and publish them in your newsletter and on your intranet. Make copies of team photos or other action shots available to the team members.

3. FEATURE VOLUNTEERS IN ARTICLES IN YOUR IN-HOUSE NEWSLETTER. MAIL NEWSLETTERS HOME. Make it cool to volunteer. Build employee pride in community accomplishments.

4. SPONSOR A HIGHWAY, GREENWAY, RIVER, OR OTHER OUTDOOR FEATURE. Kiwanis and Rotary Clubs have known for years that sponsoring and caring for a public area is good publicity. Involve employees in cleanup and maintenance. Hands-on involvement builds team spirit!

5. RECOGNIZE "SUPER VOLUNTEERS" WITH SPECIAL AWARDS. At ONEX, Inc., a high-tech consulting and recruiting firm in Indianapolis, employees involved with the community receive ONE^X pins in recognition that their efforts are taking both themselves and the community to the "X potential." At other organizations, employees receive plaques or other awards and may participate in recognition celebrations.

6. FEATURE "SUPER VOLUNTEERS" AND THEIR ACTIVITIES IN RADIO, BILLBOARD, AND PRINT ADVERTISEMENTS ABOUT YOUR ORGANIZATION. Give the public some insight into the people at GreatBiz, Inc.—and make them want to join in the fun!

7. ENCOURAGE EMPLOYEES TO MAKE PUBLIC PRESENTATIONS. One of the first things to happen whenever people address an audience is that they are introduced! If your organization has employees with public-speaking skills and non-sales messages to share, encourage them to address community groups, professional organizations, user groups, and church groups. In so doing, your company will be introduced, too!

8. ENCOURAGE SENIOR MANAGEMENT AND OTHERS TO JOIN BOARDS OF DIRECTORS. Not-for-profit as well as corporate boards of directors benefit from your employees' skills—and your organization benefits from the skills they acquire while serving on the boards.

9. ANNOUNCE AN ESSAY COMPETITION. Tell the news media. Ask involved employees to compete for financial support of their favorite organization. Select an organization to receive a $1,000, $5,000, or other donation based on worthiness as described in an employee's essay.

10. MAKE MEETING-ROOM SPACE AVAILABLE. Ask your employees if they would like to host meetings on-site. Emphasize your organization's community involvement to qualified potential new hires or potential clients by providing rooms where professional and civic organizations may meet either during or after hours. Invite the Explorer Scouts, Toastmasters, and other groups to your offices. For the cost of light refreshments, a bright, intelligent group of your employees' peers will get a tour, hear about your organization, and be able to speak accurately and well of their experience—or they may refer business leads or job candidates. In fact, they may even consider applying for jobs themselves.

11. USE ART TO BRING THE COMMUNITY INTO YOUR ORGANIZATION. Showcase a variety of local artists, your employees' children, or the children at a school that your organization has adopted. Host an open house for clients, prospects, vendors, and employees to celebrate the artists' work. Invite the artists!

12. TEAM WITH ANOTHER ORGANIZATION TO SPONSOR A COMMU-NITY EVENT. A client, prospect, vendor, or strategic-partner organization in your community probably seeks exposure to the same audience that you do. By sharing sponsorship costs, your organization may gain greater exposure and achieve a bigger impact. Select an event that matches the interests of your employees or clients—or your potential employees or clients. If appropriate, sponsor the printed programs and/or a promotional giveaway item for attendees. Depending upon your organization's focus, consider sponsoring a night at the symphony, a speaker at a business conference, outdoor fireworks, a softball team, a baseball game, a fund-raiser for a political candidate, an ice cream social, or a community dog show.

13. LOOK FOR EMPLOYEES TO SHOWCASE IN THE LOCAL MEDIA. Your employees could be newsmakers! Pitch the local media about employees with unusual hobbies or considerable community involvement, retiring long-term employees, or those with unusual success stories.

14. COMPETE FOR BUSINESS AWARDS. Most communities find a wide variety of ways to put the spotlight on businesses and not-for-profit organizations of different sizes and types. The local chamber of commerce, business development corporation, business journal, "Big Five" accounting/management firms, professional organizations, and other entities sponsor awards for "Entrepreneur of the Year," "40 under 40," or "Growth 100 Companies." A finalist attracts great media coverage—selection as the winner brings entry to an inner circle of business leaders who share opportunities and gladly work with one another. In either instance, greater overall recognition among potential hires and increased pride among current employees are a considerable payoff. Employers of Choice often win these competitions— and EOCs-to-be become Employers of Choice!

15. ASK YOUR EMPLOYEES HOW THEY WOULD LIKE TO HELP THE COM-MUNITY. Get ready to be flooded with ideas!

Brand Your Culture to Attract Prospective Employees

You want your managers, employees, potential employees, and referral sources for employees to be able to answer the question "Why work at GreatBiz, Inc.?" The answer to the question is your organization's brand. Strong brands attract high-quality job seekers and retain high-quality employees.

Whether you use a public relations (PR) specialist or a PR/marketing firm, the odds of successfully branding your culture and being featured in the local media, co-hosting a successful event, or otherwise getting in front of the right audience on a repeat basis increase with the help of a professional. PR and marketing professionals who understand branding and media relations will help you develop a message about your organization and will suggest ways to align your overall marketing efforts with your efforts to market to potential employees. They will provide direction on joining specific professional and civic organizations, competing for significant business awards, querying the appropriate trade journals, sponsoring special events, and changing your signage. They may also suggest article ideas and propose other means of raising public awareness of your organization. Hiring will be much easier when your potential candidates say, "GreatBiz? Yes! I know who they are!"

HR or senior management must team up with Marketing or Corporate Communications to tie recruiting efforts to overall marketing efforts. Selecting a PR firm to assist in building a positive reputation is not too difficult—but finding an entity that can also brand your culture may take a bit of effort. While there are individual practitioners and PR firms, PR capabilities may also be found within marketing firms or advertising agencies. In the latter case, however, PR services may not be a strong suit and may be offered solely to existing clients who are already making use of other advertising-related services. Meeting with several firms will be required. As with any other vendor, selecting a PR firm requires a little homework.

1. DETERMINE YOUR GOALS. Do you have multiple goals—marketing your product or service to potential buyers *and* attracting

potential employees? If so, you need to state these goals to potential firms and to referral sources for firms.

2. DETERMINE YOUR AUDIENCE. Whom do you want to reach/hire? Nurses? Information technology (IT) specialists? Accounting staff? Does your company need to be recognizable to a cross section of the general public in your local community? Or would attaining a high profile solely within a specific segment of the population be the key to accomplishing your goals?

3. DETERMINE YOUR IN-HOUSE CAPABILITIES. Many organizations have trained corporate communications or public relations specialists on staff. If you do—and even if you do not—assess your current capabilities and determine which skills are lacking. Perhaps you have in-house event planning skills but lack writing or strategic media placement skills. Few organizations have in-house research abilities or media relations expertise.

4. NETWORK FOR THE RIGHT PROVIDER. Lists of PR firms are of no help unless they include the names of well-known clients and the quality of the profile-raising activities on behalf of those clients is known to your organization. Rather than pick names at random from a list or the telephone book, consider other sources of referral such as

- Your local Public Relations Society of America (PRSA) or International Association of Business Communicators (IABC) chapter

- Leaders of companies engaged in a similar type of business

- Individuals and organizations that have received an uncommon amount of positive publicity

- Business reporters for your local newspaper who work daily with a variety of PR professionals

5. GET REFERENCES AND CHECK SAMPLES. If a firm or individual practitioner has experience with both raising the profile of organizations to their potential employees and "branding" cultures, references and samples will validate this experience.

6. SELECT A FIRM TO BRAND YOUR CULTURE. A brand describes the experience of working for the organization. Organizations that have already put considerable dollars and effort into branding their services and products to attract new clients understand why it is also important to brand their culture to attract new employees. Employers need to ask themselves

- What kind of characteristics do our employees display?

- What kind of relationship do we have with our employees?

- What does it mean to work here?

- How can we make our culture real to potential employees?

7. DEVELOP A PLAN, AND IMPLEMENT IT. Raising the profile of an organization and branding its culture are not overnight activities. Success requires immersing the PR or marketing specialist in information and enabling him or her to prepare a plan, get the plan approved, and put it to work.

It is critical that external communication efforts contain accurate claims so that existing employees will support and validate these claims when they speak to job candidates and referral sources. Otherwise, existing employees will react so negatively to the message that it will actually be counterproductive to attraction and retention efforts.

Crisis Reputation Management Is Worth the Effort

Whatever is printed or announced on the evening news concerning your company is what people talk about inside the organization. It also becomes what people outside the organization discuss with your employees. Long after the management of the organization has decided to put it all behind them, your employees will be asked to explain what happened, why it happened, what will happen next, and how they feel about it. If the news is negative, it casts a pall over the employees as a group. Because they identify so closely with their work, employees may ask themselves, "How can I work at a company that does this?" Clearly, negative headlines can lengthen fill times, decrease productivity, and increase turnover. EOCs work hard to create a positive reputation for their organizations—but they have a contingency plan for negative surprises.

Any employer, regardless of its service or product, can unintentionally (or recklessly) create negative headlines. Examples of negative headlines might include

- Nurse suspected of poisoning elderly patients

- Explosion rips paint storage warehouse—two neighboring businesses destroyed

- IT consulting firm sued for failed Y2K-compliance updates

- Fourth "big cat" death at zoo brings probe

- Deaths halt heart-drug testing for ABC Pharmaceutical Corp.

- Bridge collapses as new sections are put in place

- Elderly resident dies when construction company's backhoe hits gas line

- Sexual harassment suit embroils company president

- Brokerage house uncovers client account embezzlement

- Arguing patrons shoot each other outside of Sam's Restaurant

An organization with a bad reputation will have to mount a considerable, expensive, multiyear effort to regain the lost trust and overcome the "bad vibes" in the community before it can become an Employer of Choice. The effort is worth it because of the long-term positive impact on hiring, retention, and client development. Hiring a PR firm with strength in the area of crisis media management is absolutely necessary to turn around a bad reputation.

All employers need a crisis media plan in case of an emergency. Not-for-profit organizations are no less likely to be in the news than are manufacturers, government agencies, universities, or hospitals. Any employer who has had negative information in the news must take immediate action. Simply stating "no comment" is *not* an option for an Employer of Choice or any employer that desires EOC status in the future.

What basic steps are required to prevent bad news from ruining an organization's carefully developed community or industry profile? Develop a plan and review it at least annually so that all parties know their roles in case of a reputation emergency.

1. REVIEW ALL POLICIES AND PROCEDURES TO ENSURE THAT THEY ARE CURRENT AND IN COMPLIANCE WITH ALL LAWS. Remember the oil company accused of violating the civil rights of black employees? The senior executives themselves were audiotaped expounding on the illegal hiring and promotion practices of the company. This type of situation can be avoided by ensuring that your organization adheres to current legal and ethical practices.

2. ADHERE TO SAFETY PROCEDURE RECOMMENDATIONS. Cutting corners with safety is an accident waiting to happen. Safety violations cost lives and endanger the health of employees and visitors. The public (including the news media, current and potential employees, and current and potential clients) can be very unforgiving of preventable accidents.

3. PREVENT EMPLOYEE BEHAVIOR THAT PUTS ORGANIZATION ASSETS AT RISK. Train all managers on EEOC, sexual harassment, and other state and federal laws that—if violated—lead to lawsuits and headlines. Ethical leadership is critical to the prevention of costly problems. Organizations that have been found unethical have considerable difficulty hiring and retaining employees and gaining and retaining clients, investors, and vendors.

4. DESIGNATE AN ORGANIZATION SPOKESPERSON AND A BACKUP SPOKESPERSON. Educate all employees about referring media calls to appropriate spokespeople.

5. SELECT A CRISIS TASK FORCE. A cross section of senior management, along with representatives from HR and Corporate Communications, should seek input from the corporate attorney and/or outside PR firm. By gathering information quickly, the team can determine the appropriate response.

6. ESTABLISH CLEAR GOALS. Depending upon the nature of the emergency, some goals may be more achievable than others.

Obviously, a fire at a gas utility site will be on the six o'clock news—but a lawsuit does not show up on the front page if it is handled well.

7. BE TRUTHFUL WITH THE MEDIA AND ON YOUR ORGANIZATION'S WEB SITE. Lies are instantly recognized as lies inside the organization, will be uncovered by investigators or the news media, and will harm the goodwill that exists in the community. Contact your PR professional and attorney for specific scripting of answers to anticipated questions.

8. APOLOGIZE, IF APPROPRIATE. Express concern for those involved, and name a time and date when an action plan will be announced. Meet this deadline! Moving quickly is critical when errors have been committed or lives harmed. Immediately demonstrate positive intentions and take action to correct problems. Cooperation, positive action, and caring responses are appropriate. Denials, stonewalling, and righteous indignation will be costly.

Defiantly denying EEOC charges, Mitsubishi Motor Manufacturing of America, Inc., endured years of negative publicity before it finally paid $34 million to settle government charges of severe harassment of female employees. The harm to the company's sales, profits, recruiting and retention efforts, and overall productivity may never be made public. The $34 million was *in addition to those costs!*

9. COMMUNICATE INSIDE THE ORGANIZATION BEFORE COMMUNICATING OUTSIDE THE ORGANIZATION, IF AT ALL POSSIBLE. For employees, few things are harder than hearing bad news about their employer on the radio or on television—or from people outside their organization. To the extent possible, prepare employees with information and plans for action. If appropriate, solicit their input regarding action planning. Thank them in advance for their cooperation and assistance with the positive resolution of the crisis.

10. COMMUNICATE WITH CLIENTS, VENDORS, AND INVESTORS AS SOON AS POSSIBLE. Once a plan is announced, share it with all

those who can positively affect the organization's bottom line. Assure them of the intent to prevent repeated occurrences. Ask them for their input. Thank them for remaining with your organization through this trying time.

11. IF APPROPRIATE, IMPLEMENT TRAINING OR OTHER REMEDIAL ACTIONS AS SOON AS POSSIBLE. With proper training, safety violations, harassment suits, and other situations may be avoided. Rapid scheduling of remedial activities demonstrates responsibility and an understanding of the seriousness of the situation.

12. MEASURE RESULTS AGAINST OBJECTIVES. What was the tone of newspaper and other media accounts? How long were the stories? Were you able to halt or limit employee resignations? To what degree has recruiting been affected? How have clients, vendors, and investors reacted? Have any neutral or positive stories been printed? What were the actual costs of the entire sequence of events?

It is no fun to work for an organization that is repeatedly pummeled in the news media. No organization wants to experience negative headlines, but many have survived the experience. It is more fun to work for a company that is respected by friends, family, and colleagues based on their understanding of its services and products, as well as its community involvement. Proud employees are more likely to remain on staff. It is worth the effort to create positive media relationships so that EOC status can be achieved. It is also worth the effort to create a positive local reputation by encouraging community involvement among your employees.

Reputations are like bank accounts: the more frequent the "deposits," or positive results, of community activities and favorable articles, the more interest and value accrue, lessening the impact of a negative episode, or "withdrawal." A commitment to corporate social responsibility can provide a distinct advantage in the areas of attracting and retaining employees, as well as in cementing customer, vendor, investor, and regulator relationships.

PART TWO

CREATIVE STRATEGIES FOR RECRUITING TOP TALENT

▼

CHAPTER FOUR

HOW EMPLOYERS OF CHOICE ARE REDESIGNING RECRUITMENT

The recruiting process builds and reinforces the organization's image and culture, and the quality of hires determines future corporate capabilities and profitability. Employers have three choices in the hiring process:

1. HIRE PROVEN WINNERS. This strategy takes time and effort.

2. HIRE POTENTIAL WINNERS AND TRAIN THEM. This strategy takes more time and effort.

3. HIRE ANYONE WHO APPLIES—and pray that it works out!

Employers get what they expect—because they put in place processes and procedures that support the expectation. If hiring and keeping great employees is *the* strategic advantage that EOCs have over their competition, why are most policies, procedures, and actions based on the late-20th-century employment environment? Hiring anyone who applies and then using the "sink or swim" approach to assimilation results in the sinking of too many new hires. Hiring high-quality, qualified candidates is the first step in a series of processes that should result in a long-term, mutually beneficial, and profitable relationship between the employee and employer.

All turnover is costly, but new-hire turnover is the most costly. New-hire turnover refers to those individuals at any level, in any function, who do not show up on day one, who leave after day one, who leave during training—or who leave at any point in the first six months of employment. Today, new-hire turnover is recognized as being too expensive for any organization. This chapter will share the processes, tactics, and technology of EOCs who hire well, train new hires, and develop and retain current employees for longer than the statistical averages. We will discuss the procedures and tracking by which EOCs ensure that they get the desired positive results. It takes planning, processes, and accountability to prevent hiring failures.

Take Responsibility for Retention

Job seekers prepare for their interviews, dress for success, and practice interviewing. The historic overabundance of potential hires lessened the need for employers to train hiring managers in the art and science of interviewing—much less put effort into any other part of the hiring process. This lack of effort is still evident in the behavior of employers today when job candidates are sent to side entrances, left waiting for long periods in uncomfortable reception areas, interviewed by unprepared managers, and generally given the message that they do not matter as individuals.

First impressions count. Successful hiring and retention are strongly impacted by the activities of several departments, including Marketing, Administration, Facilities Management, and HR—in addition to the department with the opening. Successful hiring and retention start *prior to* the first interview with the planning of the job seeker's first impression. Job seekers start to evaluate an organization from the first encounter—in person or otherwise—and decide whether to interview based on their reactions to

- A brochure, annual report, job advertisement, and/or Web site

- Conversations with employees whom they know from church or earlier work experiences, or who are family members

- The buzz, or reputation, of the organization

- The external appearance of the the facility

- The chairs, plants, magazines, and general appearance of the reception area

- The way the receptionist greets them

- What they overhear and see while waiting for the first interview

- The information they receive about the job itself

EOCs rally the entire organization to achieve successful recruiting and retention by putting ongoing effort into

- Creating recruiting brochures with a benefits overview

- Developing candidate-oriented Web site content

- Creating a great buzz about the organization through articles, event sponsorship, and community involvement

- Brightening the appearance of the building and reception area

- Scripting the greeting guests receive both on the telephone and in person

- Updating the job description available to the candidate with additional details about the specific position

- Rewarding employee referrals on an ongoing basis

EOCs Develop Interviewing Skills

If excellent hiring is the foundation of retention, all hiring managers need to become excellent interviewers. This is a learned skill, not an instinctive ability. Training (and even retraining) is the key. Hiring managers must take the time to learn interviewing techniques, prepare questions for interviews, update job descriptions, and focus on the candidate. This is very much a sales process: the manager is selling the organization to the candidate. The candidate is buying a job and a career. Sloppy interviewing processes won't get the sale.

Interview skills training must be added to an organization's mandatory management training curriculum or arranged for managers through an external source such as the local HR association. EOCs usually require interview skills training for supervisors and managers within six months of hire and *do not allow untrained supervisors or other managers to make independent hiring decisions.*

The right person must be selected from a variety of candidates. Generating a candidate pipeline is covered in Chapters Seven and Eight. Hiring managers cannot make a racehorse out of a mule, nor can new-hire trainers wave a magic wand and turn a poor hire into a great hire. Hiring well is a must—and it can be learned.

The type and number of interview questions must be appropriate to the open position and must result in the selection of either a qualified individual or one so nearly qualified that a reasonable amount of training will quickly result in satisfactory performance. While most hiring managers know that they cannot ask personal questions such as whether someone is married or plans to have children, they could use comments about their own children to trick an applicant into discussing his or her family or family planning situation. This is foolish since many applicants know the law. Keep interview questions on target, friendly, and mutually beneficial. Ask behavior-based questions that uncover competencies for the job. Further, while past performance is an indicator of future performance, be sure to include future-oriented questions. Ask how the candidate would handle specific job-related situations, or have the candidate discuss his or her approach to a hypothetical project.

Interviewing is a two-way process. Employers must give as much information as they get. Plan facility tours, introductions to peers and key players, and opportunities for the candidate to ask questions and start picturing himself or herself working at GreatBiz, Inc. Candidates for mid-level positions and higher are routinely wined and dined, along with their spouses, by many EOCs. Some invite candidates to attend company events once a job offer has been made.

A variety of resources are available to assist hiring managers and HR specialists in developing a set of questions to be used for each position in the organization. To ensure the legality of interview questions, consult your labor attorney or any of the readily available publications and Web sites produced by the government or the Society for Human Resource Management (SHRM).

Results of Current Hiring Practices

Too few organizations have developed sucessful hiring practices as an *organizational* competency—as a result, many qualified candidates are getting away, or not even getting a first interview. Traditional hiring processes are so slow that many candidates lose interest. Long fill times for job openings also put unnecessary pressure on an organization. Overworked staff try to fill in, but deadlines slip, client files are lost, tempers flare, and productivity plummets along with morale. Today, filling open positions is a crisis equal in magnitude to the unhappy client, the overdue report, and the innumerable waiting e-mails. If not quickly addressed, turnover breeds more turnover— and even more unhappy clients, overdue reports, and unanswered e-mail.

Successful hiring goes to the swift. High-quality applicants are being landed by the first organizations to make acceptable offers. Companies with traditional recruiting processes will be left with long fill times. For the next 10 years, the pipeline of potential new hires will provide barely a trickle of candidates considering the staffing needs of organizations of all types and sizes. We will experience a severe mismatch between the number of jobs available and the number of candidates—especially candidates with technology skills. New tactics are needed to attract top technical and other needed talent.

EOCs know it is a *seller's* market for employees—and it will continue to be a seller's market during the foreseeable future. Quality candidates do not wait—and will not have to wait—because EOCs respond to their queries within 24 hours! EOCs are already interviewing hot candidates when other employers are waiting to hear back from hiring managers about candidate preferences and open interview times and are otherwise letting other business activities slow down the hiring process.

EOCs have hiring processes in place to speed the opening-to-offer cycle. Technology is playing a greater role, from enabling the sorting of résumés by keyword and date of submission to providing automated skills assessment. No matter the method used, the recruiting function must effect significant change in the area of speed-to-hire. Because organizations are competing for potential new hires with organizations of all sizes and types, as well as with much-publicized companies that are planning to move into new areas, speed-to-hire is ever more critical.

At Cisco Systems, one of the largest high-tech network and hardware companies based in California, a "buddy" is immediately assigned to a candidate who uses the company Web site to respond to openings or even casually inquire for information. The buddy matches the job seeker's age and skills with available positions in order to increase the odds that the query will become an interview. Cisco hires thousands of employees each year via its Web site. It knows that casual inquiries are serious business. Cisco also knows that by the time other employers respond to a candidate "next week," it will be well into the hiring process with the same candidate.

At Eli Lilly and Company, recruiting is a sophisticated process designed to attract both active and passive job seekers, according to Susan Burleigh, Senior Associate, U.S. Flexible Staffing, speaking at the Indiana Personnel Association Conference on October 29, 1999. The recuiting process should be documented, communicated, and reviewed regularly, and the metrics surrounding the process steps should be monitored (see Figure 5).

Susan Burleigh uses the metaphor of a funnel to demonstrate how every organization needs to review its entire recruiting process from top to bottom because the quality and quantity of leads determine the quality and quantity of hires. "Track each source to determine the resulting percentage of applications, interviews, offers, and hires," she recommends. "Further, track the ratios of applications to interviews, interviews to offers, and offers to hires." She suggests using the following figures: 70 percent of interviewed candidates receive an offer, 80 percent of those who are offered positions accept, and 90 percent of those who accept start work. "The most important figure to track is the percentage of interviews to offers," she adds. Clearly, the top of the funnel determines the likelihood that those interviewed will be qualified.

Too few hiring managers of mid-size and smaller organizations have kept current with these technology and process trends. EOCs

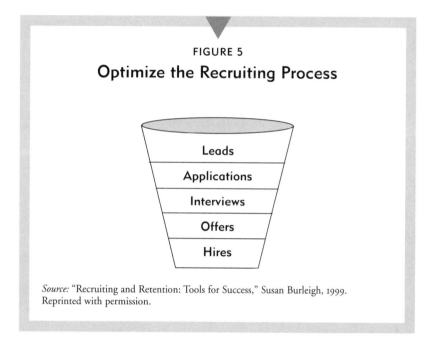

FIGURE 5

Optimize the Recruiting Process

Leads

Applications

Interviews

Offers

Hires

Source: "Recruiting and Retention: Tools for Success," Susan Burleigh, 1999. Reprinted with permission.

recognize that organizations are no longer competing for employees with direct industry competitors only—or even with same-size companies in their geographic marketplace.

Think about your most recent hires. Were they recruited from a variety of big and small, for-profit and not-for-profit organizations, both inside and outside your industry? How far away did you have to go to find the best hires? And when you review the list of employees lost to other organizations, note the diverse size and types of employers that recruited them.

Candidates themselves are seeking a greater variety of work experiences in an attempt to find a more suitable environment or to round out their careers. Some seek a *fast* company with an entrepreneurial environment. A start-up operation is their opportunity to make their mark and get in on the ground floor. This is their chance to grow an organization—and possibly earn equity in the company. Candidates with experience in small to medium-size organizations may seek a company one size up in order to stretch and build on their experience. It is not uncommon for candidates to review their work histories for transferable skills—and for potential employers to welcome the cross-pollination made possible by bringing in someone with different industry experience and problem-solving approaches. For many individuals, simply changing jobs may be a rich career development experience—and career development is the number one attraction of EOCs.

Employers are also beginning to realize that there are mini-companies (skunk works) or departments within their organizations that operate differently and might require candidates with competencies and skill sets that would not be considered fit elsewhere in the organization. A well-crafted hiring message combined with efficient speed-to-hire processes will enable a company to hire the quality and quantity of employees it needs for an unusual department.

Raise the Bar for Hiring Managers

Hiring managers must be held accountable for their significant role in the success or failure of new hires. Car sales representatives know that they have a short amount of time to interest a potential buyer. Even casual "tire kickers" can be turned into buyers if they are treated well and provided with the critical information that meets their needs. Once that potential buyer leaves the showroom, however, the odds of a sale are much lower. Car sales reps know that speed-to-sale is the key to attaining their goals. Hiring managers must learn that speed-to-hire starts with an immediate response to qualified candidates. EOCs frequently tie a portion of each hiring manager's annual compensation to his or her success in partnering with HR to significantly shorten the hiring cycle.

The traditional lengthy hiring cycle too often results in fewer candidates for initial interviews and candidates lost before offers can be made. Typically, organizations advertise in the Sunday classified ad section of the newspaper in Week One, start to review responses in the middle of Week Two, start to set up interviews by the end of Week Two, and conduct first interviews in Week Three. Not until Weeks Four and Five can they conduct second interviews, and they make offers in Week Five or later. Allowing for the amount of time the candidate needs to discuss the offer with family and friends, plus the customary two-week notice at the current job, the position is not truly filled until Week Seven or later. That is assuming the ad gets any response at all.

This is a cumbersome process fraught with disappointment. Hiring victories go to the swift! EOCs should be well into the hiring cycle and bonded with their future employees by the end of Week Two—or even within 24 to 48 hours! Quality candidates will be snapped up with the first competitive offer from an equally qualified EOC.

Speed is also important when considering internal candidates. Any employee who applies for a new position *inside* the company is close to applying for a new position *outside* the company. Internal candidates must be treated with as much respect and professionalism as external candidates. They must be interviewed even though HR and the hiring manager feel that "everyone knows" him or her. The way to keep employees is to treat them as if they were customers—or external job candidates!

For a *very* select few candidates, lengthy hiring processes should be eliminated altogether. These individuals could be the ones that got away in earlier hiring rounds (they took other offers). The select candidate may be such a noted leader in his or her field—and so well known to the key players in your organization—that all pertinent parties have agreed to the hire. Clearly, a mutual understanding of the position is required. Elimination of formal hiring procedures can backfire and must be used with extreme caution. If, however, a Nobel Prize–winning scientist is about to take another offer, you might want to eliminate unnecessary steps and make an offer today!

Reduce Cycle Time and Increase User-Friendliness

Time is a precious, non-renewable resource. Speed-to-hire is especially critical for organizations that are on their way to EOC status but are competing with EOCs in their geographic area or industry. Every day, quality candidates—including internal candidates—are being hired away by faster, more time-sensitive EOCs.

To get a real grasp of what works in hiring and what does not, survey both the candidates who accept positions and those who decline. Get truthful input from them about their decisions and your hiring processes. Consider hiring a third party to conduct the survey. Encourage the new hires as well as the ones that got away to provide confidential comments as well as answers to specific questions. Analyze the data by business unit/department and in the aggregate. Until a survey process has been developed—or even if your organization is currently surveying successful and unsuccessful hires—review the hiring process itself.

Organizations that lack a cohesive hiring process may require candidates to return repeatedly or allow long periods of time to elapse between contacts; they will lose candidates to employers with more user-friendly hiring mechanisms. User-friendliness is important to all involved: external candidates, internal candidates, and internal referral sources. Delays in the hiring process may result in frustration and lack of results.

Organizations must make it appealing for candidates to apply and interview. In real estate, this is called "curb appeal." If potential home buyers cannot see the fabulous kitchen, warm family room, and great deck out back because a fence and a barking dog bar the front door, they go on to the next open house. Job seekers do the same thing. Smart home sellers plant flowers, mow the lawn, and board the dog during the open house. Smart employers make sure that there are few—if any—barriers to applying and interviewing.

Initial face-to-face interviews may be impossible with out-of-town candidates. Time and space get in the way of fast hiring, yet responding within a week is critical to stacking the odds in your organization's favor. Out-of-town candidates and crazy schedules sometimes make in-person interviews almost impossible. Telephone interviews between the candidate and HR, and between the candidate and the hiring manager, are one effective substitute. A more complete tool is the real-time videoconference interview. Since very few organizations (much less candidates) have the necessary equipment, several cost-effective resources are available: videoconferencing services, colleges, and copying centers. Videoconference interviews can be used for recruiting students, as well as more experienced candidates.

If face-to-face interviews are feasible, make appointments quickly. Once an opening is advertised, hiring managers should block time slots for likely interviews. Some organizations' hiring managers hold specific blocks of time free *each week* just for interviews. At a minimum, interviews with both HR and the hiring manager should be arranged back-to-back for the same day.

Ideally, a panel could be set up ahead of time and be ready to interview a mid- or management-level candidate on the same day, assuming that the one-on-one interview with the hiring manager goes well. Consider including a customer if the position involves extensive customer contact. Potentially, a decision could be rendered later the same day. If additional interviews are needed—due to the high level of the candidate or the need to compare multiple candidates, or if requested by the candidate—an offer could be made quickly after the second interview cycle.

In today's leaner organizations, almost all hires are critical hires. EOCs elevate improved recruiting and retention to a high level of strategic importance and translate those goals into achievable objectives for every hiring manager. Supervisors, managers, directors, and vice presidents all have the responsibility to attain these goals.

To reduce fill times, HR must track fill-time processes. Each step must be documented and metrics applied. Automating résumé intake and cataloging will speed the tracking process and generate metrics more quickly. Tracking might include

- Date-stamping résumés upon receipt (paper or e-mail)

- Logging the date on which a résumé is entered into the database

- Calculating the time between placing the recruiting order and receiving résumés from recruiters

- Figuring out the ratio of *qualified* applicants to total number of résumés received from ads or from recruiters

- Measuring the turnaround time for a hiring manager to review and respond to résumés

Tracking the source of candidates is critical for later value evaluation. Metrics should be applied no matter how the candidate is made known to the organization. Some individuals respond to ads, while others make contact by e-mail, via the Web site, or in person. Some are referred without résumés by internal or external sources. Each day that passes without action on an interesting résumé and/or an interested candidate is a day closer to the moment the competition wins a new employee.

What if the candidate is surfing your Web site but does not have a résumé? Many organizations have added software that helps the candidate create a résumé by filling in a form. Wise organizations offer this capability on their intranet as well so that employees may also apply quickly for interesting positions. The goal is to make it easy for the job seeker to supply enough information to enable the internal recruiter to follow up appropriately. Simplified processes are the hallmark of successful Internet and intranet usage.

Hiring managers should set deadlines for responding to requests from outside recruiters or HR for approval/selection of candidates or to arrange interview dates and times. Organizations that still involve hiring managers at this stage of the process have determined that calls to candidates within 48 hours result in the greatest number of viable interview candidates. In some geographic areas and industries, even 24 hours may be too long a response time. Landing a qualified information technology or other in-demand candidate may require an immediate e-mail or telephone call upon receipt of a query. Whether HR or the hiring manager makes this first call, the objective is to contact the candidate before your competition has a chance to do so!

Many organizations have determined that asking the hiring manager to participate at this early stage is unnecessary and do not involve him or her until the interview stage itself.

If HR knows the job requirements and competencies of top performers, only qualified candidates should be invited for interviews. With access to hiring managers' schedules through online calendars, HR can screen and schedule top candidates for immediate interviews. Clearly, with this model, HR must also prepare the hiring manager with the résumé, any additional telephone interview information, and even a set of standard questions to be asked of all candidates. Preparing hiring managers to this degree results in a faster, more uniform interview process.

One of the most time-consuming parts of the hiring process is waiting for responses from job seekers once a position has been advertised. Of those who do respond, a disappointingly small percentage may be qualified. Whether the opening is for entry-level positions or more technical positions, and whether the advertising medium is a newspaper or some other means (the Web, billboard, or radio and television ads), it is possible to shorten the time spent waiting for qualified candidates to appear. Technology is the answer.

Advertisements typically are run in Sunday newspapers or in other media with the proviso "No calls, please." For organizations that hire hundreds or even thousands of entry-level or other employees (such as airlines, delivery services, healthcare operations, and retail chains), days are lost between the time the ad is placed (Week One) and when job seekers read or hear the advertisement. More time is lost between the job seeker finding out about the ad and taking action and the organization receiving résumés or other documents to indicate interest (in Week Two or Week Three). At that point, HR or a hiring manager must review the résumés and determine which candidates are most likely to be qualified. This step takes hours, days, or even weeks, depending upon the number of candidates and the available time of company representatives.

For many organizations, the first opportunity to contact qualified candidates is at the end of Week Two, but it is likely to be during Week Three. The number and speed of the responses also influence whether the organization decides to re-advertise (to grow the pool of potential candidates), or even to wait in hopes of receiving résumés from more qualified candidates. In either case, this traditional process takes too long.

Employers know that filling job openings with enough of the right people in the shortest amount of time at the lowest possible cost is critical to achieving bottom-line goals and keeping customers happy. Often, employers with call centers or other high-turnover functions (sales staff, certified nursing assistants, baggage handlers, mechanics, drivers, manufacturing employees, or customer service representatives) need to advertise the same types of positions repeatedly during a year. In some organizations, the hiring of some functions is a monthly cycle. In these organizations, there is a dearth of qualified individuals who fit the job requirements and who will succeed and stay on the job. Recruiting these employees demands relentless expenditures of resources and exerts pressure on management and existing employees. Technology is needed to speed the hiring cycle.

Advertising Management Group (AMG), a Cleveland-based firm that develops telephony and Web-enabled processes and tools, has developed AdManager™ to significantly shorten the hiring cycle and reduce employment advertising and other recruitment costs.

This recruitment placement tool is accessed through a secure Web site and enables an employer to design or modify an ad, place it, and instantly know the success rate of the specific ad if it was used previously in a particular publication or other media (billboards, for example). Because the ads encourage immediate telephone contact, and because the caller is screened for specific competencies or experience using a series of questions and automated telephone or Web processes, initial screening can begin at any hour of the day or night, whenever a job seeker responds to the ad.

Job seekers are tallied in two categories: total responses and qualified responses. Qualified callers are placed on hold while the AdManager™ service bureau staff review the employer's interview schedule and sets up an appointment for the earliest available date and time. With this system, the AdManager staff can schedule an appointment any time a caller responds to the ad, and the employer can interview qualified candidates within 24 hours of the ad's appearance. This means that hiring decisions can be made as early as the day after a recruitment ad runs!

For new ads, AdManager generates metrics for total responses and qualified responses less than a week after publication. Metrics that track cost per qualified candidate and number of qualified candidates enable more dynamic ad strategies that reflect response rates. Further, the accumulated knowledge base from previous ad placements is available to both new and experienced recruiting staff. It is easy to know which recruitment ads were successful in which publications and in which markets—and for what cost. Revamping ads quickly to increase the response rates of qualified candidates is critical. Shortening the hiring cycle is a key part of making sure an organization is able to meet its other strategic goals.

Some organizations use online assessments, questionnaires, and "mutual expectation contracts" to shorten the screening and interviewing process—and speed the bonding process. In addition to gathering a job seeker's résumé, your corporate Web site could guide high-tech and other job seekers though a skills assessment process as well as an online questionnaire that provides insights into their reasons for being in the marketplace, salary requirements, and preferred corporate culture. Such information eliminates the need for initial telephone screening and reserves the interview process for qualified candidates. As soon as solid candidates are identified, reference checks are in order. Many organizations initiate checks prior to or concurrent with initial interviews; others do not initiate checks until an offer has been extended. Don't wait! Yes, reference checks take time (and money), but they are critical to the process of building your organization into an EOC.

Minimize the Need to Recruit

Instead of focusing solely on the recruiting end of the problem, EOCs step back and evaluate alternatives. What are some of these alternatives?

1. REDUCE TURNOVER. Clearly, the most effective way to reduce the need to recruit is to keep more employees in their current positions. If the "green money" (visible) and "blue money" (invisible) costs of replacing an employee are at least one to two times the employee's annual salary, then implementing the needed retention strategies could save company dollars or at least reroute those dollars to effective use. An overall goal must be to reduce turnover. Retention strategies are discussed in detail later in this book.

2. DETERMINE WHETHER THE POSITION IS NEEDED. Organizations must reevaluate the need for specific positions whenever they lose an employee. Too many positions have been refilled over the years without thought to streamlining processes, the impact of technology on productivity, the current needs of the organization, or whether others in the department might experience job enrichment from splitting the job.

Overworking current employees is *not* a retention strategy. Career development, however, *is* a retention strategy. Serious consideration should be given to reviewing workflow in any department when a job opening appears. Small-scale reengineering of one or more positions provides variety, improves processes, leverages technology—and may save the cost of a salary.

Maximize Internal Recruiting

EOCs understand that career development is a primary attraction for both job seekers and current employees. Job seekers are attracted to organizations that are known for having long-term employees who have moved through the ranks. Employees stay when they feel confident that, at some time in the foreseeable future, they will be considered for another position in the company: up, over, or even down (if taking a step down puts them on an appealing career path).

Career development occurs within positions when stretch assignments are added or duties are shifted among employees, through job shadowing and cross-training, or when training is provided that prepares an employee for greater responsibilities. Development also occurs when an actual job change is made within the company and an employee must learn rapidly in order to succeed in the new position.

Between the impact of technology and flattened organization structures, the move is just as likely to be in a lateral direction—or even down—as up the so-called career ladder. How does an organization create a ready candidate pool from which to choose when openings occur? And how can an organization increase the number of internal hires so that career development is reality, not lip service?

1. POST ALL INTERNAL JOB OPENINGS. While this tactic seems obvious, very few employers truly post all openings—and many do not post *any* openings where all employees can easily access them. Some organizations use physical bulletin boards while others use their intranet bulletin boards. The latter enables employees to review opportunities discreetly without arousing discussion among their peers. Failure to post openings, secretive interview processes, implied favoritism (telling a select few about an open-

ing), or interviewing only external candidates causes rancor and suspicion in the organization. Even if it is known that there are no qualified internal candidates, posting allows current employees to refer qualified candidates from other organizations. This builds goodwill and enhances the chances of quickly hiring new employees who will fit into the culture.

Internal postings should include a deadline for response and the minimum job requirements, which should be the same qualifications the organization is seeking in an outside candidate. Too often, external candidates are selected who must then receive job-specific training—and no one thinks anything about it! But an internal candidate with the same need is too often overlooked. Internal candidates with above-average performance records bring with them internal and external relationships, cultural insights, industry knowledge, and a demonstrated desire to build a career with the organization! If an internal candidate requires a stretch assignment or a class in order to get up to speed, those costs are surely less than the green money and blue money costs of an external hire!

2. INSTITUTE SUCCESSION PLANNING. Annually, many organizations mandate that managers at all levels take the time to evaluate each direct report to determine the skills or competencies (behaviors) that are needed in order to consider each individual for a promotion or other job movement. This evaluation should dovetail with the developmental plan portion of annual reviews and should reflect the discussions that each manager has had with his or her employees.

Not all employees want to move up—many would rather develop deeper skills in their current fields. Particularly for technical employees—those in IT, engineering, and biotech, for example—a non-management track with significant opportunities to extend their involvement in their own areas of expertise is critical to both recruiting and retention efforts.

The cumulative outcome of the succession planning exercise should be rolled up to the HR or training department to become a road map for training courses. Many employees throughout the organization will lack the same skills and competencies, so workshops can be created or trainers brought on-site to start the learning process. For those individuals with unique needs, appropriate courses may be located through professional organizations or local colleges and universities; other resources, such as books, videotaped programs, job shadowing, mentoring, or cross-training, may also be used.

Adults learn by doing. Reading, watching videotapes, or even classroom training rarely succeeds in fully preparing someone for a new career step. It is advisable to incorporate a learning transfer mechanism to allow the employee to demonstrate his or her new skills. The employee could be required to demonstrate the new skill or competency to his or her supervisor within 30 days of attending the class in order to receive credit for attending. An e-mail or signoff process would update the internal training and development records. Alternatively, a stretch assignment that uses the new skills and competencies could be devised. The goal is to develop a ready pool of internal candidates who can logically be considered for openings in their own departments or elsewhere in the organization.

Use Competencies to Hire the Best Person for the Job

Too often, employers focus on the hard-skills portion of the job description when interviewing applicants for a position. Many of us have interviewed executive assistant applicants and focused too narrowly on computer literacy, typing speed, and telephone voice—only to discover that we have hired someone who cannot solve problems, dislikes dealing with peers, and lacks initiative or follow-through on projects. Oh, but he or she can pound out documents in a flash! Belatedly, we realize that hard skills are not enough when our new hire offends clients and employees alike and leaves projects unfinished—or uninitiated. The solution is to develop the competencies needed for each position, use the competencies as part of the interview process, and hire the best person for the job.

Sandra O'Neal, a Towers Perrin principal who spoke at the Third International Conference on Using Competency-Based Tools and Applications to Drive Organizational Performance (Chicago, September 1996), defines competencies as the combination of observable and measurable skills, knowledge, performance behaviors, and personal attributes that contribute to enhanced employee performance and organizational success. Her keynote address, "Competency Applications: Out of the Lab and into the Real World," focused on linking competencies to business strategy. She recommends defining the competencies of each position in order to use them as the basis for staffing, training and development, performance management, and compensation. Clearly, competencies can also be used in succession planning.

At the same conference, Ben Granberg, manager of global compensation for GE Medical Systems (GEMS), shared his insights into using competencies to improve the recruiting and retention process in his presentation "Making Competency-Based Pay Work: Lessons Learned at GE Medical Systems." Noting that a competency is an underlying characteristic that causes or predicts the effective and/or superior performance of an individual in a job or situation, he urged employers to develop job descriptions that contain not only job/role competencies (which include strategic requirements, work requirements, and the organization's culture) but also the personal characteristics of superior performers in the position.

Examples of competencies of top sales representatives might be resilience, persistence, relationship-building skills, listening skills, time management, reporting, and follow-through. Experience in sales alone might not be a predictor of success in another sales position. Employers are finding that training for hard skills (sales techniques and product knowledge, in this case) and hiring for soft skills (competencies) results in more positive outcomes than hiring for hard skills alone.

Employers who are frustrated with the need to continually rehire for the same positions may scoff at the idea of taking the time to uncover the competencies of superior performers in their high-turnover positions—but not doing so condemns them to the expensive, endless cycle of rehiring and retraining.

Some employers are guilty of hiring whoever applies. Their theory is that if the job seeker really wants the job, he or she will learn to perform it well. Enthusiasm or merely being there is seen as qualification enough. Most employers are guilty of ignoring the competencies of top performers and filling openings with supposedly less expensive, minimally qualified individuals whom they hope to train to satisfactory performance standards. Both groups of employers are destined to be disappointed because they make no attempt to ensure retention at the time of hiring. It stands to reason that job seekers who demonstrate needed competencies (the behaviors of superior employees) are more likely to be welcomed by peers, fit into the culture, perform well, and remain in the job or with the organization longer than those hired just because they're available.

A variety of resources—and consultants—offer assistance with an organization's competency-building process. Depending upon time and cost limitations, an employer may use focus groups, behavioral-event interviews, surveys, or expert systems to define the organization's core competencies (those skills and behaviors that set one organization's employees apart from all others in their field), as well as job-specific competencies for each position, including those of superior performers.

To maximize the value of using competencies, weave them into the entire employee life cycle:

- ADVERTISE FOR COMPETENCIES. Advertise more than the job description—describe the behaviors of superior performers.

- INTERVIEW FOR COMPETENCIES. Ask behavior-based questions—not belief-based questions.

- CHECK REFERENCES FOR COMPETENCIES. Verify competencies by asking behavior-based questions of past employers.

- REWARD PERFORMANCE OF COMPETENCIES. Use spot rewards such as tickets to performances or higher raises for consistent use of competencies.

- TRAIN EMPLOYEES TO FURTHER DEVELOP COMPETENCIES.

- USE COMPETENCIES AS THE BASIS FOR SUCCESSION PLANNING.

Remember, it is cheaper in the long run to train for hard skills and hire for competencies.

Use Simulations and Virtual Reality, so "What You See Is What You Get"

New-hire turnover is the most expensive turnover of all because the organization absorbs all the costs of recruiting—but reaps no benefits from the new hire. What can an employer do to reduce the number of false starts? There are many factors over which employers have no control, such as counteroffers or interview offers from other employers, but they can reduce the mismatch between the job as described and the job as experienced.

If the purpose of the interview process is to determine whether the candidate can and will do the job and whether he or she will fit in, then the interview must be conducted to elicit that information for both the organization and the candidate. The interview process itself must honestly communicate this message: "what you see, hear, and experience is what you will get on the job." Job simulations during the interview process should provide the necessary virtual reality—they will then "screen in" those candidates who perform well but do not interview well.

Too many interviews take place in restaurants, airports, conference rooms, or areas other than the true work environment. While this approach provides privacy, it leaves too much to the candidate's imagination. If seeing the work environment and getting a feel for the job and one's peers are not parts of the process, it is too easy for both the interviewer and the job seeker to avoid discussing the negative aspects of the job. This is particularly true in interviews for high-turnover positions. Urgency to fill open positions can also cause a rush to offer and pressure to accept without adequate information about the day-to-day realities on the job.

Often, high-turnover positions are in customer service, manufacturing, IT, sales, or other functions where large numbers of similarly skilled employees work together—although even independent contributors may have high turnover. In either case, there are always star performers whom the organization would like to clone through the hiring process. Start with a group discussion with the department head and top performers of the job in question, or brainstorm with the incumbent. Ask about the basic clusters of activities—and which are the most challenging. Gather as much information as needed to determine what type of simulation is appropriate to provide the candidate with a realistic glimpse of the day-to-day activities required to be successful on the job.

Simulations have been used to interest candidates in positions as varied as flying jets and telemarketing. What types of simulations adequately portray the job experience—and meet legal requirements? Four types of simulations allow employers to see how candidates will perform on the job:

1. REAL WORK ASSIGNMENTS. Many jobs cannot be fully explained in an interview, nor will meetings with peers and tours of the work environment suffice. Even experienced candidates may find that one job of the same description is not the equivalent of another. Too often, assumptions on the part of the employer or candidate prevent the full and honest discussion of issues such as the range of tasks, need for accuracy, and noise level of the work environment. If asked, candidates will tell you that they want the answers to the following questions: "What will be my real tasks, and who are the people I will work with every day?"

   Paid or unpaid projects, or spending a day "test-driving" the job, may provide the employer and candidate with solid information about how well the candidate fits with the work itself. (Clearly, some candidates will decline unpaid work assigned by a prospective employer.) Each party has an opportunity to experience the other's work style and quality standards.

   It is not uncommon for management-level candidates to be asked to draft a proposed marketing plan or proposed sales plan. Public relations firms often request a project in addition to writing samples. Projects can vary from rewrites of press releases or other collateral materials to research and writing. A call center might have a qualified candidate spend six or more hours listening in and actively working the phones. Initially, candidates monitor calls and hear experienced call center employees respond, solve problems, and close sales. Later in the simulation, the candidate might handle one or more calls alone.

2. IN-BOX EXERCISES. Executives and managers are often asked to complete in-box exercises as part of the interview process. In-box exercises may last for an hour or up to one day and are intended to mimic the volume and types of decisions that are required of managers within the same time period. Exercises may include handling interruptions, filling out paperwork, determining which items to delegate or defer, prioritizing, and other realistic activities. Often, external consultants score these exercises and provide a detailed analysis of the results to make the employer aware of the strengths and weaknesses of the candidate.

3. MEETING LEADERSHIP. Sales managers and other managers are often individuals with technical skills who lack the communication skills needed in group situations. Because meeting facilitation is a critical element of many management positions, some employers include a meeting as part of the interview process. Asking candidates to facilitate a meeting can be helpful for both the candidate and the organization. Clearly, this tactic should be reserved for finalists. The individual needs to be prepared with an agenda or be given enough information to create his or her own agenda.

Although it is a little different as an interview tactic, meeting leadership is very revealing. An observer must be assigned to the meeting to record the activity. Does the candidate involve everyone in discussion? Does the candidate pontificate or otherwise hog the floor? Does the candidate ignore women, people of color, or any other class? Does the candidate handle questions well? How does the staff react to him or her? Get their feedback. When a group is prepared for this part of the interview process, their feedback can be an excellent tie-breaker in the case of two otherwise equally qualified candidates.

4. JOB SHADOWING. Job shadowing is one of the most common and more helpful means of ensuring that the candidate fully understands the range of job responsibilities as well as what to expect

during a typical day or week. Often, finalists for sales positions spend time shadowing an experienced sales representative. Candidates appreciate the opportunity to discuss on-the-job issues such as schedule, necessary job skills, technologies used, and type of clients and prospects. Sales candidates in particular find it valuable to be on-site during sales calls. Job shadowing works well for a wide range of positions. The employer gains additional insights and comments from an experienced employee, and the candidate has the opportunity to learn enough about the position to make an informed decision about an offer.

Once you select a format for the specific simulation, be sure to have your corporate or labor attorney review it to ensure that no candidate will experience discrimination and that the simulation actually reflects the job itself. Make sure the candidates understand the criteria being used, the time allotted for their experience, and when and how they will be told of their results. If possible, plan to have a diverse team evaluate the results of any simulations.

Assessments: What Works, When to Use Them, and What Is Legal

Employers want a foolproof way to hire the right person for the job. Too frequently, an off-the-shelf assessment is used to determine an applicant's fit with the open position without confirming the assessment's effectiveness or accuracy. There is no silver-bullet assessment available from any vendor—if there were, it would be well known. Assessments benefit the organization most when they are used in conjunction with an interview process. In addition, selection and use of the appropriate assessment for each position are critical in order to minimize the risk of legal action from applicants who are not hired.

Assessments are intended to augment the interview process by providing information that is difficult to uncover in an interview. The interview process for a position that requires proficiency in math, grammar, or spelling but not a college degree can logically include tests or skills assessments. Rarely would a college graduate be required to take assessments for basic math or grammar, but a degreed applicant for an electrical engineering position is often expected to take a basic engineering assessment. More commonly, however, employers feel confident about verifying the candidate's hard skills through the interview and reference checking process but want more information about personality fit.

The selection process for a professional football player might include a review of his or her previous experience, personal interviews, a physical examination, a personality test, an interest test, and a simulation or tryout with the team. The selection process for a front-line manager might include a review of previous performance, at least one interview, an intelligence test, an interest test, a personality test, and a simulated in-box exercise. Selecting an appropriate testing tool is critical to the successful outcome of the exercise as well as to ensure that the applicant's legal rights are protected.

Literally thousands of personality assessments are available through catalogs, Web sites, or consultants. Very few, however, have proved both reliable and valid enough to justify any claim to accurate predictions of behavior and performance. A reliable assessment provides scores that do not change over time. A valid assessment measures what it was designed to measure. Inappropriate assessments may measure irrelevant competencies or psychological parameters. Worse, they may discriminate against racial or ethnic groups or violate candidates' rights to privacy. In order to determine an assessment's reliability and validity, ask to see the list of research studies performed on the assessment; 20 to 30 studies by recognized professionals is desirable.

When evaluating a generic personality assessment, consider the personality theory the assessment is used to measure. Make sure that it is designed to measure normal personality; tools used to measure abnormal personality may put your organization at risk from a legal standpoint. The most commonly recognized—or "Big Five"—factors in normal personality are emotional stability, extraversion, agreeableness, contentiousness, and openness to experiences. While these factors may be given different labels, most personality psychologists have reached agreement on their use.

Many service providers sell generic assessments to predict ability to achieve occupational success in fields such as sales, management, and customer service. Other providers will assist in developing a profile that is unique to your organization as a means of predicting success in a specific position.

Because each person's behavior is influenced by personality as well as environment, the personal characteristics of the top performer in one organization are likely to be different from those of the top performer in another, depending upon the corporate cultures. The result is that generic assessments may be best suited for use in organizations that do not have distinctive cultures. For example, a successful product sales representative in an organization with a numbers-oriented (daily sales-calls quota) sales strategy may have a difficult time being successful in an organization that focuses on relationship development, repeat sales, and long-term client relationships. The personality characteristics needed to succeed in one sales situation may not match those needed in another sales situation.

Too much reliance on assessment results—or the use of a tool that does not measure appropriate characteristics—may screen out potentially successful employees. An international HR consulting firm that used several assessments to determine position fit nearly declined a seasoned sales candidate whose scores differed from its profile. Entreaties by others in management, who knew the past performance of the individual, prevailed—and he quickly rose to become a regional sales star! His 10-year tenure with the company—during which he not only set sales records but also facilitated many sales training sessions for other offices in his region—is testimony to the need to use common sense along with well-known personality profiles when evaluating an individual.

If your organization chooses to develop a customized profile for specific positions, select an experienced consultant to assist with the process and insist that he or she monitor the effectiveness of the resulting tool. Using data collected in a systematic manner from top performers, the consultant should be able to create a tool that will identify the personal characteristics most critical to top performance in the specific position. Check with your labor attorney to ensure that the use of specific assessments for specific positions is on solid legal ground.

With the addition of results tracking, the organization will be able to determine the effectiveness of the assessment tool in selecting successful individuals. If you can improve the performance of new employees in key positions, the rewards of using assessments will outweigh the work required to select the correct tool.

If your organization is not satisfied with the recruiting results, a review of processes—including input from hired candidates and those who declined offers—can do a great deal to increase the chances of success. Chapter Five builds on these processes and examines them in detail.

ONLY YOU
WILL DO!

There was a time when decisions were justified by statements such as "It's not personal; it's just business." Today, it's all personal. The New Economy is all about individual possibility and the experience of work. Just as organizations are realizing that sales and marketing success depends upon individualization and customer intimacy, Employers of Choice know that their overall success depends upon specific individuals in specific positions and the organization's degree of employee intimacy. The interview process offers an opportunity to get to know the full range of the candidate's capabilities and to begin the relationship with him or her as a person.

Developing and asking the right questions are important, but a series of well-conducted interviews is not enough to sway a candidate who has several options. Filling the ranks with high-quality additions to staff—and keeping them onboard—is a fundamental element of becoming an EOC. Once the baseline interview process is in place, how do organizations differentiate themselves from other employers and land sought-after candidates to fill key positions? Starting with the interview process and negotiations, this chapter will focus on the ways that EOCs send the message "Only *you* will do!"

Wow by Wooing

Assume that a candidate is caught in a career decision face-off between equally respected EOCs. The job responsibilities are the same, the pay is the same, and the locations are similar. There is no discernible difference between the two jobs, and the candidate is having a tough time making a choice. If you were the candidate, how would you decide? You would decide with your heart!

Once the right person has been identified for a position, assume that your organization has stiff competition. A top candidate probably does have more than one offer, or a second offer is just about to be presented. Act quickly to stand out as the only logical place for this person to work! Make him or her feel wooed; make him or her say, "Wow!"

Your organization may be an EOC in the making—not yet an Employer of Choice. Your organization may not have the best location. It may pay competitive, but not above-market, salaries. You may be offering a challenging turnaround situation. Whatever your organization's situation, use the techniques of EOCs to hire top talent. Job tasks are available anywhere—but relationships are not. EOCs know how to woo—and wow—top candidates from the moment of first contact. Wow them by unexpectedly wooing them!

If your employees regularly pass through a lobby where job candidates typically wait to be interviewed, encourage your employees to greet the job seekers. A simple opener of, "You look great! Are you applying for a position here? Best of luck!" will make any job seeker feel welcome. Introduce a top candidate to (prepared) managers and executives who can comment on his or her achievements to date. A simple e-mail will alert managers of the expected time of the candidate's tour and introduction. Wow the candidate with stories of the accomplishments of his or her potential peers and recent project successes. Wow exceptional candidates with opportunities to develop specific skills, advance, and have an impact. Discuss the cross-functional teams that work on special projects with a respected member of the executive team. Assuming your organization has tuition reimbursement, discuss the option of starting an advanced degree program immediately upon hire. Ask the candidate about hobbies and interests—then introduce him or her to employees with similar interests. Let there be no question that the organization believes this candidate is the right person for the job and can see a future with him or her in it!

Wow 'em by

- Sending a limousine to pick up an out-of-town candidate at the airport

- Having the company president make the offer along with the hiring manager

- Sending Broadway show tickets with a note saying, "We'll put your name in lights if you join our team as Marketing Director!"

- Delivering a special book, plant, or flowers with an offer letter

- Having employees who know the candidate call and offer to answer questions and say how much the organization would benefit from having him or her onboard

- Inviting the candidate's spouse to tour the facilities and enjoy a quiet evening out with one or two employees and their spouses

A "wow experience" does not have to cost more than a few moments of time if it involves a telephone call from a respected colleague. It might require the cost of a book, dinner, or golf tournament tickets. Whatever it takes, it is less expensive than losing a top candidate to a competitor! When a candidate feels wooed, and when a candidate says, "Wow!" he or she is much more likely to accept your offer.

Good Save!

With today's tight hiring market, a newly filled position might become unfilled if the candidate

- Receives a counteroffer from his or her current employer

- Receives an equivalent or better offer from another EOC

- Receives offers to interview from other EOCs

- Starts but does not bond with his or her supervisor

- Starts but does not bond with his or her peers

- Finds the job to be very different from the description he or she was given during the interview process

Instead of bemoaning the fragility of accepted offers, EOCs improve the odds that the candidate will become a long-term employee by preparing themselves and the candidate for what lies ahead.

The job search process initiated by the "perfect" candidate does not magically disappear upon acceptance of your organization's offer. Frequently, job seekers send out dozens of résumés, initiate a series of networking meetings, and create a small army of people who agree to keep their ears open for opportunities. These opportunities can be immediate but are more often spread out over a few months' time. Further, quick-thinking employers may counteroffer with new or enhanced positions when key employees resign.

To lower the likelihood of losing their hard-earned commissions, recruiters routinely prepare candidates for counteroffers. New employers also need to talk to candidates about the likelihood of a counteroffer at their current places of employment when they give notice. A brief reiteration of the reasons why the candidate made both choices—to leave the old job and to join the new organization—lessens the candidate's vulnerability to a counteroffer. New employers can lessen that chance even further by requesting a commitment from the candidate.

Fending off competitors' unexpected requests to interview is another likelihood that should be addressed by savvy employers. If a candidate seems perfect for one organization, the odds are good that one or more other employers will move quickly to make an offer.

It is not idle flattery to tell a candidate that additional offers may come his or her way. Repeat the reasons why this candidate would benefit from taking the position at GreatBiz, Inc., and ask for a commitment to decline other offers.

If at First You Don't Succeed—Repeat the Offer

When was the last time you interviewed the "perfect" candidate, got agreement to hire—but missed out because a competitor's offer was extended and accepted? Last week? Yesterday? Take a deep breath, put on your friendliest face, and wish the candidate all the best—with a twist! Here is how a critical sales hire was saved for one consulting firm:

"Jane, as you can imagine, we are very disappointed for ourselves but happy for you," said the Vice President of Sales at GreatBiz, Inc. "It was a pleasure talking with you and learning so much about your capabilities. We thought you would be a great fit for our organization and our opportunities were on target to enable you to achieve your goals. I know you need to make a decision that is the right one for your career and for your family. As we discussed, we are prepared to work with you regarding your schedule [or whatever issue was presented in the interviews] and feel certain that a fair arrangement can be worked out. You have a lot to bring to the table, so I am not surprised that another employer made you an offer. Just know that we want the best for you. Let's stay in touch—and if you reconsider, call me because we continue to be very interested in working with you!"

Over the next three days, Jane received three upbeat, supportive telephone messages from other company executives who had been impressed with her accomplishments, capabilities, and potential. The calls were friendly, expressed congratulations—and offered to answer any questions she might have about GreatBiz, Inc., in case she changed her mind about accepting the other company's offer. She was cordial but distant, so the assumption was that she might not relent. She called on Day Four to ask for a meeting to discuss how her scheduling concerns might be handled *if* she decided to take the offer from GreatBiz, Inc. After brief negotiation, she declined the first accepted offer and accepted the amended offer from GreatBiz, Inc.!

Don't give up without a fight! Too many employers continue to think that if they act vague or disinterested, the candidate will become the pursuer. Not in a seller's market! Too many employers assume that if they throw enough money at a candidate, the offer will be accepted. Not when your competition is an Employer of Choice. Listen to what the candidate says about current working conditions, work styles, personality styles, goals, and preferences. Take the time to think about the individual candidate, his or her interests, and create a "wow experience" that suits the person.

EOCs know the importance of continued contact during the two-week notice period while the new hire winds down projects and responsibilities at the old organization. Invite him or her to participate in meetings, fill out benefits paperwork, inspect his or her office, meet more people, or attend a company outing. Stay in touch! This initiates the bonding process and forms a protective shield against the inevitable barrage of invitations to interview that the new hire will receive once other employers learn of his or her availability.

Good Start!

A joke that has been circulating among HR professionals goes like this:

> An HR manager dies and goes to the Pearly Gates. Saint Peter says, "We have a new policy. You must choose between Heaven and Hell. We will show you Hell first." The HR manager goes to Hell, is greeted warmly by the Devil, and is given a tour. All the people are happy and friendly; they are wearing great clothes, playing golf, and clearly enjoying themselves. Next, the HR manager goes to Heaven, where the scene is much as she had expected. Everyone is wearing a flowing robe, harp music is playing in the background, and the atmosphere is serene. Asked by Saint Peter which place she prefers, the HR manager chooses Hell. She is instantly transported there—but the scene is completely different: no one speaks to her, it is dirty and hot, and there are sounds of wailing in the background. She asks the Devil, "What happened? Hell was so terrific when I was here before." "That's because we were recruiting you," says the Devil.

New hires should not confuse their first few days on the job with their idea of Hell! EOCs plan the first two weeks of a new hire's tenure with the organization. They do not commit the cardinal sin of allowing a new hire to report on Day One to a supervisor who is on vacation. This is the extreme version of the familiar "hit the ground running" scenario that assumes the new employee—at any level—has just been hired in a pure skills-for-money trade and consequently anyone with the right skills could do the job. What a letdown! No one is likely to adopt the "orphan" employee. The "sink or swim" approach may have worked when jobs were difficult to find—but today, no one will tolerate being ignored or treated as if anyone with the same skill set could do the job.

Wise employers formally match new hires at any level with a sponsor who will make sure that the new hire assimilates well and has a sounding board for questions and concerns. The sponsor might confirm that the workspace is ready, take the new hire to lunch on the first day, and check in every few days to verify that the rest of the orientation period is going well. A sponsor could be a peer or from any level in the organization. The critical ingredient is the sponsor's *willingness* to assume these duties; he or she must also have considerable organizational pride and be knowledgeable about the organization.

Orientation

Today, every hire is a critical hire. Upon starting a new position, the new employee must have several experiences that confirm the decision to accept your organization's offer. EOCs develop an orientation schedule of at least two weeks that includes tours, introductions, meetings with key people, lunch appointments, systems training (for online calendars, phone, and email), and opportunities to provide feedback. Formal organization orientation and any necessary skills training are also scheduled. Every opportunity should be taken to make the individual feel welcome, valued, and needed. EOCs know how important it is for the new employee to bond both with his or her supervisor and with peers or other key players. Discrepancies between the job description and the reality of the job itself must be minimized.

The orientation process should enhance the new hire's sense of trust, confidence, and belonging. It should maximize his or her connections within the organization and shorten the learning curve toward full productivity. Orientation involves the participation of HR, the supervisor, and often the organization's officers. The process has five goals:

1. To create a favorable impression of the organization, its history, its culture, and its work

2. To introduce the new hire to peers, co-workers, and subordinates

3. To integrate individuals into workgroups

4. To provide an overview of benefits

5. To provide solid grounding in the new position

Coordination between HR and the new hire's manager will ensure that all critical information is covered. Many organizations use a first-day checklist for this purpose. At the end of the first day, the checklist should be signed by HR and the supervisor and returned to HR for the employee file. A sample checklist is shown in Figure 6.

Onboard and Committed

Personal attention says, "Only *you* will do!" There is nothing equal to the enthusiasm of a new employee anticipating the future with a new employer. It is a magical time for employers, too. Like fishing, hiring takes preparation, the right bait, practice, expert technique, patience, and readiness to move quickly. The best part of fishing is the same as the best part of hiring: bragging rights! In the case of hiring, however, both the "fisher" and the "fish" get to brag!

FIGURE 6

Sample Orientation Checklist

Employee Name: _____

Department: _____ **Date:** _____

Day One of employment: Please review all of the following items with the new employee; then sign and return this form to HR to be filed in the employee's personnel file.

Activity/Topic	Responsibility
Greeting: Extend a warm greeting to the new employee.	☐ Supervisor
Tour: Provide a tour of the entire facility as well as an overview of the company history, products/services, and direction.	☐ Supervisor
Introductions: Introduce the new employee to peers, co-workers, and subordinates.	☐ Supervisor
Department overview: Briefly explain the department's purpose, organization, and relationship to other departments.	☐ Supervisor
Department layout: Review the new employee's immediate work area as well as the location of the cafeteria, restrooms, closets or lockers, fire exits, etc.	☐ Supervisor
Job overview: Review the new employee's job description and essential job functions; provide a written job description; explain training availability (if appropriate).	☐ Supervisor
Phone lists: Share appropriate telephone numbers and lists.	☐ Supervisor

(continues)

FIGURE 6 (CONT'D)

Sample Orientation Checklist

Employee Name: _____

Department:_____ Date: _____

Day One of employment: Please review all of the following items with the new employee; then sign and return this form to HR to be filed in the employee's personnel file.

Activity/Topic	Responsibility
Department procedures: Review hours of work, flexible work schedules (if applicable), tele-commuting options (if applicable), lunch and break periods, general work schedules, overtime, reporting absences, telephone procedures, progress reports, and performance reviews.	☐ Supervisor
Compensation procedures: Discuss pay schedule and salary raise process.	☐ Supervisor or HR
Overview of organization policies: Provide an employee handbook, review important policies, discuss the review process and timetable; ask the employee to complete any outstanding forms; gather emergency contact information.	☐ Supervisor or HR
Employee benefits: Review medical benefits, life insurance, pension/401(k), waiting period for benefits, vacations, and holiday schedules.	☐ Supervisor or HR
Other items: Any organization-specific or department-specific items not on this list.	☐ Supervisor or HR

Day One orientation was completed on _____

_____
Department Manager/Supervisor

_____
Human Resources Representative

CHAPTER SIX

SURFING FOR RECRUITING
RESULTS ONLINE

Technology has transformed our economy. By the end of the 20th century, organizations of all sizes were reaping the benefits of decades of information technology (IT) training and hardware investment. Once basic IT skills and the PC entered businesses and homes, users of all ages were propelled onto the World Wide Web. Unlike radio, which took 38 years to attract 50 million listeners, the Internet took only 4 years to claim 50 million "clickers." The ease of use and range of information and services available, combined with the e-commerce applications from businesses and not-for-profit organizations, led very quickly to hundreds of billions of dollars in business-to-business sales. One of the first successful commercial uses of the Internet, however, was as a recruitment tool!

This chapter will look at employer Web strategies, including how to build a Web site with a career focus, how to drive candidate traffic to your site, and seven ways to e-cruit the best of the best candidates.

Employers of Choice automate as many processes as possible in order to free time for strategic recruiting activities. The explosive growth of online recruiting venues for employers has provided options that work with more speed and less expense than other, traditional means. Most important, the Internet provides ways to "push" candidates to employers, representing an important addition to the traditional "pull" methods of advertising and recruiting. Push sites invite candidates to register their résumés once to receive e-mailed notice of matching positions over time. This removes the job seeker's hassle of constantly searching the same site for job openings. Push technology benefits both candidates and organizations because it increases the odds of making a match.

While the Internet can be used as a giant shopping mall where employers can window-shop for employees at hundreds of thousands of personal Web pages, a faster and more focused method is to look at job and résumé Internet supersites and industry-related Web sites. To start leveraging the power of the Internet, however, an EOC must have a solid career Web site dedicated to posting current job openings and developing relationships with future hires.

Build It and They Will Come

It worked in the movies—but how can an organization build a terrific Web site and also push candidates to it? Most companies have a Web site that is e-commerce focused—or may have an "Internet" brochure and nothing more. How effective is this as a candidate magnet? How much candidate response is it generating? Has the site reduced employment costs or increased efficiency? No? It is time to get wired and get hiring! Here are some steps you'll need to take:

- SELECT A WEB SITE DEVELOPER. Even if you have a Web site, you may need help from specialists to produce the recruitment site. If your IT department does not have the skills—or the time—select another provider. Rates vary, so interview several companies. Go to the *Advertising Age* Internet publication *Net Marketing*, at **www.netb2b.com** to check median rates and view a list of developers in major metropolitan areas.

- MAKE THE EMPLOYMENT SECTION EASY TO ACCESS. A simple directory structure such as www.yourcompanyname.com/careers/ will speed access to job openings and online applications and bypass the home page. If your organization has multiple sites, consider enabling job searches by city.

- DESCRIBE POSITIONS IN DETAIL. Reduce unqualified responses by providing full job descriptions including needed competencies.

- PROVIDE AN ONLINE APPLICATION. Capture as many candidates as possible as quickly as possible by eliminating the need for a résumé. Be sure to allow résumés as attachments.

- REWARD APPLICANTS. Free articles, cool toys, mini-training tools, online seminars, and similar inducements are terrific rewards for submitting résumés.

- UPLOAD RÉSUMÉS DIRECTLY TO YOUR RÉSUMÉ MANAGEMENT SYSTEM. Save time and effort by linking the e-mailed résumés to your Resumix, Res Trac, or other tracking system.

- PROVIDE CONTACT INFORMATION. E-mail, fax numbers, or telephone numbers often make the difference for hesitant candidates who have questions.

- PUBLICIZE YOUR CAREER SITE. Press releases, mailings, strategic use of the company's URL address, announcements to employees, and links to career hubs such as Career Mosaic (**www.careermosaic.com**) or the Monster Board (**www.monster.com**) will generate traffic and candidates for your new career site.

- USE WORD OF MOUTH. At career fairs, professional organization meetings, and speaking engagements, tell everyone about your employment site.

- DEVELOP AN EFFECTIVE EMPLOYMENT SITE. Unattractive, clumsy, time-consuming employment sites turn off Internet-savvy candidates. In this case, time is more than money; time is candidates! Effective employer sites have five main features:
  —SPEED: fast-loading pages
  —USABILITY: ease of navigation
  —DESIGN: great visuals
  —CONTENT: comprehensive information
  —FUNCTIONALITY: interactive communication through e-mail and online applications

An organization's site makes a first impression that must not be undervalued, because the price paid in lost opportunities (lost candidates!) is too great. Hire a professional Web site developer and designer (preferably with considerable job-site experience) to ensure that your site keeps job seekers coming back.

Eight employers have been showing others what works when it comes to Internet hiring:

- Cisco Systems at **www.cisco.com** (more than 80 percent of their hires come through their site)

- IBM or Club CyberBlue at **www.ibm.com** (IBM hires more than 1,500 new employees per year through their site)

- Dell at **www.dell.com** (Dell hires more than 1,000 employees per year through the Web)

- Hewlett-Packard at **www.hp.com**

- Intevac at **www.intevac.com**

- CIDCO at **www.cidco.com**

- Silicon Graphics at **www.sgi.com**

- Texas Instruments at **www.ti.com**

These sites are attractive from a candidate's viewpoint because their designers understood that employment screening is a two-way process: candidates use the Internet to screen potential employers. There are ways to make it easy for potential candidates to "screen in" your organization.

West Coast employers were among the first to develop a strong Internet hiring presence. They matched their product and service branding efforts with the look and feel of their online hiring process. They made the hiring process cool—not stressful and mysterious. They assigned "buddies" to interested job seekers and used every conceivable means to attract new graduates and experienced candidates to their Web site.

It is easy to use your organization's Web site to provide information to interested candidates. Provide a link from the home page to the jobs page. In addition to the expected organization information (history, timeline, mission statement, and products and services overview), provide a window into the organization's culture. A message from the president is a minimum. Help interested candidates picture themselves working at your organization. Photos from company events, reprinted articles about the organization, quotes from employees, and a list of awards presented to the organization or individual employees all paint a picture of what it is like to work there. Community information, maps to your location, and parking information make the process friendlier.

Provide a list of upcoming job fairs where interested candidates may look for your booth. Use well-written job descriptions that include the competencies needed for the position. Salary range information minimizes disappointment. Make sure that you feature an Equal Employment Opportunity (EEO) statement to attract a diverse response.

Enable easy e-mail communication if the candidate has questions. Online applications and registration for future openings will encourage candidates to submit résumés. Corporate Web sites are cost-effective, reduce hiring-cycle time and push candidates to your organization for consideration. Candidates share information about great sites with other candidates and revisit the ones with the best content and ease of use.

Seven Ways to E-cruit the Best of the Best

Today, with Internet access provided through offices, libraries, cyber cafés, and home computers, employers with positions that require computer skills can feel confident that appropriate job seekers will be using the Internet as a tool. Whether an employer hires hundreds of individuals per week—as many national organizations do—or has ongoing but small hiring needs, the Internet makes sense as a time-sensitive, cost-effective recruiting tool. Use it to find the best of the best candidates. Here are seven e-cruiting tools.

BUILD LINKS TO YOUR ORGANIZATION'S WEB PAGE
Start with the right ore to make the finest steel. Recruiting is a numbers game. The more qualified candidates an organization has available to interview, the better its selection decisions will be, resulting in

a high-quality employee pool with which to grow the business. In the current low-unemployment marketplace, with so few active job seekers, employers must use every tool at their disposal to increase the number of appropriate résumés available for review. Links are an excellent tool for driving traffic and résumés to an organization's Web site.

Most employers have determined that it is in their best interests to put their Web site addresses on everything from print, television, and radio advertisements to promotional items such as letterhead and employee clothing. Customers and interested job seekers want access to organizational information 24 hours a day, seven days a week. They want information when they want it, where they want it, and how they want it—which is privately, discreetly, and without hassle. Most organizations understand that 24-hour information and response capability is crucial to both sales and recruiting success. While there will be a certain number of job seekers who know the names of interesting organizations to research as potential employers, many more job seekers find employers as a side benefit of other Web surfing. They click on a link to get information, and voilà—they enter your new career Web site.

It is relatively inexpensive for an organization's IT staff to add links to documents, lists, or articles on the Web. To maximize your organization's exposure to potential employees, consider requesting links from:

- PROFESSIONAL ORGANIZATIONS. Especially if your employees are members, professional trade groups might be willing to offer links on their Web sites to members' employers as part of their online directories or employment advertisements.

- COMMUNITY ORGANIZATIONS. If your company supports community organizations, they may be willing to offer links on their Web sites to show appreciation for your support.

- ONLINE DIRECTORIES. Online telephone, yellow-page, or community directories may be willing to add a link to your organization's Web site as a bonus for your listing in the directory.

- MAGAZINE ARTICLES. Links to organizations' Web sites are often buried in online articles. Ask for links if an online magazine publishes articles written by your employees, or if your organization is featured in an article.

- MUTUAL LINK RELATIONSHIPS. Employers that are proud of their employees' community and professional affiliations often publish on the company Web site a list of organizations to which employees belong. These organizations may allow a return link on their Web sites in exchange for one on yours. Other mutual linking opportunities exist between organizations and their vendors, who showcase each other's work by allowing visitors to one site to click over to the other site. Colleges and universities present linking opportunities as well. If their Web sites carry employer advertisements, they often allow embedded links to the Web sites of featured employers—and those employers in turn can place links to university Web sites on their intranet sites to encourage employees to explore or even participate in higher education. Think about the linking opportunities that may exist for your organization, and talk to others about linking for mutual benefit!

USE ONLINE SERVICES, CHAT ROOMS, AND LISTSERVS TO LOCATE CANDIDATES

Matching an organization's job openings with the perfect candidates has never been easy. Depending upon your business or the specific types of positions your organization needs to fill, sorting through the vast array of Internet recruiting resources can be daunting. It is vital that an organization have its own Web site, and the Web site must be candidate-friendly. And, if they are to be aggressive recruiters, employers cannot stop with just having a Web site. For recruiting purposes, it is vital for a company to locate multiple sources of plentiful candidates to fill current and anticipated job openings. The third step is to determine how to use technology to push candidates to your site—literally, how to immediately inform armies of appropriate candidates when a job opening is posted. Many employers subscribe to a variety of online services, as well as targeted chat rooms and listservs. E-mail your employees to ask for recommendations and to find out which sites interest them.

Through online services, employers are able to advertise openings and/or review hundreds of thousands of fresh résumés. The best sites offer ease of access to both employers and job seekers and allow them to sort résumés and search for openings by city, job title, educational level, salary requirements, keywords, or skills.

Typically, job seekers are not charged for registering their résumés, but employers pay fees for either advertising specific numbers of positions per month or advertising as many positions as desired for one year. For little or no cost, advertisers then have access to the companion résumé bank sponsored by the same service. Employers benefit from access to a wide variety of résumés, and candidates benefit from the employers' ease in matching jobs to their skills. Some online services provide résumé-matching services to employers (a must if there are tens of thousands of appropriate résumés to sort). Most online services do not limit access to résumés but charge higher fees to non-advertisers.

New résumé banks are springing up (and merging or shutting down!) every day, but some of the largest résumé and job banks with the greatest range of professionals in different disciplines are

- JobOptions (previously E-SPAN) at **www.joboptions.com** matches candidates to employers by using criteria submitted by the candidate. It then sends résumés to employers after the candidate gives permission; refreshes résumés after six months.

- Monster Board at **www.monster.com** posts more than 500,000 résumés and 25,000 job openings and offers weekly, geography-specific virtual career fairs for employers.

- Career Mosaic at **www.careermosaic.com** draws candidates with more than 70,000 jobs that are updated daily.

- Hot Jobs at **www.hotjobs.com** keeps great candidates coming back because of its Hot Lock feature, which restricts certain companies from seeing their résumés (current employers, for example), and creates a personal home page for job seekers.

For more information and an alphabetized list of job sites on the Web, check out Best Jobs USA at **www.bestjobsusa.com**, or visit CareerXRoads at **www.careerxroads.com** to locate both résumé and job advertisement sites. Another site that catalogs online job services available for employers and employees is the Riley Guide (**www.dbm.com/jobguide/**). Best Internet Recruiting (**www.bestrecruit.com**) lets employers create job advertisements and post them simultaneously to multiple sites.

Employers who need recruiting surveys, tools, trend information, or recruiting newsletter information may contact

- Employment Management Association (EMA, a division of the Society for Human Resource Management) at **www.shrm.org/ema**

- Interbiznet at **www.interbiznet.com**

- Recruiters Network at **www.recruitersnetwork.com**

- iLogos at **www.ilogos.com**

- Online Recruiting Strategist at **www.hunt-scanlon.com**

Quite often, highly skilled candidates do not post their résumés to Internet sites. Their telephones ring and their e-mail boxes are full anyway because they are known by other means. Chat rooms and listservs have become "Web watercoolers," where candidates and recruiters mingle, drawn by shared interests. These virtual communities are at the beginning stages, so there are few rules of conduct. While some employers sponsor chat rooms and listservs as a way of gaining exposure to candidates, others simply make good use of existing ones.

Chat rooms focus on everything from *Star Trek* episodes to specific industries and careers. If you have never used a chat room, check out **www.otn.net/chatroom/help.html** for some tips. Chat rooms often ask for your name and photograph, but these fields can be left blank if "silent" looking and listening are acceptable. Your name will be required to join a discussion (a photo is optional). Use InfoSeek, Excite, Lycos, or Yahoo to search for appropriate chat rooms. Enter keywords such as your industry or the position that is open. For more manageable results (it is possible to get tens of thousands of chat rooms in response to searches), try online services such as AOL or CompuServe for career chat rooms.

Newsgroups, or Usenet, are networks of discussion groups that can be found by searching specialized Web-based services such as

- Dejanews.com (**www.dejanews.com**)

- Tile.net (**www.tile.net/news**)

- Liszt (**www.liszt.com/news**)

All it takes to participate in a newsgroup is an e-mail account and a Web browser. Newsgroups can be very slow to reply to questions, but your questions are usually answered, and candidates can be found among newsgroup users.

Listservs are online discussion groups formed around industries or disciplines. To exchange ideas and get questions answered, sign on to an HR listserv such as HR-NET or D-Recruit, or check out **www.liszt.com** to review more than 70,000 different types of listservs. Other sources include Tile.net (**www.tile.net/list**) and the AOL Mailing List Directory (**ifrit.web.aol.com/mid/production/mid-general.html**), which has more than 3,500 mailing lists. Signing up for announcements is one terrific option for employers, so that your organization can post its own e-mail announcements, the online equivalent of press releases.

On an ongoing basis, ask your peers, recent new hires, and HR consultants for their site advice so that your organization will maximize the number and quality of candidates available via the Internet. Diversify your site investments to maximize returns. Plan to change your recruiting strategy as the Internet changes.

HIRE A DATA MINER TO DIG UP CANDIDATE GOLD

While many organizations have hired full-time Internet recruiters to surf for candidate résumés, a few have added researchers, or data miners, to seek, retrieve, and comb through databases, directories, job postings, Web site hits, and other organizations' Web pages for candidates. The goal is to produce entire lists of appropriate candidates as your job openings occur. Data miners create in-house candidate databases and combine them with subscriptions to Web databases to provide instant candidate profiles and résumés as jobs are posted.

HIRE FRESHLY MINTED GRADUATES ONLINE

College students have been driving the culture of Internet recruiting. By the fall of 1998, college seniors were telling employers, "If you're not on the Net, we don't know you exist." Access to employment opportunities through library, lab, and personal computers is so pervasive that many students ignore on-campus recruiting events because they have landed jobs months before the recruiters arrive on campus.

Many campus recruiting offices have given up on hard-copy job descriptions altogether and are opting for services such as Jobtrak (**www.jobtrak.com**). Students and alumni connect to Jobtrak through unique passwords. This free service for more than 650 college and university career centers addresses the hiring needs of more than 300,000 employers.

HIRE EXPERIENCE ONLINE

Professional organizations exist to help members hone their skills— and to facilitate career movement. Professional organizations also enable employers to target a specific population of potential new hires.

For years, most organizations published job openings in their newsletters and journals and offered formal or informal résumé matching for their members, but the process was cumbersome and slow. Too often, positions were already filled by the time of publication, or the response time of volunteer-staffed résumé-matching services failed to provide fresh résumés. Demand from members, combined with the willingness of fledgling webmasters to design low-cost Web pages and online résumé or job databases enabled professional organizations to develop excellent resources for both job seekers and employers.

Today, most professional organizations offer free résumé matching to members, as well as free or low-cost position listings to employers (members or not). Additionally, professional organizations often provide chat rooms where members may discuss topics and share resources and ideas. Recruiters who hang out in chat rooms often meet terrific candidates. Companies searching for appropriate sites may access Employer's Direct for links to the sites of professional organizations through **www.rpi.edu/dept/cdc/society/soca.html**.

Industry-specific job databases often target specific employee populations. These databases, as well as professional-organization Web sites, are perfect places for banner ads to attract interested candidates to an employer's Web site. By making its ad stand out and providing easy access to more information, an organization with one or more job openings can attract a targeted applicant population.

HIRE DIVERSE CANDIDATES ON THE WEB

Diversity, often an organizational hiring goal, can be enhanced using the Internet. Recruiting at known "diversity Web sites" enables an organization to target specific populations and job functions simultaneously. These sites allow employers to advertise openings or place banner ads to attract female, multilingual, or racially diverse employees. Consider recruiting through sites such as

- Society of Women Engineers (**www.swe.org**)
- Association for Women in Computing (**www.awc-hq.org**)
- Bilingual-Jobs (**www.bilingual-jobs.com**)
- The Black Collegian Online (**www.black-collegian.com**)
- Career Center for Workforce Diversity (**www.eop.com**)
- Careers Online (disability services) (**www.disserv.stu.umn.edu/ COL/index.html**)
- Saludos Web, which targets Hispanic job seekers (**www.saludos. com/webjob.html**)

AUTOMATE CANDIDATE SCREENING

Use of the Internet can dramatically reduce cost-per-hire because of the faster response time and the lower cost of technology compared to other people- and time-intensive means. Any steps of the initial screening process that can be automated should be streamlined to free recruiters and hiring managers for candidate relationship management, vital face-to-face interviewing, and the selection process.

Automation means reducing or eliminating the steps involving human interaction and paper résumés that bog down the hiring

CHAPTER SEVEN

FINDING NEW HIRES IN UNLIKELY PLACES

Necessity drives innovation! We no longer have time to test one potential employee resource at a time and then move on to another. We cannot rely solely on e-cruiting to bring in every candidate. The lack of qualified candidates for most positions has motivated many employers to utilize many different hiring tactics simultaneously. EOCs know that to maximize their candidate selection, they must multiply their recruiting strategies. In spite of the tight hiring market, there *are* enough qualified candidates—but they are not working for your company . . . yet!

Think about your current hiring resources. Compared to tactics used two years ago, what is your organization doing differently to fill positions at all levels? If you have not added a wide variety of resources to your recruiting repertoire, you are missing out on qualified candidates! Track results by source. Keep tabs not just on quantity but on *quality* of hires, including potential business gains—so that you know what to continue and what to eliminate in the future.

This chapter looks at 40 ways to find new hires in unlikely places. If you need quality people, these sources can help!

Recruit from Your Old Files

Old files are filled with hiring gold! Instead of just boxing them up and storing them, look at them in a new way. Use your files to re-recruit ex-employees, declines, and retirees and to reestablish contact with previously interested job seekers.

RE-RECRUIT EX-EMPLOYEES

While some employers occasionally rehire ex-employees, it is not the norm. The "Big Five" management consulting firm of Deloitte & Touche was the first organization to go public with rehiring as a national recruiting strategy in 1993. Still considered radical by many employers, re-recruiting ex-employees is one of the richest sources of competent hires.

Too often, employees who give notice are treated as pariahs and shown the door immediately upon resigning. Even those who are asked to work through their two-week notice period are frequently ignored by peers and supervisors or loaded up with assignments to complete before leaving. In either case, the unspoken message of "Don't let the door hit you on the way out" is quite clear. Many organizations have policies forbidding all ex-employees to come onto company property, including parking lots and reception areas, or have contact with current employees during work hours. While these policies may prevent some problems, they broadcast the message "And don't come back!" Everyone who is aware of the turnover can hear the organization's literal and figurative door slam shut.

It is not uncommon for managers to comment aloud to their staffs, "If John doesn't want to work here, then I/we don't want him here," or make similar statements that clearly inform current employees that once notice is given, all relationships are finished. These organizations are peopled with managers who would never consider making a counteroffer. This is short-sighted and wastes not only the organization's time and training investment but the ex-employee's client relationships and understanding of the culture as well. Organizations must leave the door open if they hope to recapture valuable individuals in the future.

Assuming that many voluntary separations are unplanned, inconvenient, and costly in terms of both "blue money," or invisible costs, and "green money," or visible costs, re-recruiting ex-employees is a winning strategy. Many organizations such as Deloitte & Touche have established policies and procedures to maximize the likelihood of successful re-recruiting.

Re-recruiting begins with civil, even caring, treatment of employees when they give notice. Supervisors at all levels must know how to respond, what transition meetings to conduct, and how to communicate to others in the department. A positive spin is absolutely necessary—with no sotto voce comments that negate the outward message.

Clearly, valuable employees should receive counteroffers. Informal conversations *held prior to formal exit interviews* may uncover issues that can be reframed as the basis of a counteroffer. Counteroffers are not necessarily about dollars; often they reflect a need for a different assignment, physical location, or other non-monetary need. Even if the counteroffer is declined, the prudent manager continues to be gracious and states aloud that the employee would be welcome to return at a future time. One or more individuals must express the organization's position that the "door is open"—because returning is so unexpected and uncommon.

Many employers take their "employee boomerang" strategy to greater heights. They form alumni clubs that sponsor golf outings, cocktail parties, and other events for company expatriates, send newsletters to alumni, and otherwise keep in touch. To ensure that ex-employees are considered for openings, many organizations create a database of ex-employees and schedule formal contacts 12, 18, and 24 months after the employee resigns to invite him or her to consider specific job openings that are available at those times. Even if the ex-employee declines, he or she might be able to refer other candidates to fill openings.

RECRUIT DECLINES

It hurts to lose in the competition for great employees, but EOCs do not let it get in the way of future hiring! Keep the résumés and contact information for candidates who declined offers and set up a regular process of contacting them. You'll increase your odds of future hiring! Consider creating a special print or e-mail newsletter that keeps them informed of corporate accomplishments. Let them know,

"We wish you were here!" Make sure they're kept apprised of appropriate openings. These individuals could be pre-approved for instant hiring, depending upon the opening.

RE-RECRUIT RETIREES

By 2005, there will be more than 21 million people over the age of 55. Retirees rarely plan their retirements, and they often find that golf or other hobbies do not hold their interest. Retiring Baby Boomers—workaholics by many standards—have an especially difficult time with full-time free time. While some individuals need to earn extra dollars, most simply cannot walk away from the routines, intellectual enrichment, and socializing they find at work. Re-recruiting retirees—your own or those of other organizations—is a winning strategy to fill current openings. Travelers Companies allows retired employees to work up to 960 hours per year without affecting their pensions, while IBM considers its rehired retirees to be an "elite corps of managers," according to an article by Barry Dym in the *Boston Globe* (1998). Consider retirees as possible full-time employees, as well as consultants, job-sharing candidates, temporary workers, or even paid mentors.

As with voluntary ex-employees, retirees should be treated well prior to their last day, and the verbal welcome mat if they decide to return should be laid out in advance. Though many retirees may decline immediate part-time, full-time, or consulting employment, the message that the door will be open in the future must be stated repeatedly in order to increase the chances that they will return. This is especially true in organizations that lack a history of rehiring retirees.

Work with your corporate or labor attorney to develop a retiree rehiring program that benefits both the organization and the individual—and conforms to the changing requirements of Social Security. Depending upon the age of the individual, and the specifics of his or her retirement benefits, different work arrangements will be appropriate. Do not lower your requirements or standards, just raise your expectations of the possibilities! To learn more, contact **www.seniornet.com.**

KEEP RÉSUMÉS FOR TWO YEARS

Too often, both the candidate and the employer assume that the other party would not be interested in the future if a current job inquiry does not turn into a hire. Nothing could be more wrong! If a candidate accepted another position, he or she may be ready to move on in 18 to 24 months—or sooner, if the new job does not measure up to expectations! Likewise, employers may decline an applicant because of other candidates or timing—only to have later needs that provide an excellent fit. Recontact previously interested candidates at least annually.

Look Closer to Home

Your stressed-out recruiters need help! In fact, they need every employee's help to fill the pipeline with viable candidates. EOCs deputize their employees and create a recruiting posse!

IMPLEMENT AN EMPLOYEE REFERRAL PROGRAM THAT WORKS

Unconsciously, your employees enhance or destroy your organization's "magnetism," or ability to attract new hires, every day when they speak with their spouses, families, neighbors, or other members of professional and civic organizations. Their choice of words, their facial expressions, and the stories they tell either intrigue or put off their listeners, who are likely to be equally skilled, equally educated potential employees of your organization. Because every employee is a walking billboard for your organization, why not acknowledge this fact and motivate *conscious* recruiting behavior?

Employee referral programs take less time and effort and produce better-quality results for a lower cost than any other method of recruitment. Employee referral programs have been in existence for many years, but too few employers maximize the potential results because their referral programs are quiet programs that may be underfunded or are rarely discussed.

While employers willingly pay recruiters 25 percent or more of the annual salary of the candidate hired, they too often put low limits on payments to existing employees. Fifty dollars is *not* a motivator! Nor is a $200 television set. Neither is enough compensation to make the employee referral program a priority in existing employees' minds.

EOCs vary referral fees depending upon the level of difficulty filling specific positions. For example, hospitals in areas that have too few nurse anesthetists may pay thousands of dollars to employees who refer candidates. Their alternative is to pay thousands of dollars to specialized recruiters. While a recruiter is often effective, employee referrals have an edge because of the relationship between the candidate and the employee. No employee will deliberately refer someone who might fail in the position or within the culture of the organization. The employee's insider knowledge of the job seeker's past work history, personality, and preferences enhances the likelihood that the candidate will be a successful hire. Further, the bond between the new hire and the referring employee helps the new hire assimilate into the organization.

Many organizations pay existing employees half of the referral fee on the new employee's first day and half after six months or more. In theory, this delay encourages the more experienced employee to spend time mentoring the new hire and increases the chances that the candidate will succeed in his or her new position.

Opinions do differ on this point, however. Some experts favor immediate, full payout. According to Carolyn Koenig, vice president of human resources for MasterCard International in St. Louis, a change from delayed to immediate payout paid off. Referrals as a source of hires jumped from 10 percent to 42 percent of all hires during the first year! Koenig told the audience at the August 1999 Society for Human Resource Management (SHRM) 51st Annual Conference in Atlanta that employees feel a responsibility to refer the best candidates possible, but it is up to the supervisor to select the right person and integrate him or her into the new position.

Referral bonuses of $1,000, $4,000, and even $10,000 are common. Gifts such as weekend stays at a romantic bed-and-breakfast, VCRs, televisions, household appliances, video cameras, or a chance to win serious prizes such as cars or trips are also used as referral rewards. In addition to reviewing the amount paid to employees for referrals, organizations must review how the referral program is communicated in order to maximize its effectiveness.

Employee referral programs should be publicized regularly through the new-employee orientation process, employee handbook, newsletter, intranet, department meetings, contests, bulletin boards, internal postings of openings, external advertisements, stuffers in paychecks, and any other means of reminding employees to keep their eyes and ears open for appropriate potential hires.

While employees will oblige by referring potential candidates, there are ways to minimize problems with the program. To ensure that the employee receives credit for referrals, add a line to the application form: "Who referred you to our organization?" If Human Resources (HR) receives a résumé through an employee, be sure to track that fact in a database so the employee is rewarded if the referred candidate is hired.

To minimize the possibility of underqualified candidates, be very clear about the minimum requirements for the position—and then abide by those standards when selecting candidates to interview. Establish the understanding that all qualified candidates will have the opportunity to interview, but the best candidate will be hired regardless of the source.

Clearly, if the organization has engaged a recruiter for a search, but the best candidate is introduced by an employee, two fees might be paid. To avoid this expensive outcome, be sure to advertise all positions internally with a cut-off date for submission of applications. If no appropriate internal candidates emerge, or if there are no appropriate internal referrals, engage a recruiting firm or advertise in an appropriate medium as the next logical step.

To ensure maximum employee referrals, put the spotlight on the best employee-recruiters on a quarterly basis and consider holding annual competitions for most candidates referred—with an additional cash or other desirable prize for the employee who refers the most hired candidates for the year. You may decide to publish in the company newsletter either a group photograph of employees and referrals together, or a list of employees and the names of those they referred that month. Annually, spotlight the top five employee-recruiters and list their successes. By making a big deal of the program, you will generate competition, enthusiasm—and more quality employees!

Finally, arm your employees with brochures that picture your organization and provide an overview of the benefits and culture. Brochures sell products and services—and they can be used to help sell your organization to potential employees. A recruiting brochure should include your company's Web site address, where interested applicants may obtain details such as a mini-map to guide them to your door, parking information, contact names, e-mail addresses, and fax and telephone numbers. You should also include the organization's mission statement, founder's vision, commitment to the community, company awards, and other information of interest to potential employees at any level. Augment these brochures with a dated slip-in page that lists current job openings.

Offer to provide these brochures to realtors and the local chamber of commerce as inserts for their newcomer packets, to internal and external recruiters, and to all employees.

Challenge each employee to refer a minimum of one new employee per year—and watch your organization grow with qualified new hires!

HIRE FRIENDS . . . AND FAMILY, TOO

Many employers in tight hiring markets have found that eliminating rules prohibiting nepotism vastly expands their choices of candidates. Clear position requirements and a policy of hiring the most qualified candidates will keep this tactic on course. Family support can also encourage top performance. To ensure that there is a minimal downside to hiring family members, discuss potential areas of conflict during the interview process. Ensure that performance reviews are timely and accurate, and let all employees know that fairness is an organizational value and applies to all employees.

HIRE VIA LETTERS SENT TO ANNOUNCE NEW EMPLOYEES

When are employees most excited about working for your organization? In their first two weeks, their elation is palpable. By encouraging referrals from new hires as soon as they walk through your doors, your organization will grow quickly with high-quality employees. Ask whom they would hire from their previous workplace. Contact those individuals.

Another way to do this is to ask new hires for electronic disks listing the names of people in their personal network—those with whom they have regular contact. Send out a letter from your organization president to the people in that network, announcing the individual's new position. Include references to your company's culture, Web site, and desire to grow by adding equally qualified employees. Whether the new hire's personal network is composed of 10 names or several hundred names, these letters work!

RECRUIT REFERENCES FROM GREAT HIRES
Track and follow up on references from great hires—and even the ones who got away—because great candidates know great future hires. During the interview, ask questions such as "Who was the best manager you ever worked for?" File the name and contact information in your candidate database and follow up with that person when an appropriate opening appears.

USE NETWORKS AND ALLIANCES
We have developed networks for our own career changes, so why not develop networks to assist with the career changes of others—into your organization, of course! Just as your organization needs a variety of alliances and partnerships to speed its sales growth, alliances and partnerships can be used to grow your number of employees. In particular, the following alliances can play a critical role in employee referrals: existing strategic partners, customers, consultants to your organization, and even professional recruiters.

JOB SHARE WITH STRATEGIC PARTNERS
Strategic partnerships give large and small organizations an edge over competitors by providing access to referrals and resources that would otherwise have to be purchased or created. A strategic partner might be the employer of someone on your board of directors, or it might sell different products or services to the same market as your organization. In some cases, strategic partners even develop products together without merging. One of the most creative approaches to recruiting is for strategis partners to share selected job openings with

each other, thereby creating the opportunity to cross-pollinate. Clearly, not every opening will have a corresponding perfect fit in the allied organization, but with every successful hire, the bond will grow deeper. These placements may be permanent, or they may be short-term opportunities for stretch assignments and development.

HIRE THROUGH YOUR CUSTOMERS
How many times have you been through a car wash, stood in line at a fast-food restaurant, or listened to music while on hold and read or heard about job openings at that business? Many organizations know that their customers may be interested in filling and qualified for positions ranging from front-line, customer service openings to high-level executive positions, or they may know other candidates to refer.

Struggling to fill 40 information technology (IT) positions, an airline advertised in its own frequent-flyer mailings and offered free round-trip tickets to members if the candidates they referred were eventually hired. The company was amazed to receive more than 300 referrals!

In order to take action, your customers need background information on your organization, an application form, and details on general or specific openings. Encourage your customers to refer potential employees (or to apply themselves!) via your invoices, your mailings, your Web site, or brochures at your business sites. Consider paying a bird-dog, or referral, fee. Be creative, but don't be shy! Your customers like your business, know your business, and feel proud to do business with you. It is natural that they might imagine themselves as employees or feel comfortable telling others about opportunities with your organization.

ASK YOUR ATTORNEY, ACCOUNTANT, INSURANCE AGENT, CONSULTANTS, AND OTHER VENDORS FOR REFERRALS
Pay a bounty for referrals from consultants, vendors, and other service providers! They are in daily contact with clients who may be ready to move on.

CREATE A RÉSUMÉ NETWORK WITH OTHER EMPLOYERS
Some networks focus on sharing the résumés of relocated or new employees' spouses. Other employer networks share all high-quality

candidate information (provided they have no plans to hire the applicants themselves). Frequently, employers have either unsolicited résumés or a surplus of excellent candidates for a current opening. Start a network and share résumés with other employers.

FORM A STRATEGIC ALLIANCE WITH A RECRUITING FIRM

At the end of the century, too few employers truly understood the value of recruiters. Instead of working with recruiters as they would like their own clients to work with them (open communication, clear direction, aligning for mutual benefit, responsiveness, and fast payment), these employers would hand out job openings to several recruiters and pit them against one another. Other employers disregarded the recruiters' rates (typically 20 to 25 percent or more of the final agreed-upon compensation for the successful candidate) and insisted upon lower rates.

Foolish, wasteful, and fruitless, these tactics often resulted in few or no candidates presented by the recruiters. Mystified employers assumed that recruiters either were not a good source of employees or that they just did not want to work. These conclusions were further evidence that employers still did not understand that the employment marketplace had totally changed into a seller's market. In this case, the sellers are the recruiters who have databases of thousands of potential employees and enjoy hundreds of personal relationships built over years of working with the top candidates in each field. Little did employers know that by the end of 1999, recruiters were so busy that they routinely ignored such negative treatment and filled orders for other, more cooperative organizations.

The so-called Big Five accounting firms were among the first to realize that recruiters are strategic resources for intellectual capital— and worthy partners and allies. While there are many ways to align with a vendor, one major accounting firm understood its need to hire the best candidates and took a very direct tack to ensure that they were presented with the *best* candidates. For every candidate hired, the firm would pay 1 percent higher than its fee for the last candidate hired—up to a ceiling of 45 percent! The fee for the first hire was 25 percent, the second hire was 26 percent, the third hire was 27 percent, and so on! Clearly, recruiting firms with multiple orders to fill for many employers—and few truly qualified candidates—presented the qualified candidates to the employer that was willing to pay the highest fee. This employer had first right of refusal, the best-quality candidates, and shorter hiring cycles. Other clients who paid less received the leftover candidates—if there were any left over!

Too many organizations try to conduct business with recruiters at a distance: electronically or solely by telephone and fax. They assume that recruiting services are a commodity, and that one recruiter's ability to fill positions is the same as another's. Wrong!

A more successful strategy is to meet with the specific individuals assigned to fill your organization's positions. Invite the recruiter(s) to tour the facility and set up a meeting with the hiring manager and peers of the employee whose position must be filled. Provide as much information as possible to ensure a full understanding not only of the organization's culture but of the hard skills and competencies required to be successful in the position as well.

To further develop your effective relationship with a recruiting firm, agree to retained searches instead of contingency searches—and ask for metrics that demonstrate the recruiter's commitment to shortening the hiring cycle (and delivering results!). Metrics are ratios of dynamics such as screening interviews to face-to-face interviews, face-to-face interviews to offers, or offers to acceptances. It is no help to you to wade through stacks of résumés or schedule days of interviews that result in disqualified candidates or declined offers. The goal is for the recruiter to have such a deep understanding of your organization's culture and position requirements that very few candidates are presented for face-to-face interviews, all of those candidates are qualified, and all offers are accepted.

Contingency, or non-exclusive, searches that are distributed among two or more recruiters do not get the same attention that exclusive, retained searches receive. This is counterintuitive, but true. Because retained searches must be filled in order to generate repeat retained searches, they are given priority. Otherwise, a recruiter could work diligently to fill a position and discover and qualify one or more candidates, only to find that the position has been filled by a competing recruiting firm! All that effort for nothing! While building a database of candidates is important to recruiters, it takes a backseat to filling orders. Furthermore, in the situation described above, the candidate may become frustrated and refuse future interviews with the recruiter to avoid disappointment.

Since shorter fill times are a goal for employers, and time is a non-renewable resource, it is in the interests of the employer and the recruiting firm to discuss fewer candidates (all of whom should be qualified) and fill the position quickly. Most recruiters track the different steps in the hiring process and can guarantee results such as résumés, first interviews, and filled positions within a specific range of weeks (or months, depending upon the complexity of the employer's hiring processes and the availability of appropriate candidates). The recruiter must not be held responsible if your hiring managers do not agree to interviews, fail to return telephone calls, or are slow to give feedback after interviews. Your hiring managers play a critical role in shortening the hiring cycle and quickly landing the best candidates. Their cooperation is vital.

Recruiters are a source of competitive compensation and benefits information. They can also assist with negotiations because of their knowledge of the candidate's true reason(s) for leaving. Recruiters with whom you have formed an alliance can speak more knowledgeably and enthusiastically about your organization because they have developed a relationship with your company. Remember that the job seekers with whom they work can select from many potential employers. Armed with their deep knowledge of your organization, its culture, and its people, recruiters working with your organization are better able to present candidates who not only will please your hiring managers but will stay longer with your organization!

Old Standbys Deserve a New Look

PAY HIRING BONUSES

Often used as a way to keep base salaries from leaping higher, hiring bonuses can tilt the acceptance decision in your favor when the candidate receives two otherwise equal offers. A hiring bonus may be the deciding factor when an organization is attempting to hire a high-level employee who will lose a year-end bonus or experience a tax loss due to the job change. One-time bonuses do not affect the base salary and are not included in annual calculations for raises. Mention of hiring bonuses may be made in the original advertisement for the position or may be added later as part of the negotiations. Some organizations with positions that are particularly difficult to fill (IT or nursing, for example) announce their hiring bonuses on billboards—much to the consternation of their competitors!

Hiring bonuses were originally used solely for IT hires, but they are now offered for any job category that employers consider hard to fill. Experienced auto repair technicians may receive $2,000 to $3,000. Air-conditioning specialists may receive $750. Executives with $200,000 base salaries may receive $50,000 to $75,000 to come onboard because they are walking away from year-end bonuses of equivalent value.

RETHINK NEWSPAPER ADVERTISING:
AD SIZE AND CONTENT, USE OF COLOR, AND PLACEMENT

Too many employers go to their files, pull out the same tired one-inch, 15-word ads they have been using for the last seven years, and express surprise when no one responds. Another low-response tactic is the blind ad, which does not identify the employer. Most curious (but employed) job seekers cannot risk accidentally applying to their own organization. Or worse, because of the greater expense, employers run large ads that generate little or no response. Your newspaper advertisement is too easily lost among the thousands of ads that run daily or on the weekends.

Why does this happen when newspapers used to be *the* place for conducting job searches? For one thing, very few people are *looking* for jobs today. They are working. The unemployment rate is low— and will continue to be low due to the greater number of openings versus the smaller Generation X and emerging Generation Y populations. The new goal must be to get the attention of the few individuals who *are* looking.

If the newspaper is one of your organization's advertising media of choice, make your ads stand out. Hire an advertising design firm. Integrate your ad messages with your branding campaign. Use humor, color, graphics, or photographs and make the text positively sing! Advertise your organization's assets: its benefits, work environment, culture, flexible hours, great customers, location, and awards—along with the hard skills needed for the job. Advertise for competencies, too, because doing so will attract individuals with these success factors and eliminate those who lack them. Give serious consideration to encouraging telephone calls to either the hiring manager or to HR, and use your Internet address or fax number to speed the receipt of résumés. Place your ad so that it stands out: on the front page of the classified section, in the middle of the stock-market pages, or in the sports or other special interest sections. Since you must pay to advertise, pay to get noticed!

USE BILLBOARDS, RADIO AND TELEVISION ADVERTISING, AND DIRECT MAIL TO REACH THOSE WHO "AREN'T LOOKING"

Billboards aren't just for fast-food franchises and apartment complexes—and they aren't just found by the road! In addition to billboards in high-traffic areas, consider using sports billboards, electronic billboards, portable billboards, and even bulletin boards to get out the word about job openings.

Radio advertising—featuring the voices of happy employees—can be very effective because it sneaks into the consciousness of those who are not looking for a new job. Radio advertisements for one car wash company are voiced by a seven-year employee who talks about a summer job that became a full-time one after college! After listening to the testimonial, the listener concludes

- The car wash hires college graduates and promotes them to management positions.

- There is more to this business than meets the eye.

- The car wash is a great place to work.

- The car wash retains employees.

- A car washed by long-term, happy employees will probably be cleaner, unscratched, and worth the drive across town.

Television recruitment advertising is often either slipped into image advertising or found on specific programs that broadcast information on job opportunities. As part of their public service requirements, many television stations make recruitment advertising available; other stations offer special advertising packages focused on recruitment. A fee is usually involved if the employer would like to have more than a generic listing.

Because so many desirable employees are not currently seeking jobs, many corporations make targeted hiring pitches during or after college football games or during early morning local news programs, with tie-ins to the television station's Web site. Alternatively, television stations are offering 30- to 60-minute segments with titles such as "The Hiring Network," which are further promoted via direct mail. Advertisers featured on Web sites and in direct mail hope to capture even more viewers by cross-advertising through recruitment-focused television segments.

Direct mail can be an excellent means of attracting target populations. Use first-class postage, stamped versus metered mail, and hand-addressed envelopes versus self-mailers. Enclose a Web site address, reply card, or other means of response. Use billboards, radio and television advertising, and direct mail to lead potential candidates to your Web site, and be sure to provide detailed information about job openings there.

GROW YOUR NEXT HIRE THROUGH INTERNSHIPS AND APPRENTICESHIPS

While these are tried and true strategies, they are underutilized by too many organizations. Internships are available year-round. Interns from local colleges and universities (or even the younger siblings or children of employees who attend college outside of your area) provide a steady stream of eager, intelligent employees who can focus on projects and move your department's goals forward. Advertise in the school newspaper and contact the appropriate departments of local colleges and universities to tap into their internship programs.

Interview interns just as you would other job candidates: prepare a job description with detailed responsibilities, set a competitive pay range, and ask behavior-based questions to determine that the intern has the competencies needed to perform well on the job. Allow employees who will work closely with the intern to interview the best candidates.

Make sure that you have adequate workspace, a telephone, and a computer for each intern. Consider hiring two or more interns per semester and each summer, but be sure that each is adequately supervised. Be prepared to write a letter of recommendation at the end of the semester or summer so that the intern can more easily find future internships or full-time employment upon graduation. Clearly, good interns are good potential employees and should be encouraged to apply to your organization after graduation!

As the economy continues to evolve into an information rather than a manufacturing base, some employers have begun to educate future employees through apprenticeship programs. Starting early in the education cycle—high school—is an excellent way to locate immediate talent as well as future employees. Apprenticeship programs have been used primarily by manufacturers to train high school students to run equipment and learn how to make or repair equipment or products safely. Team up with a local high school or technical school to start an apprenticeship program, and ensure a steady stream of potential future hires!

CONDUCT OPEN HOUSES AND ATTEND JOB FAIRS

An open house is a recruiting affair conducted at the employer's facility. Balloons, signs, refreshments, tours, speeches by executives, and a combination of group and individual experiences await the applicant. Organizations with ongoing needs for call center staff, manufacturing staff, or simply entry- to mid-level employees benefit from open houses. Consider offering a $1,000 signing bonus to attract attendees.

A job fair provides a forum at which dozens or even hundreds of employers are able to meet with interested prospective employees at a neutral location (such as a convention center or college). Job fairs are publicized via radio advertising, newspapers, the Internet, and professional organizations. These events frequently attract people who want to change careers. Successful job fairs offer convenient hours (consider scheduling tours for the end of the day and early evening, as well as on weekends), clever giveaways, free trips and other desirable door prizes, refreshments, and even free training as lures to build attendance.

CONDUCT COLLEGE RECRUITING

Any organization that hopes to hire the top students in a class must raise its profile with the professors who influence the top students. While colleges actively encourage employers to interview graduating students through on-site job fairs, advanced college recruiting gives employers an edge because they hear about the top students *before* the annual career fairs are scheduled! Some employers become better known to professors who are trusted referral sources for students by taking the time to meet with appropriate professors and sharing company or job-specific information, offering to teach one or more class segments, and raising the organization's profile through advertisements in alumni publications. Another strategy is to invite professors and their students to tour your facility and talk with your organization's scientists, engineers, and other relevant specialists.

If experienced graduates are your target hires, the university and college alumni associations are your allies. Alumni résumé databases, left over from the tough hiring times of the 1980s, can be tapped by employers. Put out an e-mail to all employees in your organization requesting assistance from college alumni. Their alumni status may bring special attention to your request to tap résumé databases. Additionally, consider placing advertisements that list employees who are alumni, along with their graduation years, in alumni newsletters. School spirit attracts and bonds individuals.

Expand Your Recruiting Resources

CALL IN THE ARMY, THE NAVY, AND THE MARINES!

Yes, call in the air force, the reserves, and the coast guard, too! For years, we heard the message that our armed services were "looking for a few good men—and women!" We competed with them for the best and the brightest candidates, and depending upon the world situation, we won some but lost many to different branches of the service.

How do the various service branches work with employers to meet mutual goals? Employers can benefit from hiring individuals before —and after—they enter the service. One tactic used by the army and other services is to promise recruits the assignment of their choice.

Recruits often must wait up to nine months for an appropriate opening once they have passed their physical examination and other entry requirements. Speaking at the Workforce Solutions '99 Conference (Indianapolis, January 28, 1999), Bob D'Orso, HR manager for Fazoli's Restaurants, stated that hiring recruits during their waiting period is good business. The recruits provide a steady stream of high-quality hires in a business known for high turnover and a sparse field of qualified candidates. Working closely with the armed services has eased the quality issue.

Major Rick E. Ayer, Chief of the Marketing Research and Plans Division of the U.S. Army, pointed out in a presentation at the same conference that soldiers who finish their tours "go to college, get higher grades, and finish faster" than other students—qualities that translate well into most work environments. Smart employers work closely with the discharge offices of the various service branches to link with potential employees before they serve their last day in the military.

OFFER $500 HIRING BONUSES FOR REFERRALS WHO ARE HIRED

A few smart employers are putting hiring bonus information in their ads and offering to pay other job seekers—or anyone—for referrals.

HIRE OLDER WORKERS

As Baby Boomers age, more will cross the 45-year threshold that is generally regarded as the cut-off between older and younger employees. Studies released by the American Association of Retired Persons (AARP) show that older workers are often bypassed in favor of younger hires. Even employers who know that negative stereotypes about older employees are untrue (inflexible, unwilling to learn, unfamiliar with technology) discriminate against them.

In many cases, employers would enthusiastically hire older employees but hold back because they fear the higher healthcare costs associated with seniors. Wellness programs, which have been around for years, are underutilized as a powerful means of reducing or maintaining the present cost of benefits for employers. One Midwest bank engaged a wellness program provider to investigate the source of its uncommonly high health insurance rates. Prepared for the usual explanations of employee age, smoking, and weight problems, the bank's management was surprised to learn the real basis of its benefits costs. The hunters among its employees were driving up the benefits rates due to accidents in remote locations! A new company education program involving first aid and CPR classes, gun safety training, plus general wellness program components was successful in containing costs.

While some employers demur, Wal-Mart sets a *hiring goal* for job candidates over 55 years of age and believes that the company's bottom line benefits from doing so. An Indianapolis not-for-profit food bank has a forklift operator who is over 80 years old! A frustrated "older" IT specialist in California set up a database of job seekers over the age of 55 and received more than 10,000 résumés in the first year!

Does your organization need punctual, capable, educated employees who use good judgment with your customers, meet deadlines, attain goals, and aren't bored? The human brain does not stop learning at an arbitrary age; enthusiasm is not confined to younger years. Experienced older employees are not as motivated to job hop, and they make excellent full-time and part-time employees. Organizations benefit from diversity in age, sex, race, religion, and culture.

USE MERGERS AS AN EMPLOYEE ACQUISITION STRATEGY

Clearly, this is a big step to take to achieve rapid growth. Rather than building your employee base, you can buy it. This is a common strategy for high-tech firms facing a tight development deadline. They purchase one or more software companies with 50 to 100 employees that are on the brink of launching commercial products. Due to short product life spans, acquiring new product teams is the logical alternative.

Many EOCs have successfully acquired competitors or complementary organizations and, in so doing, have grown overnight into a company with the number and quality of employees they need. It is not, however, a foolproof way to add staff. Cultural fit must be taken into account when selecting a merger target. In a tight hiring market, the best employees in the acquired organization can easily find new jobs. Careful handling of the new employees, as well as of your existing employees, is critical. Consider engaging a top-notch HR consulting and outplacement firm to assist with communication and retention strategies that will enable you to keep as many of the desirable employees as possible.

CONTACT HR DEPARTMENTS OF MERGED COMPANIES
Mergers usually mean staff consolidations and layoffs of good people. Do not wait until the public knows about the merger or acquisition, or many other employers will be ahead of you.

RECRUIT FOREIGN WORKERS
While this idea may seem radical at first, historically, America has opened its borders to foreign workers whenever the number of job openings has wildly exceeded the number of available employees. Waves of immigrants from a variety of foreign countries have helped to build everything from highways to high-tech products.

While many engineers, scientists, physicians, business executives, teachers, and programmers enter the United States to work for American companies, importing workers is not a strategy used exclusively for upper-end hiring. For many employers, apparently low-level positions are sometimes the most critical hires because of the impact these employees have on customers.

In the mid-1990s, Marriott Corporation in Des Moines, Iowa, hired 20 Bosnian refugees to plug the gaps in its housekeeping staff. This was a win-win strategy for all involved. Marriott worked closely with the new employees to improve their language skills and train them for their new jobs. Safe from the dangers of their war-torn homeland, the employees thrived in their new city.

SEEK ENCLAVES OF IMMIGRANTS
Contact churches and existing employees to locate groups of immigrants who are interested in new jobs. Be prepared to assist with language difficulties and consider offering courses in English as a second language to ease the transition and increase productivity.

RECRUIT AMERICANS OVERSEAS

Another twist on hiring foreign workers is to hire Americans who are currently living outside of the country. The state of Nebraska has sponsored trips to Germany to recruit retiring army personnel to settle in the Cornhusker State. Many of these individuals have moved so many times that they are very comfortable about making the decision to live in a new city.

HIRE THOSE WITH DISABILITIES

In your area, there are several organizations that train and place disabled individuals and work closely with organizations to ensure that the matches are successful. The stereotype of disabled employees as suited primarily for heavy telephone or seated assembly work is not borne out in reality. A disabled employee presents the same wide range of skills as any other employee and may be able to fill a variety of positions, such as attorney, psychiatrist, medical transcriptionist, home healthcare specialist, machine operator, shipping or stock clerk, patient account representative, computer programmer, and more. Organizations must open their collective minds to take advantage of the numerous talents and skills available from disabled employees.

USE STATE EMPLOYMENT SERVICES
AND UNEMPLOYMENT OFFICES

Cost-effective state agencies provide prescreening and testing with no fee to the employer. This resource may be best for filling entry- or lower-level positions.

HIRE WELFARE-TO-WORK CANDIDATES,
SOCIAL OUTCASTS, AND CONVICTS

Employers in tight hiring environments must use "outside the box" thinking in order to serve banquets, fill production orders, build furniture, staff call centers, and more. With little or no response to their job postings, these employers need new sources of employees. Frantic to fill spots even for one day, hotel banquet managers have been known to literally grab people off the street, put them in tuxedos, and have them start serving dinners to conventioneers. This gives new meaning to the phrase "Anyone off the street could do your job." Barely.

If new hires show up for work late, are unkempt, or leave quickly after training, the employer loses money, time, and probably customers. What is a practical method of finding individuals who meet deadlines, provide quality service for customers, and stay on the job for years? Hire trained welfare-to-work candidates, social outcasts, and convicts.

In 1968, a well-known brewing company in Golden, Colorado, started hiring felons, workers from low economic backgrounds, and those lacking high school diplomas—and reports a 70 percent retention rate. Their keys to success are extensive training, support, and advancement. In return, employers receive loyalty and low turnover.

Prisons around the country provide workers, either on-site at the employer's workplace or off-site at the prison, to staff call centers or manufacture a variety of products. Employers report low tardiness and absenteeism rates, quality output, and long-term employees who know their products and services and are grateful to have paying jobs after their release.

Goodwill Industries, the Private Industry Council (PIC), many churches, and other not-for-profit organizations provide both hard-skills and life-skills training that can turn non-working adults into promising employees. Additionally, adult literacy programs link employers with new readers who have acquired useful skills.

CONTACT RÉSUMÉ-WRITING COMPANIES OR OUTPLACEMENT FIRMS

Go where the job seekers go! Job loss or the anticipated need to conduct a job search can motivate employees at all levels of an organization to seek professional assistance with their search. Organizations that provide services to job seekers can be excellent sources of management and non-management candidates. Do not expect them to screen candidates for your organization, as this would put them in the position of discriminating against some of their own clients.

CONTACT CHURCHES

Pastors know who is ready to make a change, who is underemployed and frustrated but unaware of options, and who is retired but ready to return to work! Whether your organization seeks carpet cleaning staff or a CFO, churches are an inexpensive resource. In addition to enlisting the assistance of pastors, you may be able to tap into other church communication mechanisms in order to contact potential new hires. You might use church Web sites to advertise your openings, place ads in their bulletins, post ads on bulletin boards, or go through your own employees who are members and willing to network within the church to find potential employees.

Never Give Up! Never Give Up! Never Give Up!

RECRUIT CONTINUOUSLY

To be successful at hiring the best of the best, every manager and recruiter must recruit continuously and create a pool of preselected, viable candidates. This requires attending conferences and meeting presenters, calling article authors and interesting individuals featured in articles, becoming active in local/regional/national professional organizations, carrying business cards at all times, and continuously stating your organization's goal to hire the best of the best.

GET TO KNOW YOUR CANDIDATES

The "best" have no reason to quit their jobs to come to work for your organization—unless they know about your current projects and future goals. To hire the cream of the crop, you must make an effort to meet them, know them, and be *desired by them*. Cultivate a relationship. Send them e-mails, invite them to attend open houses or seminars, call occasionally, meet for lunch, or ask them for feedback on your organization's Web page. Create and send an e-mail newsletter that tells them about organization activities, projects, and triumphs. Invite prequalified candidates to participate as speakers or serve on panels at your organization's special events or for professional or community organizations. Consider hiring them as weekend consultants, if doing so would not be a conflict of interest.

KEEP IN TOUCH WITH YOUR CANDIDATES

EOCs maintain communication with their candidates, often using e-mail to stay in touch. Try setting up an e-mail mechanism to automatically inform prequalified candidates about appropriate open positions.

IF YOU DON'T HAVE A JOB OPENING, CREATE ONE
Many EOCs will hire the best even without a specific opening (or accelerate the creation of a position) when they receive a signal that this person is ready to make a move.

BE READY TO JUMP
To maximize the benefits of having a pool of prequalified candidates, be sure to call when your organization has open positions of interest to them, and be ready to hire quickly!

DON'T ACCEPT "NO" FOR AN ANSWER
If a candidate whom you consider one of the best of the best says "no," stay in touch, and call again in a few months. Let him or her know you're still interested, and mention the changes in your company that might make it worthwhile to talk again.

TRACK YOUR HIRING PROCESS
For employers, there is no such thing as using too many resources in the current low-unemployment marketplace. Tracking the effectiveness of each source is important in order to determine how many candidates for which types of jobs are recruited through which source. It is also important to calculate cost-per-hire from each source. Perhaps the most important analysis is to track the *quality* of hires from each source.

PART THREE

COMPREHENSIVE STRATEGIES FOR RETAINING TOP PERFORMERS

▼

CHAPTER EIGHT

UNDERSTANDING WHY EMPLOYEES LEAVE

A report entitled "Attracting and Retaining Employees," by William M. Mercer, a global consulting firm, discusses the results of a Conference Board survey of 273 HR executives and 243 CEOs, CFOs, CIOs, and other general managers from 373 companies in 33 countries. Mercer's analysis points out that turnover factors are "organization specific" and that influences on attraction and retention fall into three categories:

1. EXTERNAL: regional labor market, economic climate, competition, and location

2. ORGANIZATIONAL: programs, policies, practices

3. INDIVIDUAL: age, work history, family responsibilities

In light of this research, employers need more than one tactic if they are to make significant progress in reducing turnover. "One size fits all" solutions should be replaced with flexible or even individual responses. The rest of this book is devoted to the mind-set, strategies, and tactics a company needs to reduce turnover by accelerating the process of becoming an Employer of Choice.

Why do supervisors and other executives automatically and repeatedly cite pay as the deciding factor in an employee's decision to leave? In many cases, it is because the employee, when asked about motivators in a face-to-face exit interview or other conversation, states that a pay increase influenced his or her decision. In follow-ups to exit interviews, however, deeper issues unrelated to compensation often emerge.

It is critical to know why employees are leaving your organization or—closer to home—your particular department. The reasons may vary widely. New hires have one set of reasons, while experienced employees have another. In both cases, the employer has the resources to turn the situation around before, during, or after the resignation. In this chapter, we will look at new-hire and experienced-employee turnover, as well as effective employer responses to turnover at three points in time:

1. BEFORE NOTICE IS GIVEN. Your best solutions are retention committees, employee opinion surveys, focus groups, and chat rooms.

2. WHEN NOTICE IS GIVEN. We will look at what to do when an employee resigns.

3. AFTER NOTICE IS GIVEN. Exit interviews provide the best opportunity for employers to respond to a resignation.

This chapter focuses on fundamental turnover tactics. It is important to understand that tactics are absolutely necessary—but they work much like the little Dutch boy's finger in the dike: they prevent the dike from bursting. Some employers truly have an organization that is leaking employees as if there were no barrier at all. The dike represents strategies, while the boy's fingers represent tactics. No matter what your rate of turnover, your organization needs that Dutch boy (managers and HR personnel) plugging holes with his fingers when the dike springs a leak. Once the wall is strengthened through the implementation of EOC Foundation Strategies, a variety of tactics are still necessary as part of the "quick action" tool kit for savvy employers. Later chapters discuss how to strengthen the dike so the Dutch boy doesn't spend *all* of his time plugging leaks and can get back to other activities.

Four Reasons Why New Hires Leave

In the Introduction, we discussed formulas to calculate turnover, including the increasingly frequent problem of new-hire turnover.

Why do new hires leave just when they are getting started—and, even more bewildering, why do some of them fail to show up for work on the first day? Exit interviews (which may require persistence to secure from short-timers) provide considerable insights. When asked why they leave after such a short time with an organization, new-hire respondents provide valuable guidance to employers, who can then anticipate and reduce negative outcomes. Though common, the four main causes of new-hire turnover too often surprise employers.

COUNTEROFFERS
This retention tactic is being used more frequently than ever before. Counteroffers in the form of career progression, flextime, monetary compensation, or other adjustments cause a surprising number of new hires to return to their previous employers. To minimize this effect, hiring employers should talk openly about the possibility of a counteroffer and ask newly hired individuals to commit to resisting counteroffers from their former employers.

SECOND OFFERS
Individuals conducting active job searches often generate multiple offers one after the other. Even if the second offer is equal to the earlier accepted offer, the candidate may accept the second for other reasons. Again, interested employers should prepare candidates for this possibility and attempt to uncover any outstanding needs so that a competing job offer is likely to be declined. Before completing the interview process, ask, "Is there any other issue at your current workplace that we should discuss now?"

ON-THE-JOB EXPERIENCE DOES NOT MATCH
THE INTERVIEW JOB DESCRIPTION
Too often, the new employee is confronted with a dramatic mismatch between the culture, job, working conditions, manager, or peers described during the interview process and the actual experience on the first day of work or during training. Employers would be wise to use job shadowing, simulations, tours, and informal meetings with prospective peers to ensure that top candidates have a complete understanding of the job, work conditions, and co-workers.

One sales executive described a sales meeting he attended on his first day at work that clearly demonstrated the open warfare existing between the executive office management and the rest of the staff. One year after a merger, low morale and blatant sabotage were so obvious throughout the company that the new hire resigned that day. Later, when senior management admitted they had neglected to fully disclose the poor sales record of the office, the new employee felt vindicated in walking away from the promised $100,000 in total compensation—and potential career disaster. This employer could have realized a better outcome by being truthful about the sales figures and the need to turn the office culture around.

A purchasing manager quit after her first day when she realized that her employer had deliberately hidden working conditions from her. She had always been interviewed off-site or in conference rooms, away from the actual purchasing department, and was stunned to discover that her office had four glass walls and was situated in the middle of a factory floor. Literally all eyes were on her. Unable to work under such circumstances, she quit during her first morning on the job. If a candidate declines because of the working conditions, the employer has the option of changing those conditions, thus enlarging the pool of candidates.

One call center employer in Indiana was so familiar with high new-hire turnover that it routinely hired a specific percentage of individuals in excess of the actual number of openings. It gambled on hiring 85 call center employees in a month, so that 80 would make it through training and become productive. After several years of using this tactic, the company realized that its hiring process needed to better demonstrate the real-life conditions of the job so that new hires could truly participate in a mutual selection process. Dollars saved by *not* doing the additional interviewing, reference checks, orientation, and training for five people per month could be used elsewhere. Today, this company hires one employee for each opening.

POOR ORIENTATION PROCESS AND/OR LACK OF BONDING

Employers have two weeks maximum to reinforce a new hire's decision to accept employment. What happens in the first two weeks on the job either confirms your organization's EOC status or encourages the new hire to continue the job search. Today, there are so few qualified candidates and so many open positions that no new hire at any level is unaware of his or her marketability.

Rethink your organization's orientation process. New hires should feel welcome and confident that they will succeed, that they will be trained, and that they have made the right decision. Formalize the orientation process and make it mandatory. Discourage arguments from managers about new-hire attendance, involve senior management, and schedule the orientation within two weeks of the employee's hire date. Whether you have a number of new hires each month or just one, each employee needs formal orientation to the company and its history, its industry, the department, and his or her new job responsibilities.

Many companies use video and/or their intranet to communicate orientation information. While these are good tools for reinforcing specific parts of the orientation process, extensive personal contact in the beginning of the employment process pays off. Involve your corporate officers. Encourage the members of each orientation class to get to know one another. Match new hires with a buddy or a mentor in the organization. Be sure to allow new hires to evaluate the orientation process, and adjust it in response to suggestions. Remember that new-hire turnover is *avoidable turnover*. If your executives spend time during the orientation process creating bonds between new hires and the organization, the company will save turnover dollars.

The personal touch is also needed within the department, between the new hire and his or her co-workers and between the supervisor and the new hire. Especially in departments with high turnover, building relationships between new hires and their co-workers helps reduce turnover. If no one cares enough to make new people feel welcome, how can the organization expect them to care about staying? If they don't feel connected or important to the company, they won't care or stay! Another employer will probably offer an equivalent job at equivalent wages and will treat these new employees as if they were valued.

Eight Reasons Why Experienced Employees Leave

Long-term employees have different reasons for leaving. In a presentation titled "Employee Retention: 25 Keys to Keeping the Right People," Dr. Rick Cartor, Vice President of Consulting Services for PeopleTech, listed eight common reasons why good performers leave:

- Don't see a link between performance and pay
- Don't see advancement or growth opportunities
- View their work as unimportant
- Don't feel appreciated
- Are not using their real (or all of) their abilities
- Perceive unclear/unrealistic management expectations
- Feel they have no (or limited) support/resources
- Will no longer tolerate "corporate abuse"

These responses zero in on the lack of management skills among supervisors as well as the need to update compensation practices and development options. Each of these topics is covered in depth in the chapters that follow.

Employers of Choice understand that isolated turnover anecdotes are not quality data on which to base policy changes (including management skills training, increased compensation ranges, added benefits or changes in working conditions, for example). Anecdotes, however, often compel employers to uncover the true root causes of turnover through more objective and standardized methods. EOCs use information from retention committees, employee surveys, focus groups and chat rooms, and exit interviews to determine how to reduce turnover before, during, and after resignations.

Turnover Prevention Tactics

RETENTION COMMITTEE

Too few organizations focus on solving the real reasons for turnover. Although every employee wants to get involved with growing the organization by referring potential hires to appropriate hiring managers, few want the responsibility for reducing turnover. Just as the growth of the organization will be enhanced by the participation of all, so will the reduction of turnover. The retention committee is responsible for making strategic recommendations and augments the individual retention-reduction responsibility shouldered by each manager.

Though HR has been conducting exit interview analysis and making retention recommendations for more than a decade, too few employers have responded with comprehensive strategies and tactics to reduce turnover. Instead, senior management continues to assume that HR alone is responsible for ending turnover, or that the problem is unsolvable. The turnover crisis is real—and its causes and solutions can be found throughout the organization. Turnover begets turnover. Departments with high turnover are doomed to repeat the rehiring process if no one is authorized to analyze the real causes and make changes. One answer is a retention committee with clout.

A cross-functional retention committee with the ear of senior management can make objective recommendations on a monthly or quarterly basis so that negative trends are stopped early and action is taken before entire departments experience turnover of 50 percent or more. Each business unit should be represented on the committee, preferably with a mix of management and non-management representatives.

The committee should work closely with HR to ensure that exit interview tracking produces better information than "quit" or "better offer." Successful actions require a more detailed understanding of the underlying issues. In some cases, this committee might be empowered to conduct, or engage a consultant to conduct, post-employment interviews to provide the in-depth information needed to reduce or eliminate serious turnover.

Selection for and participation on the committee is usually seen as a career-enhancing activity. Information discussed is confidential and must be handled with care. Recommendations from the committee must be articulate and specific, and the outcomes of its recommendations should be documented for later evaluation.

EMPLOYEE OPINION SURVEYS

Employee opinion surveys are conducted for a variety of reasons, including to measure employee satisfaction with a variety of programs and policies and with their jobs. Individual confidentiality is critical because survey responses can be tracked by department, function, length of service, and sex. In order to provide honest responses, employees must feel certain that their individual identities cannot be discerned by any means, including by handwriting or the order in which forms are collected. Many independent survey providers will group the responses of small functional groups (fewer than five to seven employees with a particular job title, for example) to disguise individual responses.

Employers of Choice have the courage to add three questions to employee opinion surveys:

1. In the last six months, have you considered leaving the organization?

2. In the last three months, have you taken action (updated your résumé, started networking, or been interviewed) to leave the company?

3. Why have you been dissatisfied? (Leave space for a written response, or list the reasons given most frequently in exit interviews. Also, allow space for additional comments.)

Combined with the answers to other survey questions, these responses will reveal *where* and *why* there are troubled areas in your organization so that management can take action to address the issues. Prevention of turnover, in addition to reduction of turnover, is an EOC strategy.

FOCUS GROUPS AND INTRANET CHAT ROOMS

The purpose of gathering information from *existing* employees is to prevent turnover instead of documenting it. Organization-focused intranet chat rooms often allow issues to surface and can provide a forum for discussion of potential solutions. Focus groups are more controlled mechanisms for gathering information, brainstorming solutions, enabling increased participation in decision making, and strengthening the bonds between the organization and its employees.

By augmenting and amplifying the information available through exit interviews and employee opinion surveys, employers can improve the focus of the resulting retention strategies. Select an external consultant to facilitate the focus groups if your organization is experiencing a period of very low trust or if HR lacks credibility as an internal consultant in the organization development area.

Technological advances have given organizations new means of assuring anonymity and enhancing information gathering. Some organizations conduct surveys using software that replaces the verbal portion of traditional focus groups. The participants gather in computer-filled rooms or work independently at terminals to provide input. Questions are asked verbally or online, and responses are tallied in real time. Participants know their answers are confidential, and results are available immediately.

Additionally, many organizations routinely use their intranets as a means of surveying their employees. The input can be handled confidentially, and employees appreciate the ease of use.

"Quittin' Time" Tactics

Sometimes, a resignation takes management by surprise. A valued employee asks for a meeting and announces his or her intention to take another position. Quick action is the key to turning this situation around.

A valuable employee is the one who makes others want to say, "Only *you* will do . . . in this job." "You" may be the lead sales representative whose clients send letters filled with kudos. "You" may be the receptionist who gets compliments because callers hear the smile in her voice. "You" may be the indispensable administrative assistant who can manage projects and untangle schedules. "You" may be a key research scientist who has developed two new drugs. Or "You" may be the e-commerce guru whose idea saved the company thousands of dollars.

Take positive action if your response to an employee's quitting is "Oh, no!" Instead of recoiling from an employee who announces his or her departure, consider the value of recapturing your organization's investment, and take four steps recommended by T . J. Rogers, founder and president of Cypress Semiconductor Corporation in San Jose, California.

1. ACT FAST. "Fast" means within five minutes—any delay is coun-terproductive. Cancel the next meeting on your schedule and focus on the individual.

2. KEEP THE NEWS A SECRET. Fear of embarrassment may prevent the employee from changing his or her decision, so keep others *out* of the loop.

3. LISTEN HARD—THEN FIGHT HARD. The employee needs to know that the decision to leave is a mistake and that you will work to make sure the mistake is rectified. Ask for reasons—and then ask for more reasons. Listen for more than money because money is the easy response and may appear to be the easy solution for what is possibly a very different issue or set of issues.

4. CALL IN THE BIG GUNS. When a key employee resigns, call in the employee's mentor and/or the person who referred the employee to the company. (This information needs to be in an accessible database.) If appropriate, call in the president or other corporate officers. If big guns are needed, use them!

Turnover Reduction Tactics

EXIT INTERVIEWS (VERBAL AND WRITTEN)

Every organization experiences turnover. While a small percentage of employees who leave are not missed, all turnover is expensive. It is important for the organization to know why employees are leaving and which departments have the highest turnover (and why) in order to determine the policies and procedures needed to reduce future turnover.

Once an employee gives notice and sticks to it, an exit interview must be scheduled. The resulting information, together with re-sponses from other exit interviews, becomes a tool for change within the organization. An exit interview—verbal, written, or both—must be conducted for any employee who is leaving by choice.

Organizations with high turnover rates frequently lack an exit in-terview process. In order to speed the process of providing manage-ment with valuable data, some organizations engage a consultant to locate and interview as many of the past year's voluntarily terminated employees as possible. Concurrently, they implement an exit interview process for all voluntary terminations.

Ideally, an interview should be built into the exit process checklist: returning keys, ID badges, computer passwords, and employee handbooks. The goal of an exit interview is to collect truthful, useful information that (individually or in the aggregate) will validate or support a change in policies, procedures, pay ranges, or even staffing.

Typically, exit interviews take 20 to 60 minutes. A neutral person should conduct exit interviews. The individual selected should not be the employee's direct supervisor, as this person may actually be the reason for the employee's departure. If an HR specialist is not available, another neutral individual should be selected who will also handle the majority of the exit process and can be trusted with confidential information. This person must ask the same questions of each employee in order to develop comparable data points for different positions and departments.

It is advisable to use a standard exit interview form as part of the exit process to guarantee that the same information is collected from all exiting employees. To the extent possible, put the employee at ease by selecting a private area for a discussion and by offering the usual amenities of coffee, soda, or water. Thank the individual in advance for his or her input and candor. Use a standard format (see Figure 7) for the questions so that responses may be compared with those from different departments and from others who have left the same department. The person conducting the exit interview must be prepared to respond without emotion during what can be a very emotional meeting.

While substantial information is garnered from exit interviews, the desire for a positive reference may minimize the employee's willingness to talk about the real factors in the decision to leave. Poor management of the employee, harassment, dirty or unsafe working conditions, or a negative culture may be too sensitive for the employee to discuss with supervisors or even HR staff face-to-face. Respondents often share new or more detailed information when they participate in mailed exit interviews or anonymous surveys about their reasons for leaving.

FIGURE 7

Sample Exit Interview Questions

Name: _____

Position: _____

Supervisor: _____

Hire Date: _____ Termination Date: _____

What made you decide to leave your current job?
(Check all that apply.)

Primary	Secondary	
❑	❑	Secured a better job
❑	❑	Returning to school
❑	❑	Issues with supervisor
❑	❑	Issues with peers
❑	❑	Family issues
❑	❑	Safety issues
❑	❑	Problem with hours
❑	❑	Not satisfied with wages
❑	❑	Disliked type of work
❑	❑	Professional level of job
❑	❑	Quantity of work
❑	❑	Physical conditions
❑	❑	Working conditions
❑	❑	Transportation problems
❑	❑	Lack of advancement opportunities
❑	❑	Other

What did you like most about your job?

What did you like least about your job?

Were training opportunities made available to you?

Was your current supervisor fair and reasonable? If not, please explain.

FIGURE 7 (CONT'D)

Sample Exit Interview Questions

Were you given access to and realistic consideration for promotional opportunities within the organization?

Were your contributions appreciated by your supervisor and others?

Did you request an internal transfer? If so, when and for what position?

Did you and your supervisor discuss your desire to leave? If yes, describe the response. If not, why not?

Was there a specific incident or event that changed your feelings about your job and/or the company? Please describe.

Did you have the appropriate equipment and resources necessary to perform your job?

Was your salary satisfactory for the job you were performing?

Were you satisfied with the employee benefits provided?

Was the physical work environment comfortable and conducive to productivity?

Was the job realistically presented to you when you were hired or most recently changed positions?

What suggestions do you have for improvements?

Are there any changes that could have been made to prevent you from leaving?

Would you recommend (this company) as an employer for friends and family? If not, why not?

Would you consider returning to (this company) in the future, if an appropriate position and conditions were offered?

Nothing substitutes for caring, personal attention during an exit interview. But employees may provide the most detailed (and possibly most truthful) exit information if they are given the option of responding from a distance. The employee should be informed that he or she will receive a written questionnaire with a stamped return envelope in the next two weeks, and that further input would be greatly valued. While you may receive the questionnaires back from only 50 percent of the exiting employees, the quality of the information will be worth the extra effort. The mailed questionnaires are far more likely to contain information that many individuals would be uncomfortable about volunteering verbally: sexual or other harassment, illegal activity, drug use, or even personal businesses operating inside your organization. Results of all exit interviews should be documented and analyzed by department, manager, tenure, ethnicity, and sex.

Keep Employees and Keep Customers

While it is important to know why employees leave, it is even more important to use the information to prevent turnover. The best way to motivate employees to stay is to treat them like customers every day. What does that mean? If a potential customer seemed hesitant about buying from your organization, how would your sales team react? If a current customer were unhappy with a product or service or did not plan to make another purchase, how would your customer service and sales teams react? If a current customer pulled the contract or stopped a project from being completed, how would your sales and management teams react?

Employees are *internal* customers. Like your external customers, they want to feel special, they believe that their needs are unique—and they are in demand by your competitors. Woo them and wow them to get them in the door, and then treat them like customers to keep them coming back. Pull out all the stops to keep them because there is a bonus that comes with employee retention. When you keep internal customers, it is easier to keep your external customers.

CHAPTER NINE

MANAGING AND LEADING
FOR RETENTION

Imagine what would happen if an organization applied a focused team of employees—sales, research and development, internal communication, e-commerce—to a problem for one year. Now imagine a different organization with the same problem doing the same thing, with one difference: the second company has high turnover. The result? The first organization, with the advantage of team continuity, would make twice as much progress as the competing company with high turnover. How an organization is staffed, managed, and led—and the culture that exists as a result of high-quality management and leadership—has tremendous impact on retention and profits.

According to management guru Peter F. Drucker, quoted in *Strategy & Business Noteworthy Quotes,* "The only things that evolve by themselves in an organization are disorder, friction, and malperformance." In other words, a competitive, well-managed, high-performance, profitable Employer of Choice organization is an intentional outcome—it doesn't just happen.

Instinctively, we all know that our organizations would be more profitable if our supervisors and managers had better skills and if we could harness the ideas and discretionary effort of our employees. We also know that the more closely an employer weaves relationships among employees (and between employees and the organization), the harder it is for them to imagine working elsewhere. We also know that the variety of employees—Boomers, Gen X'ers, and ethnically diverse employees—requires a higher level of skill on the part of managers at all levels. Each day that we do not address these issues, competitors with more highly trained supervisors and more participative cultures widen the performance gap and steal both our clients and our employees.

Toxic companies with their "lean and mean" structures and management practices are not positioned for success in the 21st century. The new business environment—heavily impacted by globalization, changing technology, and the growth of the service industry—requires new approaches to management and culture in order to meet customer and employee demands. The eye-popping cost of turnover, combined with a realization that the talent marketplace has changed forever, presents a powerful inducement to management organizations in new ways.

EOCs and emerging EOCs recognize the organization-wide need to attract and retain top talent in order to achieve organizational goals. EOCs understand that holding on to top talent requires highly developed management and leadership skills throughout the organization and an organizational culture that will fuel its future success. No organization can become an Employer of Choice if its management is driving talent out the door. Other EOC strategies have no chance to take effect unless management skills are developed throughout the organization and an employee-friendly culture results.

This chapter focuses on the new psychological contract between employees and employers. It also discusses the EOC management, leadership, and cultural practices that attract top talent, minimize turnover, and maximize achievement of organizational growth goals.

Managing and Leading with the New Psychological Contract

The work relationship between employer and employee has changed as a result of decades of corporate reorganizations and the altered demographics of the workforce. This is a time of paradox: employees are seen as both an expendable commodity (their work could be

TABLE 4

The New Psychological Contract

Baby Boomers' Expectations	Gen X'ers' Expectations
Reciprocal dependence	Self-reliance
Linear career path	Multiple careers
Workaholism	Balanced work/family life
Career growth within an organization	Career growth through multiple organizations
Organizational identity	Self/professional identity
Commitment to organization	Commitment to self
Strong organization loyalty	Weak/no organization loyalty
Want to be managed	Expect to be coached
Want homogeneity	Expect/respect diversity
Expect retirement at age 65	Expect early retirement before age 50—or extended employment beyond age 65

automated, outsourced, or sent overseas) and a key competitive advantage. Our 1980s policies and inconsistent employee treatment reflect this paradox and drive the resulting employee behavior. Changes in employee expectations are best illustrated when age is used as a parameter (see Table 4).

Gen X'ers—the children of Baby Boomers—have taken their parents' experiences to heart and decided to work in new ways. There is a clear focus on independence and self-reliance among Gen X'ers, while Boomers will sacrifice for the good of the organization. Instead of working late and on weekends like Boomers, Gen X'ers will leave at 5:00 P.M. to coach Little League or lead a Scout meeting. Boomers may want more management than managers would like to give them, but X'ers prefer discussion and advice with the right to make their own decisions. Boomers are not job hoppers. Instead, they expect to be promoted after several years in the same position. After witnessing the human toll of mergers, acquisitions, and the accompanying job losses, Gen X'ers have taken their careers into their own hands. Changing companies in order to get a faster promotion is not seen as a problem. These employees believe that their development is their choice and responsibility, so changing jobs is a growth opportunity, not a risk.

In a seller's market for your employees' skills, old-style management and toxic cultures just speed your employees out the door. To keep valuable employees of all ages, toxic employers must make five fundamental changes.

REVERSE THE "US VERSUS THEM" MENTALITY

A Web site poll of *Fast Company* magazine readers posed the question, "Is your workplace toxic, or are people truly valued?" Results:

> My workplace is toxic: 48%
> My workplace values people: 52%

The "Us versus Them" mentality demonstrated in a toxic workplace is destructive in both management and non-management arenas. As the above figures show, the company's mentality seeps into the employees' perception of the workplace. Adversarial thinking consumes mental resources that could otherwise be utilized for customer service, innovation, and other ultimately profitable activities. Both land-based and Internet-based organizations understand that the old "command and control" days are gone. Taking the approach that employees are not hired to think results in malicious disobedience and stunted profits. Today's leaner organizations require the participative management, leadership attributes, and thinking contributions of every employee at every level in order to build a culture that can respond to changes in the business landscape. EOCs value, utilize, and build on the backgrounds, experiences, connections, and ideas of every employee.

There are many new characteristics of 21st-century companies that demand a change in management style, including flatter organizations, Web-based competition, fewer quality candidates available to fill positions at any level, a need for rapid decision making, and the pressure for profitability—as well as considerable research data on successful organizations. In his book *The Human Equation: Building Profits by Putting People First*, Jeffrey Pfeffer suggests that senior managers take a long, hard look at their company's management practices to determine whether they do the following:

- Encourage employees to apply their skills and knowledge in discretionary effort (will employees choose to *work harder?*)

- Enable employees to build the skills and competencies needed to enhance performance (do employees have what they need to *work smarter?*)

- Reduce administrative costs by placing more responsibility and decision-making power at lower levels in the organization (will employees *work more profitably?*)

EOCs know that implementing high-performance management practices requires a serious commitment to doing things differently. Trust is missing in organizations with toxic cultures based on "command and control" management practices, and it is almost impossible to implement effective new practices in an atmosphere that lacks mutual trust and respect. Lip service and cosmetic changes are out. Gradual change takes too long. "Business as usual" won't do. Rethinking the entire management and leadership approach—with a focus on building trust between management and employees—is needed to ignite employee discretionary performance and transform your organization into an Employer of Choice.

Let's look again at Jeffrey Pfeffer's studies of the five-year survival rates of initial public offerings, profitability, and stock prices from large samples of companies in the service, semiconductor, automobile, apparel, steel manufacturing, and oil refining industries. He found seven common characteristics of high-performance organizations.

1. SELECTIVE HIRING of new personnel

2. EXTENSIVE TRAINING

3. COMPARATIVELY HIGH COMPENSATION contingent on organizational performance

4. EMPLOYMENT SECURITY

5. REDUCED STATUS DISTINCTIONS, including dress, language, office arrangements, and wage differences

6. SELF-MANAGED TEAMS AND DECENTRALIZATION OF DECISION MAKING as the basic principles of organizational design

7. EXTENSIVE ORGANIZATION-WIDE SHARING of financial information

In Chapter Two, we said, "Hire well—or not at all." In this chapter, we will look at the retention factors of management style (including Pfeffer's points 6 and 7 above) and culture (Pfeffer's points 4 and 5). In Chapters Ten and Eleven, we will discuss training and compensation (Pfeffer's points 2 and 3) in greater detail.

HARNESS GROUP CAPABILITY WITH SELF-MANAGED TEAMS AND DECENTRALIZED DECISIONS

Flat organizations—either recent start-ups or survivors of the downsizing age—have become decentralized and networked just like the Web. A company with a well-communicated organizational vision, mission, objectives, and goals needs fewer people to supervise employees. As a result, many organizations are turning to self-managed teams to get the work done. Training in effective group process, problem solving, facilitation skills, and conflict resolution is a critical part of the success of self-managed groups.

According to Pfeffer's research, virtually all high-performance management organizations are made up of self-managed teams. Peer control is often more effective than hierarchical control because employees do not want to let their co-workers down. Peer pressure stimulates an increased sense of responsibility and greater effort while reducing absenteeism and other negative behaviors.

Self-managed teams use brainstorming and pool their ideas to maximize the likelihood that problems will be successfully addressed. Mechanisms to regularly gather ideas are also utilized to continually evaluate processes and procedures. Some organizations use 800 numbers and focus groups, while others use anonymous e-mail and suggestion boxes. In his book *The 8 Practices of Exceptional Companies*, Jac Fitz-Enz makes the point that this collaboration among functions "enhances cohesiveness across functions and [provides] a solid front against attacks from the outside."

Self-managed teams also reduce operational costs by removing layers of hierarchy and absorbing tasks previously handled by specialized staff. Decisions can be made closer to the action by front-line people who are in the best position to do so and who must live with those decisions on a daily basis.

Trust once again becomes a key success factor. Management must trust carefully selected and trained employees to make the best possible decisions. Members of self-managed teams must trust that mistakes will not be fatal to their careers. Learning must come from both successful and unsuccessful decisions. One of the best ways to ensure good decisions is to provide fast and accurate feedback. Ongoing feedback is critical to the rapid correction of errors and the timely recognition of positive behavior and innovation. Regular reports and meetings, with opportunities for interaction and encouragement, build the trust necessary to change direction, or flex, in response to changes in business or client needs. Sharing financial and performance information on an ongoing basis is another important form of feedback that's too often overlooked by organizations.

SHARE FINANCIAL INFORMATION

EOCs know that the traditional contract between employers and employees is gone. The old approach of information shared on a "need to know" basis keeps employees from committing fully to the success of the business. This arm's-length approach encourages employees to act as if the organization rents their bodies for eight hours a day but does not value their minds, abilities, efforts, and time. No organization will grow, develop innovative services and products, or conquer new markets if employees are not fully engaged. Fully engaged employees think like owners and tap into their discretionary performance abilities. Full engagement requires information—and lots of it.

In *The 8 Practices of Exceptional Companies*, Jac Fitz-Enz points out that EOCs have an extraordinary commitment to communication, and they use all available media to link information with employees and other stakeholders. They know that it is not effective to merely share information without training employees to understand what they are reading. Ongoing training—from new-hire orientation to one-hour "lunch and learn" sessions, or even financial FAQs (frequently asked questions) on the company intranet site—should be available to teach employees how to read a financial statement. The goal is to ensure that employees understand the links between their individual efforts, the productivity of their department, and the monthly company profit-and-loss statements that are shared with them.

Several organizations have used "open-book management" to accelerate growth. Jack Stack, CEO of Springfield Remanufacturing Corporation (SRC), coined the phrase when he led the 1983 turnaround of an old International Harvester plant. He used shared financial information to encourage employee-originated cost-cutting and process-improvement activities. Stack details the process in his 1994 book, *The Great Game of Business: Unlocking the Power and Profitability of Open-Book Management*. Iams Company, the innovative pet-food manufacturer in Dayton, Ohio, shares quarterly financial information and connects it to the compensation plan and performance management program. In *The 8 Practices of Exceptional Companies*, Fitz-Enz describes how Iams pays above-average compensation and rewards employees based on a combination of personal performance and corporate results.

If knowledge is power, then shared knowledge is shared power. Shared information builds trust. Teamwork is undermined when lack of information or misinformation causes trust to dissolve. Fear that sharing information will result in leaks to the competition must be tempered with the realization that the competition probably already knows. They get their information after hours by listening in on conversations at the hot local bars or by calling former colleagues. What the competition is unlikely to have, however, are your organization's specific top talent, adaptive culture, and participative management practices. Those elements open the door to discretionary employee effort and are EOC differentiators.

ELEVATE TALENT MANAGEMENT
TO A TOP-MANAGEMENT PRIORITY

Attracting top talent and developing "bench strength," or strength in reserve, are critical to achieving organizational goals. When recruiting and retention are part of the organization's written strategic plan, and when senior management as well as supervisors at all levels have adopted the formal goals of recruiting and retaining top talent, then everyone in the organization will work toward the same goals. Top management must not only preach the message that recruiting and retention are priorities but also "walk the talk" of developing and using high-level management and coaching skills—and make doing so a requirement throughout the organization down to front-line supervisors. Otherwise, those supervisors who are not held accountable for developing and using management and coaching skills will have significantly higher turnover among their staffs. Accountability must be balanced with recognition and rewards for supervisors who spend time developing their skills and attain subsequent retention results.

Using their communication, coaching, conflict-management, organization, planning, and delegation skills, supervisors at all levels determine the day-to-day satisfaction of employees. These skills are so crucial to success and the reduction of turnover that a company *must* invest in training to ensure that those with supervisory responsibilities are well equipped. Management skills lead to the creation of an organization of leaders.

CREATE AN ORGANIZATION OF LEADERS

We all know that leadership at the top of an organization is critical in providing the vision and inspiring employees to achieve organizational goals. Successful acquisition and retention of the intellectual capital (people) needed to carry out the organization's mission, however, rely on the skills of supervisors at all levels (vice presidents, directors, managers, and front-line supervisors) to recruit, manage, coach, and lead their reports. The primary relationship that determines job satisfaction is the employee's relationship with his or her supervisor. That individual determines assignments, work pace, development opportunities, and raises. While loyalty to an organization may be weaker today than it was in the past, loyalty to an individual supervisor continues to be as powerful as ever. Loyalty is granted to leaders.

Supervisors must have the attitude of a leader and must help their direct reports develop into leaders. The degree to which they accomplish these two goals has a significant influence on whether employees stay or go. Supervisors—from front-line managers to vice presidents—need to function at Maslow's fourth level (self-esteem) in order to exhibit the behaviors they need to grow leaders. Leaders— employees who think like owners—exhibit five characteristics:

1. EMOTIONAL SECURITY. First and foremost, leaders at all levels must believe in themselves.

2. INTEGRITY. Leaders are the same on the inside as on the outside and can be trusted.

3. INFLUENCE ON OTHERS. Leaders are able to persuade, gain commitment and support, and mobilize others.

4. A SENSE OF PRIORITY. Leaders can separate the important from the trivial.

5. VISION. Leaders can grasp the bigger picture and do not simply react to circumstances.

According to an article in the June 1999 issue of *Fast Company* magazine, entitled "Make Yourself a Leader," management-level leaders develop employee leaders by modeling and encouraging several behaviors:

- Listening (leaders do not have all the answers)
- Brainstorming and bringing people together

- Building staff stamina through encouragement
- Fostering teamwork
- Reinforcing organizational values
- Determining changes needed and providing the tools to deal with change
- Learning from mistakes
- Coaching others
- Networking with leaders inside and outside the organization
- Leading by example and walking the talk

Leadership involves the hard work of mobilizing people to take on today's tough business challenges. It is not enough to have a technically skilled staff. Employees who display leadership qualities are willing to step up to the plate and swing the bat. Management-level leaders throughout the organization must develop employee leaders in order to create the innovative, future-oriented workplaces that are known as Employers of Choice.

Cultures of Employers of Choice

EOCs know that culture is a powerful management tool—and that there is no one right culture. EOCs have cultures that can flex in response to client demands, technological change, and people's needs. With an ever-increasing array of business drivers such as globalization, e-commerce, Web-based competition, and technology that provides 24-hour, instant communications, organizations either have adaptive cultures—or they die.

Research by the Saratoga Institute and others has shown "the power of culture on everything from motivation to retention and productivity." According to Jac Fitz-Enz in *The 8 Practices of Exceptional Companies*, "the BHAMs [Best Human Asset Management companies] understand that if they align their strategy and systems with their culture, they will obtain numerous benefits."

In *Built to Last,* by James C. Collins and Jerry I. Porras, the authors found that in 17 out of 18 pairs of companies studied, visionary companies were driven more by ideology and less by profits than the matching company—and in all cases, the long-term profitability of the ideologically oriented company exceeded the profit-oriented company. "[W]e did not find maximizing shareholder wealth or profit maximization as the dominant driving force or primary objective through the history of the visionary companies," the book states. Yet the visionary companies were more profitable.

With so much client, marketplace, and technological change exerting pressure on organizations, EOCs are focusing on aligning their culture with their goals even more than they have in the past. The pursuit of alignment will be an ongoing process.

The CEO drives the organization's culture by communicating beliefs and values. (Values hold steady no matter how the marketplace changes, but the services, products, and strategies used to achieve the vision can vary over time.) Assuming that the CEO's vision and strategies are adaptive and market driven, the resulting culture will be adaptive and responsive to internal and external client requirements. It is important that the vision encompass more than meeting today's client needs; the business landscape is changing too rapidly to focus narrowly on the current marketplace. A focus on the future is needed.

The CEO must articulate his or her vision on a regular basis and relate today's results or challenges to the central message. The executive team must repeat the message and emphasize the ways in which department or business unit activities support the vision. All supervisors need to reinforce the vision by linking the responsibilities of individual employees to departmental and organizational goals. It is only when employees understand how they fit into the bigger picture and can affect the bottom line that they apply the discretionary effort necessary for the organization overall to excel.

Reinforcing and aligning the culture is challenging in a typical organization, but today's wired New Economy is changing both the definition and the configuration of work. Most employers would like full-time, on-site employees with uninterrupted job tenure, who can work independently and be job-centered. According to an *HR News* article by Robert W. Thompson, entitled "Recruiting for High-Tech Jobs May Mean Nontraditional Benefits," technology and the tight hiring marketplace have introduced new work landscapes, which include the following features:

- Fluctuating work times

- Multiple work sites

- Full-time or part-time telecommuting

- Interrupted tenure

- Jobs with a non-exclusive focus

- Work that focuses on skills and tasks

- Interdependent work

- Higher turnover than preferred by the organization

Turnover is a concern in more traditionally configured organizations, and it becomes an even greater challenge when off-site employees have fewer opportunities to bond with one another and with the company, and when the employer's culture is not experienced and reinforced regularly. It is no easy task to manage an organization with employees who work in a variety of configurations, yet there will be no choice if employers are to be adequately staffed with the talent they need to meet their goals. For many reasons—employee preference, profit pressures, or client needs—there will be more telecommuting and non-traditional work arrangements. Communicating the organization's values effectively will be critical to maintaining the management team's overall work goals. It will also be an important factor in holding down turnover levels.

Whether they telecommute or work a regular shift, employees will continue to have twin human needs: to belong and to feel proud. An organization that is founded on values that give meaning to the work has an edge over those organizations that are purely profit-driven and merely rent their employees as production units for a few hours a day. EOCs understand that employees are attracted to bonding together and bonding with their organization through values and culture. Four steps will enable discretionary employee effort to emerge.

INCREASE PRODUCTIVITY WITH EMPLOYMENT SECURITY

According to Jeffrey Pfeffer's *The Human Equation: Building Profits by Putting People First,* "employment security" does not mean organizations should retain employees who underperform or do not work effectively with others. Performance matters—period. If a new hire does not function as required in spite of orientation, training, and assimilation into the organization, or if a longtime employee's performance declines and development efforts fail, the company must respond with reassignment or termination—or risk the lowered performance or turnover of other employees.

"Employment security" does mean that the organization will not use layoffs as its first response to a downturn in business, so employees are not in constant fear of losing their jobs. Fear of job loss automatically shoves employees to the bottom of Maslow's Hierarchy, and they go into survival mode.

In *The 100 Best Companies to Work for in America,* one requirement for inclusion among the book's best companies was a written or implicit policy against layoffs. Layoffs may provide short-term relief to the bottom line but result in long-term costs due to loss of talent and difficulty in recruiting top talent in the future. Alternatives to layoffs such as retraining, redeployment, hiring freezes or slowdowns, or attrition should be used. An organization that offers employment security will recruit sparingly and well, develop talent, pay competitively, offer challenging work, share information, and, in return, expect the very best thinking, decisions, and effort from each employee. Trust is reciprocal. Organizations cannot expect the best from their people if they do not offer the same in return.

REDUCE STATUS DISTINCTIONS
TO INCREASE UPWARD COMMUNICATION

In *The Human Equation,* Pfeffer points out that the egalitarian movement toward fewer status distinctions in the workplace began on the West Coast when formal business attire gave way to "business casual," and hallways and offices were replaced with open-plan "cube farms." The "Us versus Them" mentality fades when organizations use terms such as "associates" or "team members" instead of "employees." Some organizations have gone so far as to remove titles from all business cards—even those of corporate officers. Reserved parking spots—except for the Employee of the Month—are disappearing, as are executive dining rooms. The unspoken message matches the spoken message: All employees are valued.

By reducing status distinctions and adding communications mechanisms, the top management of EOCs has significantly increased the upward flow of ideas that improve processes, lower costs, create new markets, and develop new services.

CHANGE BEHAVIOR TO CHANGE THE CULTURE

Entire books have been written on culture change, so we will not go into the subject in depth here. Often, an external consultant must be engaged to assist with widespread culture change. While large-scale change frequently is at least a three-year process, any change starts with building a case for better ways of doing business. Once top management has made the case for refocusing (in this case, on becoming an Employer of Choice), the fastest way to change a culture is to change specific behaviors, according to "The Fast Track Approach to Changing Organizational Culture" by William Hagerup.

Feelings and values change more slowly, but changing behavior patterns is an achievable first goal. Describe the desired outcome and the desired behavior that will produce that outcome; then reward the use of new behavior. Training is one potential way to accomplish the change. Symbols can also help reinforce change. For example, buttons bearing the words "That's the Way We've Always Done It" enclosed in a red circle with a slash through it keep employees focused on the new direction. This is one approach described in an article by Scott Kirsner (1998), entitled "Designed Innovation," in *Fast Company* magazine. Repeat the message of the desired outcome and the desired behavior. Focus a positive spotlight on employees who demonstrate the new behavior, coach those who are slow to adopt it, and punish and/or terminate deliberate cultural violators. Consistency is critical.

REINFORCE THE EMERGING CULTURE
WITH CULTURE COMMUNICATION TOOLS

The true culture of an organization is seen in the way employees behave when no supervisor is watching them. How do managers treat employees, and how do employees treat one another? How do employees treat customers? Employees who want to get ahead exhibit behavior that embodies the values of the organization. Depending upon the values and rules of the culture, and assuming that the employees fit the culture, their behavior will either create negative feelings in co-workers or customers or ultimately improve the organization's financial performance. Culture determines how goals are to be attained. If organizational goals include growth and profitability, it is important that employees understand what kind of behavior is approved and is expected to deliver results. Communicating and reinforcing organizational values and desired behaviors is an important management activity.

Culture is evident in all verbal, non-verbal, written, and symbolic communications emanating from an organization. These include, but are not limited to,

- The organization's vision, mission, and strategic goals

- Employment, product, and image advertising

- Web site content and design

- Newsletters, e-mails, flyers, and intranet and bulletin board postings

- The frequency, format, and content of meetings

- Orientation processes

- Handbooks and policies

- Benefits and amenities offered

- Compensation structure

- Training offered

- Recognition programs

- Rewards

- Company-sponsored employee gatherings

- Mailings to employees' homes

- Decor, including wall colors, furniture, art, plants

- Style of employee workstations

- Annual reports

- Employee attire

- Direct mail, e-mail, and faxes to prospects and clients

- Receptionist's greeting to newcomers

- Condition of buildings and grounds

If any one of these culture-communication mechanisms does not match the intended message, the message gets muddied and possibly lost. For example, if fun is part of the culture, a subdued decor and non-personalized workstations are inconsistent. "It's a great day at GreatBiz!" should be said as if the receptionist means it. A stressed or indifferent receptionist can make an otherwise cheery greeting sound false. An EOC regularly reviews its culture communications and refines the message on an ongoing basis.

Recruiting success, retention, and growth—these are the benefits reaped by EOCs from their ongoing investment in both the training of their leaders and the conscious development of their culture.

CHAPTER TEN

RETRAIN, DEVELOP, AND PROFIT

New graduates crave continuous learning. While they do not join organizations specifically because of career development programs, they make it clear that they will not join organizations that *lack* such programs. Employees who entered the workforce in the 1990s will change jobs an average of nine times before they reach the age of 32, according to "America @ Work: The 1999 Workforce Commitment Index," released by Aon Consulting, Inc. To stay in a job, employees of all ages must feel excited about their work and the organization. Two of the best ways to create those feelings are to ensure that employees see the results of their efforts and receive attention from management. Succession planning, performance reviews, and development plans do just that.

The dominant competitive weapons of the 21st century will be the education and skills of the workforce, according to Lester Thurow, quoted in *Strategy & Business Noteworthy Quotes*. The best employees seek the best career opportunities. This ongoing quest is true for both job seekers and current employees. They know that their current skills will be outdated in less than five years. Restrictive or toxic organizations whose management teams are not interested in employee development discourage high-quality job seekers and lose the best employees. Only employees who are less motivated or feel trapped due to economic or other factors will remain. Over a short period of time, this depletion of employees ruins an organization's ability to compete.

Today, this country faces deficits not only in more sophisticated technological skills but in fundamental skills such as reading, writing, math, and reasoning. Futurists such as Tom Mahan, vice president of the Saratoga Institute, predict that in the decade ahead, 60 percent of all jobs will require skills possessed by only 20 percent of today's workforce. Due to the overall shortage of employees, and the great discrepancy between skills and job requirements, employers must be open to the idea of hiring the competencies (desired behaviors, habits, and attitudes) of superior performers and then teaching them the hard skills needed for the job. This is altogether different from hiring a body for the job. Appropriate candidates have experience and can demonstrate the desired competencies. A body breathes, occupies space, and just hopes to make it through a few pay cycles before moving on to the next shortsighted employer.

Organizations often fall behind their competitors due to a lack of trained employees. To prevent this, employers must plan for, budget for, and conduct the skills training needed by new hires as well as existing employees. Budgeting $500 per employee for training is inadequate and exacerbates the problem. Companies need to budget realistically for training, depending on the skills involved. Pretrained employees are not going to magically appear. Do not wait 90 days to train, and do not use training as a perk at the end of a good year—a good year is impossible with an unskilled or untrained new hire. Collaboration with other employers is one way to reduce overall training costs, as is the use of training offered through professional organizations. As the saying goes, "If you think training is expensive, check out the cost of ignorance." It is cheaper to train and retain employees than to replace them.

This chapter looks at the top motivator for attracting and retaining employees: career development. Ten development options are reviewed, as well as suggestions of how development and performance management support each other.

If You Won't Train Them, Someone Else Will!

There was a time when many employers hired only pretrained employees for their open positions. Although this practice lengthened fill times, it saved training dollars that were tracked in the budget. Typically, these same employers refused to train existing employees because they felt they would just be training them for someone else. Yet, according to the "1999 Workforce Study" by Tom Mahan, vice president of the Saratoga Institute, with training and development, 12 percent of employees will leave in 12 months. Without training and development, 35 percent will leave in 12 months!

Employers' reluctance to train new hires became untenable once technology hastened all business practices across the board. The number of trained users fell dramatically behind the number of job openings requiring specific skills. With the surge of interest in e-commerce and other strategic uses of technology, chances are very slim that organizations can buy or hire all of the skills they need to meet their strategic goals. Instead, they must budget to build, or train for, the skills that are needed. Extensive training is a characteristic of high-performance organizations, according to Jeffrey Pfeffer, writing in *The Human Equation: Building Profits by Putting People First.* Retraining current employees or training new employees has become the faster—and more reliable—alternative to waiting for pretrained hires.

In survey after survey, career development always ranks in the top three characteristics of an Employer of Choice. It's been referred to by many different names, including "training and development" ("America @ Work: The 1999 Workforce Commitment Index"), "intellectual challenge" ("Hot Technologies Survey"), "promise of doing innovative technical work" (ICEX Survey), and "treatment of employees" ("Corporate Character"). No matter what it is called, career development is still career development. And it has become so important that without a solid commitment to it, few employers succeed in hiring top talent.

Career development is a process—not a one-time event. Employees are not photographic film that requires a dunking, after which the individual is developed. Adults develop skills by practicing them in real-life situations. To truly build staff bench strength, so that the organization has many internal candidates from which to choose, Employers of Choice implement a variety of cutting-edge strategies: formal classroom training with cross-training, job shadowing, temporary assignments in different business units, and as many opportunities to learn the business as possible.

Increase Development and Decrease Turnover

Employers that develop employees enhance retention *and* performance. As educational level increases, so do satisfaction and loyalty to the organization. In addition, employees' feelings of being trapped decrease, according to the results of the "National Employee Relationship Report," a study conducted by Walker Information and sponsored by the Hudson Institute. Employees who feel trapped are unlikely to unleash their discretionary effort. Too often, organizations focus on training for entry-level employees or provide development experiences for senior management, but they neglect the mid-career employee with three to ten years' experience in the organization. Turnover statistics for such organizations often mirror the lack of development at specific levels within the organization.

"Employees who stay in the same position for an extended period of time are more likely to leave," according to Joanna Robbins, executive vice president and director of corporate human resources for Fleet Financial Group. "External departures within the managerial ranks breed higher turnover—almost double the expected turnover rate—for employees reporting to that manager," even if the manager is replaced with an internal hire, she added. Depending upon the level of the manager who leaves, the length of the fill time, and the subsequent turnover of direct reports, the business unit may be unable to implement its growth strategies. Clearly, retention of managers increases the ability to meet business unit goals, and the development of their skills within the position is key to encouraging them to stay. Managerial development is particularly important as a strategy to reduce turnover.

"Employers of Choice are going to be the ones who excite and retain their employees by investing in those employees," according to Ed Galvin, partner and head of entrepreneurial advisory services practice at PricewaterhouseCoopers LLP, quoted in an article headlined "Keeping It Current," in the November 15, 1998, *Chicago*

Tribune. This investment in employee training requires more than one or two days' training per year.

The same article pointed out that Motorola, for example, operates Motorola University, a free-standing educational division that offers business courses in software development, foreign languages, project management, and other subjects, as well as lifestyle courses such as personal finance and personal communication. Employees are required to complete 40 hours of training per year, but some employees take up to 120 hours.

While not every employer can offer a university, an EOC does at least provide substantially more training at every level than other organizations and uses the full range of innovative training practices and media. High-performance work settings call for learning that occurs formally as well as just when and where it's needed. Development makes employees more attractive inside the organization as well as outside it—and development also makes employees more resistant to recruitment.

It is much easier for a recruiter or a representative of another organization to interest your employee in making a change if your employee's supervisor has not been vigilant about discussing development needs and aspirations, or has not scheduled or completed an expected review meeting. Since smart organizations use a variety of means to recruit new employees, such as networking, churches, and professional organizations, your current employees are on the receiving end of regular pitches, urging them to discuss how they might contribute at a new organization. To increase their resistance to the onslaught of opportunities, your organization must apply a variety of retention strategies. Career development is an integrated approach that includes "skill needs" forecasting, succession planning, performance reviews, and development activities—and it is one of the strongest strategies for re-recruiting employees on a regular basis!

Groom High-Potentials and Build Bench Strength with Succession Planning

Growth depends upon the quality and quantity of existing as well as potential employees. If senior management believes that no current employee has the skills needed to move the organization forward, then external recruiting is the only answer. However, this must be augmented with a concurrent effort to raise the skill levels of current staff. An exercise must be conducted to identify internal employees who could replace key executives, managers, and professionals. After identifying these individuals, development programs are needed to prepare them for moving into higher positions.

If—as indicated by the 1999 Walker Information "National Employee Relationship Report"—the average length an employee stays in one position is 2.7 years, then old-style, three- to five-year promotion cycles are obsolete, and they could be a deterrent to successful recruiting and retention. Shorter tenure per position must be built into the development plan of any company aiming for EOC status, as should processes to speed the development of key individuals. And definitely, more support must be given to newcomers in key roles.

To uncover development needs, succession planning should be conducted for all levels of the organization, from the top down. Succession plans guide the grooming of high-potential individuals, bond them to the organization, and provide for greater continuity during career movement. Clearly, individuals selected for development are on the fast track.

Fast-trackers are the lifeblood of any organization. They demonstrate their leadership with co-workers and customers every day. The core competencies of a fast-tracker include

- Customer focus: is committed to meeting or exceeding customer expectations and maintaining strong customer relationships

- Results focus: is not happy until the job is done; motivates self and others to get needed results

- Technical focus: has the know-how to get the job done; is intellectually inventive

- Learning focus: is able to learn new skills and competencies quickly; can assimilate what he or she learns to fit potential company or client needs; open to change; enjoys learning

High-potentials are also distinguished by these four qualities:

1. Their desire to contribute to the growth of the organization

2. Their enthusiasm for the organization and their role

3. Their appreciation for hard work

4. Their maintenance of high personal standards

Clearly, fast-trackers are in great demand in any organization. Once succession planning has identified employees for future leadership positions, individual development plans must be determined.

Unless an organization wants to become the farm club for other employers, individual development plans are needed for *all* employees. Knowledge is developed through training, but talent is developed through work experiences. Often, new leaders emerge from the ranks of those not originally selected for future leadership roles. Be ready to augment their development with accelerated learning opportunities.

Performance Reviews and Development Plans

Performance reviews look back on an employee's performance to date, including criteria such as projects completed and service provided, but development plans look to the future. As the pace of business continues to speed up to reflect the effects of technology and the changing business environment, more emphasis has been placed on ongoing input and development plans (or ongoing development) than on performance reviews. Because raises are frequently tied to past performance, most employees are eager for both reviews and development plans. EOCs build systems to ensure that the review-development process is not delayed or forgotten. Many EOCs make the timely conduct of performance reviews a specific objective for which managers at all levels are held responsible.

Successful performance depends upon the shared understanding of expectations between an employee and his or her supervisor—yet only two out of five employees say they know what those expectations are. A performance plan, used as the basis of a performance appraisal, is a professional development tool that focuses attention on the key individual contributions that ultimately enable an organization to achieve its business goals. Ideally, individual performance plans fit into departmental budgets and goals, support the organization's overall goals and objectives, and align with its values, mission, and vision.

Performance reviews are usually held annually. However, many organizations offer biannual or quarterly reviews under certain conditions, such as if the employee is new, the organization is very project oriented or undergoing radical change, or more communication (and subsequent positive motivation) is desired.

The best way to enhance human performance is to provide input in three areas:

1. What is expected

2. How performance will be measured

3. What support management will provide

Together, the employee and supervisor should develop clear, measurable objectives, as well as an individual development plan to enhance the employee's business and professional skills. Efforts and results should be documented to provide the foundation for a company strategy of pay-for-performance (immediate compensation adjustments as well as career growth opportunities).

Many employers call this development of performance objectives a "contract" between an employee and a supervisor that spells out performance objectives. Objectives should be specific, measurable, attainable, and output-oriented. Examples of measurable standards are quality, quantity, cost, and timeliness. Typically, individuals have two to five broad areas of responsibility with one to three performance objectives for each responsibility.

Development plans are often omitted from performance reviews—yet they constitute the number one key to employee retention. Typically, development plans focus on the hard or soft skills needed either to perform the current position at a higher level or to prepare for a future position. (Movement into new responsibilities or positions should not be promised unless the move is imminent and the individual has been selected for the position.) Skills should be developed one at a time. Training, cross-training, rotational job assignments, stretch assignments, written materials, videotapes, and other means of learning new hard and soft skills should be planned. Set deadlines for completion so that development is not forgotten in the crush of business.

Performance tracking is easier if regular meetings and reports are an ongoing part of the employee-supervisor relationship. For both the employer and the employee, these meetings and reports provide an opportunity to discuss project progress on a regular basis and form the framework for the quarterly, semiannual, or annual review. Other sources of input include direct observation and third-party or feedback reports. Ongoing feedback is preferable—and more motivating—than sparse feedback, with an annual review as the centerpiece of employee-supervisor communication.

A cardinal rule for performance reviews at EOCs is "No surprises!" Unexpected negative input or omission or delay of expected performance appraisals or development plans is often the cause of soured relationships between employees and supervisors, which loosens the ties between an employee and the organization. On a monthly basis, many EOCs publish lists of employees who are due for reviews. HR departments often provide assistance with difficult reviews so that underperforming employees have a better chance of improving and competent employees continue to be motivated.

Ten Development Options

EOCs forecast the future—especially business cycles and changing client needs—and start recruiting and retraining for necessary skill sets. Different combinations of these 10 development options are often used together.

IN-HOUSE TRAINING AND DEVELOPMENT

To attract and retain high-potential employees, organizations must offer a targeted range of courses and resources that build core career skills. In-house curricula typically include the following.

- Company overview, which is often covered as part of new-hire orientation. This learning experience provides the employee with company history and financials, internal structure, and future goals, plus a technology overview, policies and procedures overview, supplier and customer overview, and competitive strategies.

- Mentoring and networking opportunities that encourage learning from as well as teaching colleagues. EOCs provide multiple opportunities for employees to participate in group activities, intranet discussion groups, and professional, formal mentor relationships.

- Technical training, including knowledge of current technologies, best practices, and external business drivers, all of which are needed if employers are to meet and exceed customer expectations. The nature of technical training will vary widely according to the needs of the employee.

- Project-based development, or learning transfer into the workplace. Project management skills combined with other learning enables the individual to work cross-functionally as well as to achieve departmental goals.

Each organization requires its own training-and-development plan and structure. Ongoing assessment of needs, as well as development or purchase of course curricula, ensures that the plan's content meets the needs of the greatest number of employees. However, not all learning occurs in classrooms, and an organization should not restrict itself to any one particular educational method.

CONSULTANTS AS TRAINERS

Many organizations hire a consultant or a team of consultants, but they fail to get the most from the experience because of what they do not write into the contract. The consultants arrive, complete their projects, turn in their reports, and leave—without transferring their knowledge to the selected employees. This is a missed development opportunity!

Instead, organizations must get the most from their consultants by demanding knowledge transfer to their employees. By teaming with consultants, the employees can learn how to gather information, how decisions are made, and why specific alternatives are better than others. Write into your contract with consultants that all processes, models, and techniques developed during the project will be shared with employees so that they may carry forward the results of the project.

DEVELOPMENT EXPERIENCES

When an employee at any level believes that he or she has no more to learn, bonds to the organization weaken. Use the availability of development experiences as a retention tool. Adults learn by doing. As a reward for your excellent employees,

- "Loan" an executive to the United Way or to your city's government for 6 to 12 months

- Free project managers and others who have transferable skills to work on business-process reengineering projects elsewhere in the organization

- Cross-train employees within a group or between two groups

- Exchange employees with a strategic partner

- Team your employees with those of a strategic partner to develop a new product

- Allow a paid or unpaid sabbatical of 3 to 12 months, with the opportunity to return to the same or a similar position

Publicize the development opportunities in process so that other employees know what is available. For example, employees at Opus, a nine-year-old marketing agency in Richmond, Virginia, are encouraged to take a "radical sabbatical" on the company's dime. Employees have gone rock climbing or attended chef's school—and the director of marketing plans to climb Mount Everest, according to an article by Liesa Goins in the September 1999 issue of *POV Magazine*. The goal is to stimulate thinking and innovative ideas.

TUITION REIMBURSEMENT

Tuition reimbursement is fast becoming one of the keys to successful recruiting and retention because neither the external candidate nor the current employee has to use the benefit for it to work its magic! Given two equal offers, the candidate will take the one with tuition reimbursement—even if returning to college has not been a consideration to date. Just having the option is very enticing. Once college classes are initiated, few employees will leave their current employers if they will then have to pay 100 percent of their tuition.

In seminars around the country, my audiences have shared their various approaches to tuition reimbursement. While the trend leans strongly toward 100 percent coverage of course work at an accredited college or university, with immediate eligibility and no other restrictions, alternative approaches include

- Reimbursement of fixed amounts such as $1,500 per year, the cost of one to three classes per semester, or a set percentage of the cost of classes completed

- Reimbursement for grades of A or B only

- Reimbursement only for course work in pursuit of degrees that could be useful in the organization

- Reimbursement only for classes in degree studies, not development classes

- Requirement that the employee pay back a percentage of the cost of the degree if he or she leaves the organization within one year of completing any class

Since these types of restrictions can be very tough to monitor, many organizations apply tuition reimbursement only to course work at an accredited college or university.

In 1999, to encourage recruitment of night-shift employees in Indianapolis, UPS used billboards to publicize its offer of 100 percent tuition reimbursement with no payback. It worked! Many employers find that classes cost much less than other recruitment techniques— and less than long fill times. To encourage voluntary participation and further bond your employees to your organization,

- Each semester, print a group photo of employees who are in degree programs

- Showcase your employees in your organization's newsletter or at your intranet site when they complete degrees

PAID MEMBERSHIPS IN PROFESSIONAL ORGANIZATIONS, USER GROUPS, AND ROUNDTABLES

Paid memberships should be listed as a company benefit because they are such strong retention tools. Professional organizations, high-tech user groups, and function-focused roundtables are some of the least expensive resources for training employees.

User groups and roundtables create peer relationships that facilitate problem solving, brainstorming, and resource sharing. While user groups are open to users of specific software or hardware, roundtables are usually by invitation only. Roundtables typically are made up of senior-level members of IT, HR, or other departments from different, non-competing organizations.

Frequently, training takes the form of speakers who provide industry, professional, or other trend or skill overviews. Guest speakers convey a bounty of valuable information that can be put to immediate use in your organization. Additionally, employees who are encouraged to take leadership roles in organizations learn management skills, such as how to chair a meeting, prepare an agenda, follow *Robert's Rules of Order*, or influence other volunteers.

To encourage voluntary participation and further bond your employees to your organization, publicize it when employees

- Join organizations or renew memberships

- Take leadership roles in professional organizations

- Become certified through professional organizations

PAID MEMBERSHIPS IN COMMUNITY ORGANIZATIONS

A surprising percentage of your employees already belong to one or more community organizations. While it has been traditional for executives to do so, according to Gen X surveys, younger employees feel a strong desire to change the world and make a difference. Joining and becoming active in Kiwanis, Rotary, Lions, the American Cancer Society, United Way, and other community organizations are among the activities toward which employees gravitate after work. Clocking out at 5:00 P.M. often means attending committee meetings, organizing or participating in fund-raising activities, tutoring students, rocking sick babies in hospitals, or otherwise giving back to the community.

Even small organizations can make a big impact on their communities while developing and bonding with employees. ONEX, Inc., a high-tech consulting and recruiting company in Indianapolis, allows each employee up to $200 per year pay for membership in a professional or civic organization. In 1999, ONEX employees were represented in more than 200 civic organizations (and 101 professional organizations) at a time when the company had approximately 190 employee. ONEX employees provided 16 team captains, who recruited 10 teammates each, for one American Heart Association fundraising run. Community involvement is just one strategy for building relationships among employees and with the company and for keeping turnover rates to less than 10 percent.

To encourage voluntary participation and further bond your employees to your organization:

- Pay community organization dues and costs for lunch or dinner meetings

- Encourage voluntary participation in fund-raising events from within the organization

- On your Web site and in your newsletters, list the names of organizations to which your employees belong

- Provide special recognition for "super volunteers" in the form of pins or newsletter articles

CERTIFICATION PROGRAMS
Ours is an educated world, and it is becoming more so by the day! As the emphasis on upgrading skills increases throughout an organization, there will be more pressure in many fields to demonstrate levels of proficiency. For example, some organizations will do business

only with ISO-certified vendors. It is worth paying for professional certifications if your employees will benefit from software or other technical training. Some employees may want to pursue CPA (public accounting), APR (public relations), PHR or SPHR (human resources), or other certifications. Still others may need to attend seminars to receive continuing education units (CEUs) to maintain a license.

Having certified employees is an advantage from a marketing standpoint as well as from a recruiting and retention standpoint. To encourage voluntary participation and further bond your employees to your organization,

- Add certifications to employee business cards

- Showcase your employees in your organization's newsletter or at your intranet site when they complete certifications

- Add a certifications field in your employee database so that others may serve as information resources for interested non-certified employees

GENERAL EDUCATION DEVELOPMENT (GED) PROGRAMS

Many employers have one or even dozens of employees who have not received high school diplomas. Often, these individuals also lack critical skills such as reading, writing, math, and reasoning and are promoted less often than other employees. Turning even one individual around will encourage others to step forward and learn to read or do whatever it takes to finish their high school equivalency work.

Employees with GED certificates are better able to accomplish their tasks and are promoted more readily. Employees who believe that they have an employment future are likely to be loyal. With a GED certificate, these experienced employees can be retrained to use emerging technologies so that they can move to higher-value positions. To encourage voluntary participation and further bond your employees to your organization,

- Make GED completion available and easy

- Contact the nearest local high school and obtain a schedule of the courses

- Investigate television-based courses that could be provided on-site or viewed at home

- Ask whether instructors are available to teach classes in your training or conference rooms at times that are convenient for your employees

- Allow employees to attend classes on company time, if necessary

- Pay any costs associated with completion

- Make a big deal out of completion of GED programs—building pride builds loyalty!

ENGLISH AS A SECOND LANGUAGE

The United States has a great need for entry-level employees but lacks native-born young people. Eager potential hires from the Balkans, South and Central America, Asia, and Africa have entered this country ready to work—but do not have the requisite reading and verbal skills. Offering classes to existing employees and new hires will improve their productivity and is likely to improve their loyalty. Some organizations are offering mini–English classes at open houses as part of the array of organization benefits.

To encourage voluntary participation and further bond your employees to your organization,

- Provide English as a second language classes free of charge

- Survey your employees on the best times to offer classes; be willing to provide classes on-site before, during, or after normal work hours

- Provide certificates, group photos, and other forms of recognition for graduates

LIBRARIES FOR CONTINUOUS LEARNING

Access to learning is a key retention tool. Technology has accelerated change in so many fields that keeping up means not only building skills but understanding the industry overall, trends, national or international marketplaces, and more. Further, employers and employees alike are expecting more of individual employees. How can employees keep up, stay competitive, and broaden their knowledge of hard and soft skills as well as business issues? Corporate libraries—online or hard copy—are the answer!

A corporate library need not be complicated—but it must be easily accessible in order to be effective. The goal is to spark interest and facilitate learning in a variety of areas. Employees welcome the opportunity to acquire information about their specific industry; management and team skills; parenting, stress, and time-management skills; and more. The corporate library might include

- Weekly or monthly online publications

- E-mail about new articles or new books in the library

- An online connection to city or university libraries for articles, periodicals, and books

- A bookcase filled with industry publications

- A room with periodicals, books, and audio- and videotapes to be used on-site during lunch or other breaks

- A self-serve library where employees use simple library software to check out publications or other resources

- A full-fledged library with a degreed librarian and Internet access, including resources available in a variety of media such as books, periodicals, microfiche, and articles on the company intranet

Dual Career Paths

In addition to offering development opportunities for all, retention of some special groups of employees requires a different approach. High-performing technical and scientific employees often desire career growth opportunities without management responsibilities. People management is not for everyone—as many organizations have discovered after promoting apparently logical candidates based on their tenure within the organization, expertise with project management, or even their desire for the position. Too often, a solid performer with great depth of knowledge and an excellent performance record is thrust into a mid- to senior-level management position without adequate training or experience. This mistake may cost the organization both the new manager and his or her direct reports. Turnover is too costly: it's more sound financially to invest in the development of individuals. Development investments result in increased profitability.

Alternatively, non-management-track employees need development opportunities and career paths that enable them to deepen their skills and advance within their professions. Failure to develop these technical or scientific employees will encourage them to promote themselves out of the organization. Paying attention to the fit between the organization's needs and the needs of the individual is more important today than in the past. Flexibility and creativity will be needed to ensure that needs of both are met.

Development Encourages Qualified Promotion from Within

Without a substantial effort to develop internal employees, the organization has no choice but to hire from outside. Total elimination of external hires is not an EOC goal, but EOCs know that succession planning and promotion from within build loyalty. Once an employee is overlooked twice for what seems like a logical move into an available position, he or she infers (correctly or incorrectly) that an internal job change is not likely. When a larger pattern of external hires is established, especially for replacements at a management level, the message is very clear: the organization does not have an internal development plan in place, so employees desiring career movement should look elsewhere.

Assuming that training and development are available and are being utilized throughout the organization, the next step to increase the quality and quantity of internal candidates is to post all job openings internally. Even senior-level positions with no apparent internal successors should be posted to enable employees to refer candidates.

Fewer than half of the employers attending my seminars post all job openings, yet even unqualified employees may know excellent candidates. Internal postings should include minimum skill and experience requirements, the salary range, cut-off dates for application, reporting information, and contact information. Since many internal candidates may lack a résumé, it benefits the organization to allow either online or in-person completion of the application and perhaps even to assist with the résumé. Many EOCs also provide interview technique workshops on a regular basis to improve the skills of internal candidates.

Career development is not a luxury; it is a necessity if an organization intends to win the talent war. Employees know that their skills must be developed, augmented, and even obsoleted. Since the best employees seek the best career opportunities, ongoing development must be available. EOCs use development opportunities in their recruiting, in their internal communications, and in their performance standards to strengthen the organization's ability to compete.

CHAPTER ELEVEN

NEW COMPENSATION AND BENEFITS STRATEGIES

"Compensation is perceived to be one of the top three causes of dissatisfaction among high-turnover employee populations," according to a 1999 Mercer Fax Facts study entitled "Turnover—How Does It Affect Your Business?" Low turnover, on the other hand, is not perceived as mostly compensation driven. In other words, low compensation may drive away good employees, but fair compensation alone may not be enough to keep them.

"Everyone has a price," as the saying goes—but is it in dollars and cents? It is important to pay your people fairly *and* to understand what is important to them. The only way to know what is important is to listen—something that Employers of Choice do well.

Earning as much as possible drives some employees. For a few, pushing themselves to the limit is a more powerful incentive than competing with others. For other employees, title, position, and recognition play a bigger role. Having the ability to influence others is important to yet other employees. Still other individuals are attracted to an organization where they can do work that contributes to the public good. Not every organization will have all of these types of employees, but most organizations do have employees who are motivated by a variety of rewards.

Clearly, if Maslow's Hierarchy holds true, meeting basic needs of food, shelter, clothing, etc., is a motivator for all employees. What differs is how we define the dollar amount needed to meet our basic needs and how that pay is structured. There is no one way to structure compensation or benefits; a variety of pay and benefit programs work well in different organizations. In fact, it is common for organizations to offer multiple compensation programs that vary from department to department. As can be expected, this time of sweeping business changes is resulting in sweeping compensation and benefits changes.

The last two decades have been characterized by profit pressures and the popularity of the "hire the best brains for the least amount of money" approach—or simply a policy of hiring for the least amount of money. A high priority for HR and others in senior management has been to ensure pay equity within the organization, with little consideration for the strategic value of either individuals or departments or for the value the external marketplace assigns to the same employees. The overall belief was that organizations could either make money or make people happy—not both.

EOCs have known for some time that the combination of compensation and benefits (total compensation) is a major key to their success. Frequently, EOCs pay at or above the marketplace mid-range for all employees—but they also select employees carefully, set high performance goals, and utilize extensive employee development and performance-management programs to ensure that the organization receives an excellent return on every individual. EOCs want to make money *and* make their employees happy. This is a much stronger long-term strategy than the knee-jerk response to the tight hiring market of some employers: using compensation to hold on to all employees—even non-productive employees—because replacements are so hard to find. "Golden handcuffs" bind the employee—and the employer. Neither underpaying nor overpaying employees across the board will achieve the goal of attracting and retaining high-quality employees. If employees do not see a relationship between level of performance and reward, they may either leave or quit on the job.

This chapter looks at the importance of a well-understood compensation and benefits philosophy, the variety of effective compensation approaches and types of benefits, and the worth of communicating total compensation value.

Paying Peanuts? Expect to Hire Monkeys

Today, savvy employees know about pay ranges for their positions and in their industries. Employees talk to other employees about their compensation. Salary surveys are readily available through professional organizations, business publications, and a variety of Internet sites. While compensation does not rate as the number one reason that a job seeker might take a position, or that a current employee might leave, compensation is a strong factor in both decisions. Below-market compensation usually knocks out all but the highest-profile employers (such as Disney or Microsoft). According to "Basic Compensation" by Robert M. James, employees expect their compensation to do the following:

- To be competitive relative to other organizations

- To be competitive relative to similar jobs in the organization

- To be commensurate with their performance

- To include a balance between base pay and incentive pay

- To reflect their individual or departmental efforts toward incentive goals

21st-Century Philosophies

Compensation strategy is based on a set of philosophies, beliefs, and plans for the organization. Typical objectives might include

- To attract and retain the highest-quality employees in order to attain corporate growth goals

- To encourage team achievement of corporate goals

- To provide total cash compensation at average or substantially above-average marketplace levels

- To motivate employees to meet or exceed the organization's short- and long-term objectives

- To promote the appropriate balance between sales and service to the customer

The dearth of candidates overall—especially technical, administrative support, and customer service candidates—has magnified the need to retain employees. In the past, salaries were often based on tenure. Today, salary increases are based on employees' increased value to the organization. Therefore, employers must use employee development strategies to improve employees' productivity and quality. Up-to-date employee skills are a must if the organization is to receive a return on compensation.

According to the "1999 Compensation Planning Briefing," a presentation by Steve Jones of William M. Mercer, Inc., at the Human Resources Association of Central Indiana, as organizations turn away from pay-for-tenure pay practices, they have added different approaches, including

- Team-based pay (27 percent)

- Broadbanding (21 percent)

- Cash profit sharing (19 percent)

- Skills-based pay, including pay for certifications (17 percent)

- Competency-based pay (15 percent)

- Gain sharing (12 percent)

- Multi-rater performance management

- Stock options for executives, groups of key employees, or all employees

"The companies that are most successful attracting and retaining top-performing employees often offer perks that are similar to start-ups," says Mark Oldman, co-founder of VaultReports.com, an independent publisher of insider guides to companies, quoted by Drew Friedman in *POV Magazine*, September 1999. Specifically, he pointed to stock options, frequent salary reviews, and faster promotions based on performance.

EOCs know that they will be unable to build competitive organizations if managers cannot reward top performers. If your organization is paying all employees with the same job title the same amount, you are probably underpaying your top performers and overpaying your poorest ones. Increasing pay for no reason except tenure sends a negative message to top performers: extra effort and results are not measured or recognized. In a blind attempt to reduce turnover, employers may increase pay without streamlining processes, implementing technology, or improving the skills of employees. Today, this strategy will backfire. Overpaid, underproductive employees contribute to narrowed profit margins, which have resulted in mergers and closures.

All employees deserve to be paid based on their contributions to the organization's success. Understanding the cost of replacing your current employees will be an incentive to review all compensation so that you can increase the salaries and other benefits of any employees whose rates are lagging behind the marketplace. If the pay rate of an employee or group of employees is significantly below the market standard for the position(s), the organization should first determine why this mismatch has developed. Is it a factor of job performance, low starting pay, past small merit budgets, or improper job classification? Once this question is answered, a decision on how to address the difference can be made. Salary surveys, salary information from candidates, and other marketplace data sources will be valuable tools in helping you make your decision.

Additionally, special attention should be put on key employees. Key employees in your organization might include a senior scientist, the entire sales force, call center employees, nurses, multilingual management employees, specific executives, or those with technical skills. Ask yourself which individual or departmental loss would also result in the loss of

- Key clients

- Critical project-management skills

- Knowledge of core products/services

- Critical skills

- Innovative thinking

Not only should the organization have a documented succession plan for these individuals, but their total compensation should be reviewed to ensure that it is competitive. Particularly in regions of the country where technical, nursing, or other skills are in considerable demand, compensation survey data should be checked twice a year.

Measuring Return on Compensation

According to "Basic Compensation" by Robert M. James, return on compensation can be measured in two ways:

1. The ability to attract and retain needed talent

2. The ability to motivate employees to perform at superior levels and deliver quality results on a consistent basis

For the majority of employees, compensation is composed of base salary, benefits, and possibly some incentive pay. For every dollar of total compensation, the mix is typically

• Base salary: 65–70 cents

• Benefits: 20–25 cents

• Incentive pay: up to 10 cents

For more risk-tolerant groups (sales representatives or the executive teams of high-tech start-ups, for example) within the organization, incentive compensation plays a much greater role in the overall compensation package. For these individuals, compensation packages may include gain sharing, cash profit sharing, group or team incentives, stock options, and individual bonus programs.

Total compensation is a combination of direct cash (wages or salary), including short-term incentives or commission and long-term incentives or bonus, plus benefits and perks. Perks might include a car, membership at a country club, or access to corporate apartments when traveling. Pay is rarely 100 percent commission, but if a commission structure is offered and the goals are realistic, the individuals could earn considerably more than they would make with a more conventional pay structure.

In some organizations, individuals with unique or critical skills may command unique pay levels and programs. Organizations pay whatever it takes to attract and retain these individuals. Often, while they receive more base pay than many other employees, a large component of their compensation is made up of bonus and incentive pay to ensure that the organization receives equivalent value and a degree of equity is maintained.

Does a 4 Percent Increase Fit Your Organization's Compensation Philosophy?

Employees who have been working for 15 or more years may recall receiving increases of at least 10 percent. For the past decade, average increases for satisfactory performance hovered around 4 percent. Supervisors have had to make tough decisions about whether to reward superior performers or simply share the allotted funds among all employees. For employers who use a "performance matrix" approach for annual merit increases of 4 percent, the differential between average performers and high performers has been around 3 percent. Even with rating grids, low cost-of-living increases, and efforts to explain the reasons behind the range of performance increases, the increases themselves have been too small to be characterized as a motivating force in many organizations.

As a means of supplementing the traditional salary increase process and level, many EOCs have decided to

- Create greater disparity between rewards for expected performance and rewards for superior performance

- Bring employee pay to range midpoints and use incentive or spot bonus programs to motivate superior performance

Establishment of the appropriate base-incentive mix is critical. Employees will accept a lower level of base pay only if the incentive component is viewed as achievable and it rewards the organization's desired behavior. Effective incentive plans provide targets beyond the market rate for the position, with higher rewards for even greater levels of performance. According to Roger Herman, in *Keeping Good People,* the level of incentive pay should be based on

- The age of the company

- Industry practice

- The competition

- Motivational stretch required

- Organizational culture

- The company's compensation philosophy

Today, employers have many ways in which to create compensation programs that are more tailored to employees' needs and to achieving organizational goals. Variable pay programs are being used to motivate employee performance. Team or small-group incentives, non-cash awards, spot cash awards, individual incentives, gain sharing, and cash profit sharing are being used by an increasing number of employers, according to the "1998 Compensation Planning Briefing," a presentation by Robert Roeder of William M. Mercer, Inc., for the Human Resources Association of Central Indiana.

Additionally, employers are reevaluating the frequency and amount of salary increases for vulnerable groups such as information systems employees, engineers, and others who work in critical occupations; they may also consider adjustments to the salary structure itself to redefine the minimum, median, and maximum pay points. If your organization is undergoing this reevaluation process, be sure to design and upgrade compensation plans throughout the organization so that everyone—including administrative support staff—receives the message that he or she adds value.

The area of compensation is undergoing rapid change in response to the changing business environment. Work teams, start-up companies, and other business realities are driving the search for better approaches to compensation.

Announcements of changes to the compensation plan are often met with resistance and resignations. When developing compensation plans, the organization must integrate market-competitive pay ranges and performance-related increases in order to better the new program's chances for acceptance. Although using a task force approach to develop the new system may take longer, employee acceptance is more likely at all levels.

New compensation plans should not be implemented via memo. The best person to deliver a new compensation plan to employees is their own supervisor. This means that HR or an outside consultant must train the supervisors to make sure they understand both the plan and the presentation. Expect to develop printed support materials, schedule multiple group meetings, and follow up with individual meetings. By doing it right the first time, you will avoid anger, frustration, disappointment—and turnover.

To ensure that you have the best guidance in this complicated area, engage a consultant to assist your organization with a marketplace survey and/or the development of a more effective compensation plan. Consultants may be contacted through your local HR association, the American Compensation Association or by word of mouth from other colleagues and business associates.

Compensation Survey Resources

Compensation surveys are an important tool in the development of appropriate pay programs. If at all possible, use multiple sources to verify information. It is important to know the source of salary information for each survey. Newspapers and business magazines tend to survey employees instead of organizations. Did payroll or compensation specialists provide the data—or did they come from employees (who tend to inflate figures)? Reliable sources for surveys include

- Professional organizations

- Chambers of commerce

- Pooled information from area employers

- Temporary agencies

- Recruiting firms

- Compensation consulting firms

Because of the time lag between the gathering of information and publishing, cross-check any survey information with your own interview results. (What are candidates saying about their current compensation? Are you losing good candidates because your offers are too low?) For positions that are particularly difficult to fill in your region, share information with area employers or conduct a survey yourself to get the most accurate information. Be sure to inquire about benefits, too! Competitive total compensation is a mix of pay and benefits.

Benefits Are Half the Equation

McDonald's and Starbucks made strategic decisions in the late 1990s that set them apart from other employers competing for the same employees: they decided to give benefits to *all* employees—full-time and part-time. McDonald's does not require a waiting period and also has flexible hours. Starbucks offers stock options to full- and part-time employees.

When a candidate is evaluating a job offer, he or she evaluates not only the compensation but the benefits provided by the organization. In order to attract and retain employees, the benefits portion of the equation must meet the needs of the evolving employee population. Many benefits programs were designed in the 1950s—and are overdue for review.

Though too rarely articulated, every organization has a benefits philosophy. This philosophy determines which benefits will be offered, what amount the organization will pay, and desired perceptions of the benefits offered on the part of employees. Management may also want to discuss whether the level of benefits provided by other employers is of concern, how much control employees should have over the form of their benefits, and how internal administrative capabilities will drive the design of benefits programs.

By developing a benefits policy statement, the organization will have a blueprint for designing an appropriate plan. Standard benefits may include medical and dental coverage; short-term and long-term life insurance, including dependent life insurance; short-term and long-term disability insurance; retirement benefits, including defined contribution savings plans such as private sector Section 401(k), not-for-profit Section 403(b), or government employee Section 457 savings plans and/or defined benefit pension plans; vacation time and holidays; sick pay and personal days; vision and hearing care; prescription drug coverage; accidental death and dismemberment (AD&D) insurance; relocation compensation that pays all costs, a percentage, or a flat amount and up-front moving bonuses and retiree medical or death benefits.

Benefits are not restricted to those listed above, nor are all of these benefits offered by all employers. Additionally, while some employers pay all or a portion of the cost of some benefit plans, other employers simply make benefits available. One retention strategy is to pay a greater percentage—or the full benefits costs—for longer-tenured or retired employees.

More employers are taking a look at their list of benefits and finding ways to add to it. Employers are starting to get creative to meet employee needs. Many organizations offer matching donations to 401(k) plans, profit sharing, and paid time-off (PTO) plans. Some employers allow employees to either "buy" extra vacation days, roll over vacations days to the next year, or contribute unused vacation days to a reserve for other employees who lack enough sick, personal, or vacation days to cover emergency illnesses or other family situations. Many employers have decided to offer four weeks' paid vacation in recognition of their high-stress, high-demand work environments.

In the 1950s, when many benefits programs were originally designed, the typical family had two parents and one breadwinner. Today, many households are dual income or may include single parents with one or more children. Many Baby Boomers are caring for aging parents—and sending children to college. Gen X or Gen Y employees may have different priorities and needs. With such variety among employees, many organizations offer flexible plans that enable employees to select the range of benefits that suits their individual and family needs.

Most employers seek ways to continuously upgrade their benefits offerings while controlling costs. The expense and variety of benefits can make decisions difficult. Small employers are now exploring the use of professional employment organizations, or PEOs, which co-manage their employees, provide a competitive range of benefits, and administer the benefits as well as assist with other HR functions. Because of the variety of laws covering benefits plans, the availability of taxable and nontaxable benefits, reporting requirements, and the need to communicate certain mandatory information to employees, it is advisable to work with a benefits broker, consultant, or attorney to develop the plan design.

Employee- and Family-Friendly Benefits

Many employers acknowledge that their employees work hard, work long—or just deserve to feel special. While employee- and family-friendly benefits do add costs, they build loyalty and garner great local public relations. Consider

- Adoption assistance ($1,000–$5,000)

- Long-term-care insurance

- Daycare cost vouchers or on-site or company-owned daycare

- Flexible spending accounts for childcare or medical benefits

- Wellness programs

- Educational assistance (all costs, a percentage, or a flat amount)

- Prepaid legal insurance

- Benefits for domestic partners

- Lawn care

- Parental leave for up to one year (for new mothers and fathers)

- Physical examinations

- Vacation bonuses ($350–$1,200)

- First-class air travel for all employees on company business (over a certain distance)

- Shoulder massages

- Academic scholarships for employees' children
- Summer camps and vacation retreats
- Paid week off at Christmas
- Fridays off in May (or another slow month)
- Brainstorming trips to Disney World
- Home computer
- Leased car with fully paid insurance after one year on the job
- Camping gear and snowboard rentals
- Discount sports tickets
- Low-cost or no-cost loans
- Monthly housecleaning after three years on the job

While benefits may be determined by senior management, using an employee task force to generate ideas and offer input may be a valuable way to ensure that the benefits offered will meet the needs of your various employee populations. The task force should provide suggestions that are cost-effective, valued by the workforce, and leading edge—and will position your organization as an Employer of Choice.

Low-Cost or Lifestyle Benefits

While many benefits are commonly offered, the *uncommon* benefits are making headlines as employers respond to changes in the workforce. Long commutes, different family configurations, time pressure—and the desire to stand out among other employers—are driving the addition of benefits.

Low-cost or no-cost benefits might include

- Casual dress on Fridays or every day
- Pickup and delivery of dry cleaning and laundry
- ATM machines on-site

- Checking accounts through one or more banks
- Credit union membership
- Flexible working hours
- Fruit
- Coffees, lattes, and espressos
- Lunch
- Movie passes, oil changes, and car washes
- Company products or services
- Flu shots
- Work clothes
- Shuttle service for employees working odd hours
- Haircuts
- Breakfast donuts
- Ice cream bars on a hot day

  The sky is the limit!

Benefits-Survey Sources

Benefits-survey information is valuable for employers because it provides information that leads to better decisions. Employers may conduct or participate in surveys of organizations that share their standard industrial classification (SIC) codes, or they may conduct or participate in surveys of employers in their geographic area who compete with them for employees. Depending upon your products or services, one or both of these alternatives will make sense. While business magazines often provide benefits information, their sources may not be credible. General benefits-survey information is available through benefits-oriented professional associations such as the Society for Human Resource Management (SHRM) at **www.shrm.org**, Certified Employee Benefits Specialists (CEBS), the American

Compensation Association (ACA), the Association of Benefits and Compensation (ABC), or the International Foundation of Employee Benefits (IFEB). Additional sources include

- Recruiting firms
- Benefits consulting firms
- Benefits brokers

Communicate the Full Value of Total Compensation

Few employees understand or appreciate the value of the compensation and benefits packages offered by their employers. To help employees understand the organization's investment beyond the payment of base salaries, many organizations provide an annual benefits statement in a one-page format. Typically, all benefits are listed along with the annualized dollar value. These figures may be presented individually or for the entire company. Social Security, workers' compensation, and unemployment insurance should not be omitted. Many benefits brokers and third-party administrators provide individualized employee reports as part of their services.

The benefits offered by an organization are a powerful recruiting tool, but they may be too numerous for your employees to recall when speaking to a friend who might be a prospective employee. Arm your employees with recruiting brochures, or consider printing your more unusual benefits on the back of company business cards.

BECOMING AN EMPLOYER OF CHOICE

The soft issues have become the hard issues.

Ten years ago, the interviewer asked, "Why should I hire *you*?" Today, the job candidate asks, "Why should I come to work for *you*?"—and the employee asks, "Why should I stay?" Today, candidates need a compelling reason to join and stay. Talented people shop for the right organization, the right culture, the right supervisor, the right colleagues, the right projects, the right pay, the right perks, and even the right location.

We—and our employees—are bombarded with advice and the opportunity to change jobs. Active job seekers still use newspapers and the Internet to conduct a discreet job search, but even happy employees are inundated with career options. Tonight, they (your employees among them) will sit in traffic reading billboards that promise $10,000 hiring bonuses. They are being recruited weekly when they attend church, parties, meetings of professional organizations, and conferences because their peers' astute employers are paying them significant referral bonuses. Your employees hear radio advertisements and watch television ads that offer open positions with great benefits. The cartoon pages, filled with Dilbert and Dilbert clones, remind employees that working for Toxic Corp. is a joke. Their mail includes envelopes stamped with "Join the Free Agent Nation" in red block letters. Magazine covers urge employees to "Quit Now" (*Working Woman*, October 1999) or offer to coach them on "Which Job Offer Should You Take?" (*Fast Company*, October 1998) and "50 Ways to Leave Your Employer" (*Working Woman*, December 1999). Articles describe employers with "The highest pay. The perkiest perks. The coolest environment." (*POV Magazine*, September 1999). Employers are rated in a variety of media for their career development, pay, benefits, vibe, culture, company performance, and location. Readers are urged to consider the article as a "blueprint for the American Dream job." Salary-survey information is one click away on the Internet or available annually through professional organizations and business publications. Everyone from fresh college grads to seasoned executives expects to negotiate up all offers they receive.

Today's competition for *intellectual capital* requires a stronger battle plan than does the competition for banking or venture capital. Great companies are built with top talent—and top talent *chooses* its employers. Recruiting and retention can no longer be given lip service as business issues—they have become the organization-wide mission for Employers of Choice. As part of this mission, turnover must finally be seen as a cost to be measured, controlled, and reduced.

As if guerrilla tactics to hire away your employees were not enough to deal with, raw demographics limit the selection of potential hires. The new employment reality is that demographics have American employers in a vise-like grip: Slow population growth and high retirement rates ensure that the number of available employees will continue to be vastly overshadowed by the number of open positions in the years to come. Workforce increases at 1 percent per year between 1996 and 2005 will mean slower economic growth unless worker productivity improves sufficiently to compensate, according to *Workforce 2020*, written in 1997 by Richard W. Judy and Carol D'Amico. The few available potential hires can be augmented only if the government opens our shores to immigrants or if millions of older Baby Boomers delay retirement. Neither of these options appears likely.

Becoming an Employer of Choice is the logical, comprehensive approach to stemming the loss of intellectual capital and focusing on organizational growth. EOCs raise their profiles in their various communities and become known as great places to work. They invest in management skills for all supervisors, develop and bond with their current employees, use compensation and benefits as a retention strategy, communicate their culture, cultivate relationships with their customers—and are profitable as a result. Employers of Choice turn away from reactive tactics such as looking for reliable sources of replacement hires and embrace a multifaceted proactive strategy that increases retention and enables them to add staff to grow their businesses.

What is the financial advantage of reducing turnover? Remember SAS, the international software development company with 5,400 employees, which reported saving more than $65 million in one year—money that they were then able to put into EOC benefits such as training programs, an employee gym, two on-site daycare centers, and more? Clearly, even with annual savings of "only" hundreds of thousands of dollars, retention of current staff is the key to successful future recruiting, improved profits, and long-term viability for organizations of any size or type. To melt your own iceberg of hidden turnover costs and transform your organization into an EOC, you will need a new vision.

The EOC Vision: Candidates Competing to Work Here

There was a time when employees competed to work for organizations, but they were motivated by their need for work, not by choice. Today, the mismatch of job openings per available candidate has reversed the direction of competition. Organizations now battle for intellectual capital. Top talent chooses employers, not vice versa. Though employers cannot re-create the days of abundant job candidates, they can rethink their approach to recruiting and retention. Success depends on it. We must become Employers of Choice—the employers chosen by top talent.

Hiring is a two-way selection process. Hiring the right person for the job is critical whether the candidate is inside or outside the organization. The specific individuals selected reinforce the organization's image and culture. The skills and learning ability of hires determine corporate capabilities and profitability. To ensure that your organization is staffed with the best of the best, you need a pool of high-quality candidates. Top talent is available—but attracting employees of choice requires more than just deciding that becoming an Employer of Choice is part of your strategic plan. It requires accountability and improved processes throughout your organization. Recruiting and retaining top talent must overlay all other strategies.

Employers of Choice have expanded their vision to encompass more than providing services or products for their external customers. EOCs include their employees—internal customers—as a critical part of the vision and thereby make their dual focus a cornerstone of their strategic plans. By adding the goal of top talent competing and choosing to work for your organization, you will lay the foundation for the practices needed to recruit and retain the best of the best.

Recruiting and retention have been tough issues in traditionally structured, hierarchical organizations, but thanks to demographics, technology, and global business competition, organizations in the 21st century will include—and compete with—opportunistic virtual teams that come together to execute a project and then go on to form different alliances when the project ends. This flexibility can most easily be accomplished with the highly trained, highly trusting employees found at EOCs.

Although technology and customer needs are reason enough for businesses to implement rapid change, a long-term view as well as an ongoing commitment to communications is needed to transform an organization into an Employer of Choice. It takes time to see the results of adopting EOC practices. Training and development take time to plan, develop and execute—and take more time to pay off. The research, design, explanation, and implementation of new, competitive compensation and benefits plans take time—and then take more time to affect recruiting and retention. A positive buzz about an organization's community reputation takes time to develop—but starts to pay off as soon as employees and candidates begin to get positive feedback about their connection to their organization's activities and publicity. Perhaps the most time-consuming—but critical— EOC strategy is training supervisors at all levels and developing leaders throughout the organization in order to change the culture. This is the key to unlocking productivity levels that—along with technology—will help compensate for the reality of fewer numbers of available employees.

There is no magic bullet or shortcut—just strategies that work. Hesitation has no reward. Minimalist recruiting and retention tactics are doomed by demographics to result in even fewer candidates from which to choose, even longer fill times, even lower productivity, even more turnover, and even smaller profits.

Employees at all levels know that the same positions are available in a variety of organizations. They also know that the reputation, culture, development opportunities, compensation and benefits, experiences, and relationships they desire are found only in those organizations that make becoming an Employer of Choice a priority.

Reputation = Employee Magnet

Americans *are* their jobs. Given a choice, we would all like to work for an organization that builds our sense of pride. Today, employees do have a choice. To enhance retention rates, even small companies can instill pride in their employees by raising their organization's profile in the community.

Employees may feel proud of their organization's business conduct, its treatment of employees during a downturn, its support for the arts or the community, or its reputation as "a cool place to work." EOCs seek publicity, employee involvement, and other means to raise their profile and create a reputation that bonds employees to one another and to the organization. This, in turn, attracts new employees. Employment with a highly regarded organization confers status—and status is a type of psychological income. A positive reputation also opens doors with prospects, vendors, and sources of capital as well as other strategic relationships.

Management and Leadership Style

If organizations are only as good as their people, and if loyalty to an organization has been replaced with loyalty to individual supervisors at all levels, then employers must do all they can to develop effective leadership skills in management. Few supervisors are born people managers—but management and leadership skills can be learned and encouraged throughout the organization.

Top-down management is rapidly fading from all businesses. So many employees are leaving traditional organizations for more collaborative, egalitarian environs that even boards of directors are taking note and pressing for more employee participation in management decisions. Many old-style leaders and layers of hierarchy are being replaced with self-managed teams and 360-degree feedback systems. Employers must do more with fewer employees, so igniting the discretionary effort of employees is critical. Open-book management as well as other high-performance management practices not only improve retention but can also increase profitability.

Culture

Culture is made up of the unspoken and spoken rules about "how we do things around here." The CEO determines an organization's culture. Culture can be a powerful tool that either guides people to perform well and improve the organization's competitive advantage—or puts up barriers to opportunities by validating behaviors that alienate customers, extinguish innovative approaches, and maintain the status quo. The negative culture imposed by an organization's leader has caused many talented individuals to leave and start their own businesses.

"When it comes to attracting, keeping, and making teams out of talented people, money alone won't do it. Talented people want to be part of something they can believe in, something that confers meaning on their work and on their lives," according to Xerox Parc guru John Seely Brown, quoted in Robert B. Reich's article "The Company of the Future." This opinion is echoed repeatedly in results from interviews conducted with thousands of organizations and more than 5,500 executives as presented in the variety of research discussed in Chapter One.

Culture is the glue that binds employees to one another and to their organization in spite of the changes in the workplace. Organizations of the 21st century must offer a combination of free agency characteristics, such as development through experiences, compensation linked to contribution, and flextime, as well as the values, camaraderie, and mutual commitment that build trust, retention, and continuity.

Career Development

Top talent joins an organization to learn. Recruiters dread receiving job orders requiring three to five years (or more!) of experience that's identical to the descriptions of the job opening because it is so difficult to interest candidates. Lateral moves that do not include growth in skill or mental stretching are of little interest to capable people. Rapid boredom and rapid turnover are likely to follow the hiring of thoroughly pre-trained employees who can hit the ground running— in their sleep. Instead of paying for inevitable turnover, budget for training that develops hard and soft skills and readies current employees for advancement. Increased knowledge makes an employee an even more valuable asset. Conduct succession planning to assess training and staffing needs. Review employees in a timely manner and include development plans. Offer a variety of educational experiences, from classroom learning to mentors and projects. Develop career paths that offer flexibility. Ask employees whether their development opportunities have produced real improvement. Their answers determine whether they will stay—or leave to be developed elsewhere.

Compensation and Benefits

Today, employees take it for granted that their rewards will be commensurate with their contributions. After years of sticking with employers through the tough times, employees expect to be compensated fairly during better times. Paying competitive wages and benefits is always less expensive than paying the turnover costs of rehiring and refilling positions. Competitive compensation and benefits are the critical tools used by EOCs to attract and retain the quality and quantity of employees needed. With so much data available about pay ranges as well as standard and work-life benefits, it is foolish for employers to believe that their employees are unaware of competitive pay standards. Survey information for competitive pay and benefits is readily available, as are experts to assist with the development of appropriate plans.

Making the EOC Goal a Reality

Alignment of processes and increased communication of goals, objectives, and responsibilities keep EOCs on track. Not only does each employee have specific responsibilities—from referring new hires to accountability for retention—but senior management must agree to review the support processes (such as rewards, recognition, or exit-interview and turnover information) to ensure that they are refined over time to reflect the changing marketplace. Tracking turnover costs by department, tailoring turnover and recruiting strategies to the affected population, and celebrating recruiting and retention victories are all part of reinforcing the EOC mind-set.

The EOC Result: Profitability

Just as turnover begets turnover, retention begets retention. Employers of Choice understand that they must use excellent personnel practices in order to retain employees and attract new ones. They know that the quality of their employees determines their ability to attract and retain external customers—and achieve profitability! Employees must know that they are valued through the words, career development opportunities, compensation and benefits, policies, programs, recognition, and treatment they receive from management. Just as customers experience the organization's brand through every interaction with the organization and its services or products, employees experience their employer's cultural brand through everyday experiences. Actions must match words. An organization will not succeed in advertising itself as an EOC if it treats its employees poorly and has high turnover.

EOCs have discovered that basing policies and procedures on the negative platitudes of toxic organizations will only increase recruiting and retention misery. Organizations that focus too narrowly on prof-its rarely achieve their full bottom-line capacities because they view employees as costs and treat the very activities that promote develop-ment, pride, and low turnover as luxuries. Relationships, fun, inge-nuity, and change are regarded with suspicion. These same organiza-tions frequently fail to recognize the contributions of all employees and create the "Us versus Them" distinctions that are anathema to EOCs.

"Growth, profitability, and stakeholder value are the natural re-wards for developing a valid and effective operating strategy and exe-cuting it," according to Jac Fitz-Enz in his book *The 8 Practices of Exceptional Companies*. Profitability results from EOC practices because employees of EOCs (as in any organization) treat clients and customers exactly as management treats them. Year after year, posi-tive treatment of employees leads to repeat customers, customer referrals, and business growth.

EOCs translate the well-known but obsolete phrases left over from an earlier, employee-rich era (see the Introduction) into the 21st century. They reprogram old thinking for the current employment reality (see Table 5).

EOCs express gratitude to employees for consistently doing their jobs, referring their peers as new hires, developing themselves, con-tributing ideas, and staying. EOCs are known for profitability because they go beyond traditional cost-containment methods to speed recruiting, increase retention, and encourage the discretionary efforts and productivity of their employees.

Retention rates of 100 percent are neither realistic nor advanta-geous. Replacement rates of 10 percent or less, however, allow a pay-back for recruiting and training costs and stimulate the organi-zation's growth through the infusion of new-hire and experienced employee skills, ideas, and synergies. The alternative—high turnover—results in chaos: too many new hires, each in a different learning curve, trying to develop new skills, responsibilities, and rela-tionships with customers.

Jeffrey Pfeffer, in his book *The Human Equation: Building Profits by Putting People First*, makes the point that while "capital and machinery make it possible—people make it happen." Employers of

TABLE 5

Then and Now

Then	Now
Lean and mean	Lean and nice
We don't have time to train people.	We budget to train people.
We want to hire people who can hit the ground running.	We want to hire people who can learn.
Career development is up to the employee.	Career development is up to the organization and the employee.
If you don't like it here, leave!	If you don't like it here, why?
You should be grateful just to have a job.	Thank you—your contribution matters!
Anyone off the street could do your job.	Only *you* will do!
(If someone gives notice) Don't let the door hit you on the way out.	(If someone gives notice) If you must leave us, we hope you will join our alumni club and play golf with your old friends in the spring.
It's not personal; it's just business.	It's all personal.

Choice know that their practices enable the recruiting and retention of top talent, the ones who make profitability happen. We are what we have been in the proces of becoming, and becoming an EOC is a process. Change direction and your employees will thank you—and so will your customers.

RETAINING INFORMATION TECHNOLOGY BRAINPOWER

Technology has transformed our economy: Information technology is now the universal tool for getting work done. IT has so infiltrated every business department that it is no longer a support function; it is now strategic. It is woven into accounting, operations, HR, marketing, and production—every aspect of running a business. Today, your business growth is limited by the quality of the IT skills, ideas, and leadership in your organization.

Understanding the importance of attracting and retaining IT employees with specific skill sets and capabilities is imperative for service providers of all types because the valuation of a service organization in the new wired economy is calculated in human capital. One-half to one-third of the stock market value of many companies is now based on the specific individuals who work for the company. Organizations in the process of issuing an initial public offering, or IPO, are now listing their employees' résumés, speaking engagements, and published articles as part of their assets.

Too few employers have brought their policies, practices, and culture into line with the reality of the IT shortage. Companies must retain and develop existing employees overall—but especially IT employees—or face turnover, the subsequent loss of organizational productivity, long fill times, and higher expenses. In the case of IT turnover, companies could easily face Web site and database problems, or product development slowdowns, with resulting missed sales and lost customers.

The IT field is changing so rapidly that keeping up is a stiff challenge for IT professionals. It makes sense that those who do keep up will be in very short supply. The revolution of the IT function has created such strong demand for IT professionals that recruiting and retention of quality employees has become the issue of greatest importance within the overall tight hiring market. This is the Golden Era for IT.

The New Economy is one of information, speed, and extraordinary growth. We are experiencing the benefits of three decades of business and personal investment in high-tech equipment, technology training, and personal computers. In 1994, 3 million people used the Internet—but by 1999, 200 million users were "surfing." Radio took 38 years to claim 50 million listeners, but in only 4 years the Internet got 50 million clickers—and Internet traffic has doubled every 100 days since! E-mail and voice mail have so increased our expectations of communication, it is no wonder we all look to technology to equally transform other business processes.

Today, the IT function looks beyond the internal needs of an organization to the external needs of clients. E-commerce has transformed business. Now, we talk of Internet time, fast companies, 24-hour customer service, and infinite shelf space. Speed-to-market matters. By 2002, the Internet is expected to generate $300 billion in business-to-business commerce. That does not include the purchasing of items such as groceries, stocks, clothing, books, vacations, and rental cars by consumers—or the bill paying and banking performed on personal computers and other high-tech devices.

The technological transformation of the economy (and our lives) has created a demand for high-tech skills that has outstripped the capacity of our technology schools, colleges, and universities. A 1999 survey conducted by the META Group (**www.metagroup.com**) revealed 400,000 open jobs for systems analysts and computer scientists. Other reports, cited in *Time* magazine in August 1999, placed the number at 500,000 openings. The April 2000 ITAA survey uncovered 1.5 million new jobs to be created that year. Approximately 850,000 of those high-tech jobs were expected to go unfilled. Even though these jobs will pay 64 percent more than the average private-sector job, shortages of IT staff are expected to last well into the first decade of the 21st century. To a large extent, the shortage will continue because our schools are turning out only 36,000 technical graduates a year, which includes a large number of foreign transfer students. This serious shortfall of trained IT specialists versus the number of open jobs means employers must rethink their entire IT recruiting and retention process—or risk having their businesses fall rapidly behind the competition.

The Ongoing IT Talent Shortage

In its April 1999 issue, *Information Week* magazine published the results of a survey of 13,000 IT staff professionals, which revealed some startling demographics, including the following:

- Half are less than 33 years old

- Half have spent less than 8 years in IT

- 41 percent are currently looking for new jobs

- 69 percent have been contacted by recruiters in the past 12 months

- Of the 69 percent who have been contacted, half have been contacted at least 3 times in the past 6 months

If 41 percent of its IT professionals are actively looking for new positions, that's a crisis for any organization. Today, because of the availability of technology, disgruntled teams of IT professionals are instantly able to make themselves available for hire through recruiters and other Web services.

The Cost of IT Turnover

The quality of your IT staff controls the limits of your business. If IT staffers invent a new product or process, or develop a terrific e-business application for your organization, your business will grow. If they do not, your business will shrink. Eric Schmidt, CEO of Novell, writing in *Fast Company* magazine, likened IT employees to pro basketball players. "In a power relationship with management, they have more in common with pro basketball players than they do with average workers," he said. Think of your IT staff as gods—your competition does!

In Chapter One, we estimated the cost of turnover at between one and two years' annual pay and benefits. We also discussed how the costs of turnover add up due to "blue money," or invisible costs, and "green money," or visible costs. The scarcity of specific hot IT skills can drastically lengthen the hiring cycle—and thus, the cost of turnover. Further, organizations that do not have considerable hot technology to offer the IT professional find that they have very few interested candidates. An organization's competitive edge for hiring technology employees is directly related to how far along it is on the technology curve.

Assuming that turnover for the IT function is still at least 16.4 percent of what it was in the Fall 1998 study by Davis and Neusch of "Hot Technologies," let's do the math on the cost of replacing an average IT professional with an annual salary of $65,000:

- If actual replacement costs are 1.5 x annual salary = $97,500 to replace one person

- If actual replacement costs are 2 x annual salary = $130,000 to replace one person

- If the company has 50 IT employees and a 16.4 percent turnover, then 3 IT professionals will leave in a year. This results in a loss to the organization of $292,500 to $390,000!

Add to these astronomical figures the cost of lost sales, lost customers, and missed marketing windows, and you will have a sense of the importance of reducing IT turnover! Turnover dollars and replacement costs (recruiters, advertising, and transition meetings) could be spent far more profitably by investing in retention strategies that fuel the growth of the organization.

Alternatives to IT Turnover

What matters to employees, and, specifically, what matters to IT employees?

Clearly, the attitude of "You should be grateful just to have a job" is not one that works in this time of a seller's market for certain skills.

In many organizations, the need for specific skills and the realization that certain policies, procedures, and types of culture will attract technically trained individuals have led to organization-wide changes that benefit all employees. EOCs align their policies, practices, and culture with the reality of the IT staff shortage.

The five top-rated characteristics of an Employer of Choice are valued by IT staff as well as by general employees: development, compensation, community reputation, management and leadership style, and corporate culture. However, Employers of Choice make an extra effort to hold on to their IT employees. In a William M. Mercer Companies survey, employers stated that the most effective retention tactics for keeping experienced IT professionals are

- Challenging work assignments

- Well-defined career development opportunities

- High-quality supervision and leadership

- Favorable work environment

- Appropriate financial incentives

The CIO Communications/ICEX Survey (**www.cio.com**) revealed that the top three company attractions for IT professionals are

1. The reputation of the company's IT function

2. The reputation of the company

3. The promise of doing innovative technical work

While the promise of doing innovative work may not be a surprising attraction, the desire to work for an organization with *a reputation for its IT function* is a tall order for many organizations—but IT EOCs can do it!

Another consideration in IT retention is the age range of IT professionals and the effect of demographics on expectations, preferences, and needs (see Table 6, on p. 234).

With so much to take into consideration, how do Employers of Choice reduce IT turnover and hire the candidates they need? IT EOCs use the same EOC Foundation Strategies:

TABLE 6

Baby Boomer Versus Generation X Expectations

Baby Boomer	Generation X
Workaholics	NOT workaholics
Expect to be managed	Expect to be coached
Results = job satisfaction	Fun = job satisfaction
Exchange hard work for good pay	Exchange hard work for good pay *plus* training and development

Source: "Generation X and Workforce Strategies," Mary Walk, 1999.

- Make improved retention part of the organization's written strategic plan (otherwise other goals may not be met)

- Tie a percentage of compensation for each IT supervisor, manager, director, and CIO to the achievement of specific retention objectives

- Build and communicate a top-employer reputation

- Hire well—or not at all

- Treat employees as if they were customers

- Retrain and develop current employees for tomorrow's needs

- Build support processes to ensure ongoing success of the EOC Foundation Strategies

Once each supervisor understands his or her specific retention goal and performance rewards are in place for achieving that goal, a range of tactics must be implemented. While no one organization may be able to engage in all of these activities, the more you can do, the greater the likelihood that you can reduce turnover to 10 percent.

Career Development Tactics

IT is under more pressure to stay current than any other organizational function. For an IT professional, being assigned to a project that requires old skills to keep legacy systems running is IT Hell. When an IT professional is not learning, he or she is falling behind. To increase your organization's IT retention power,

1. DEVELOP TWO CAREER PATHS: ONE FOR TECHNICAL AND ANOTHER FOR MANAGEMENT-TRACK EMPLOYEES. Enable technical staff to deepen their skills and reward them for doing so. Many do not want to become managers but need recognition, rewards, and careers that move. Build a dual career ladder and consider adding titles such as "Distinguished Engineer," which can only be bestowed by peers. Peers have much tougher standards, so this type of title has clout.

2. CONDUCT SUCCESSION PLANNING EXERCISES. Ask all IT supervisors, managers, directors, and the CIO to identify the missing skills (written or verbal communication? project management? conflict management? delegation?) that prevent the internal promotion of their direct reports. Use this input to design a training curriculum. Ensure that employees not only have the opportunity to participate in needed training but are recognized for doing so. Additionally, all supervisors must be held accountable for enabling the development of their staff.

3. CONDUCT TIMELY PERFORMANCE REVIEWS. Late or poorly prepared reviews send the message that employee efforts are not appreciated. Unappreciated employees have no reason to stay. Include development plans (both technical and soft-skills training) with deadlines. Hold supervisors responsible for ensuring the ongoing training of their staffs.

4. DEVELOP TALENT THROUGH EXPERIENCES. Use rotational assignments and stretch projects. Enrich current assignments or initiate a new career path within IT.

5. PROMOTE FROM WITHIN AS MUCH AS POSSIBLE. If succession planning results in training needs being met and the overall skill

level of the employee pool rises over time, more employees should be eligible to move up.

6. ENCOURAGE—OR EVEN REQUIRE—PARTICIPATION IN IT USER GROUPS, PROFESSIONAL ORGANIZATIONS, AND ROUNDTABLES. Do not restrict membership to one representative per group. Some technical fields are so complicated that having more than one organizational representative in a user group might be the key to solving software or hardware problems.

7. CREATE TECHNOLOGY HEROES WHO ADDRESS GRADE-SCHOOL, HIGH-SCHOOL, AND COLLEGE-LEVEL CLASSES. Get out in the community and discuss how IT is changing business, saving money, and even saving lives. Fight the negative image of nerds, and increase the number of students who choose IT as a career.

8. PROVIDE SABBATICALS—PAID OR UNPAID—AFTER ATTAINMENT OF CERTAIN SERVICE LEVELS (FIVE YEARS? EIGHT YEARS?) Allow the individual to return to the same or a similar position.

9. COLLABORATE WITH OTHER ORGANIZATIONS TO OFFER TRAINING AT LOWER COST. Talk with strategic partners, neighbors in the same office building, other members—of professional organizations, etc., to uncover similar training needs and collaborate to reduce costs.

10. DEVELOP NON-TECHNICAL STAFF INTO IT SPECIALISTS. Grow your own staff solutions. Since the number of IT graduates is far below the number needed, offer tuition reimbursement and special training to current employees who are not IT specialists. Second or third careers benefit from earlier work experience.

Compensation and Benefits Tactics

While compensation pressures abound, new approaches are working for many organizations. In one survey of IT professionals cited in *HR News*, 65 percent were satisfied with their compensation, but 20 percent were not. That's a lot of dissatisfied employees, and that dissatisfaction could be a big problem if it leads to turnover. To increase the chances of offering competitive compensation and benefits,

1. TWICE A YEAR, CONDUCT OR PARTICIPATE IN SALARY SURVEYS. In many markets, information in so-called current salary surveys may be nearly a year old when it is published. In the volatile IT field, upward pressure is continuous for aggressive base pay.

2. ACCELERATE RAISE SCHEDULES, OR TIE RAISES TO THE COMPLETION OF PROJECTS.

3. OFFER SHORT-TERM INCENTIVES. According to a 1999 Mercer study of 1,930 executives, 45 percent of the organizations surveyed use short-term incentives to reward IT staff.

4. OFFER LONG-TERM INCENTIVES EQUITY, IF POSSIBLE. If equity or stock options are being offered to the top tier of the company, consider including key employees. According to the same Mercer study, 25 percent of the organizations surveyed offer long-term incentives for IT employees. They expect to share in the wealth they create.

5. OFFER SPOT CASH AWARDS AND NON-CASH AWARDS. Surprise is the key element in the success of this program.

6. OFFER IMMEDIATE BENEFITS—NO WAITING PERIOD. The 90-day wait can be a "deal killer" when negotiating for IT staff.

7. PAY A SIGNING BONUS. According to the same Mercer study, 64 percent of respondents' companies pay signing bonuses for IT staff.

8. INCREASE THE PERCENTAGE OF BENEFITS PAID IN RELATION TO TENURE.

9. OFFER NEW BENEFITS:

   - Long-term-care insurance
   - Stock purchase plans
   - Benefits for same-sex partners
   - Subsidized childcare
   - Concierge or errand services

Reputation-Building Tactics for the Organization— and the IT Function

Who wants to work for an organization that no one has heard of— if there is an alternative? It *is* easier to hire and retain employees of all types if their association with your organization results in murmurs of approval and exclamations of, "Really? You work there?" How do employers become IT EOCs? They make their *people* the centerpiece of their strategies.

1. HOST OR FOUND INFORMATION TECHNOLOGY–FOCUSED ROUND-TABLES. Often by invitation only and focused on the management rungs of the IT ladder, roundtables are a terrific source of ideas, resources, solutions, and staff.

2. ENCOURAGE SPEECHES AND ARTICLE WRITING. An IT employee at any level may have a message to offer his or her peers. The message might be "10 Sins of a Web Site," or "Beyond the Web Site: Backroom Capabilities Make the Sale," or "Installing an ERP System? Go Vanilla!" If your staff has conquered a big IT problem, tell the multitudes about their victory!

3. SUBSIDIZE COMMUNITY INVOLVEMENT AND MEMBERSHIP IN PRO-FESSIONAL ORGANIZATIONS. Raise the profile of your organization through the activities of your IT staff—and raise their skills at the same time!

4. FEATURE IT STAFF IN RECRUITING ADVERTISING: WHY I LIKE WORKING AT GREATBIZ, INC. Radio, print, billboards, and Web site ads will be more effective if an employee is featured.

5. PROVIDE BOOTHS AND SPEAKERS FOR CAREER FAIRS AND TRADE SHOWS. Or sponsor an event yourself. Don't let your competition steal 100 percent of the "mind share" of great candidates.

6. SHOWCASE IT STAFF AND PROJECTS IN IN-HOUSE NEWSLETTERS, EXTERNAL RECRUITING, SALES, OR PR PIECES. Give credit where credit is due. If your IT staff saved millions in operating expenses with the installation of an ERP system or developed a new downloadable tool for clients, tell the world!

7. USE YOUR WEB SITE TO BUILD YOUR IT EOC REPUTATION. Showcase your culture, IT accomplishments, management philosophy, and unusual benefits on the careers area of your Web site.

Management and Leadership Style Tactics

If half of the IT professionals are Gen X'ers who prefer to be coached and half are Baby Boomers who want to be managed, supervising IT professionals is one tough job. Coaching skills, after all, are very high-level management skills indeed. Assuming that supervisors at all levels have stronger technical skills and training than management skills and experience, much attention must be focused on ensuring that supervisors have the tools (management and coaching skills) they need to be part of the retention solution.

Managing projects and managing people are different tasks that require different skills. To be successful as an IT EOC,

- Require annual management training for IT supervisors, managers, directors, and CIOs.

- Require development and use of coaching skills among IT management.

- Set measurable, attainable retention goals based on past turnover for each supervisor. Make a portion of compensation contingent on attaining the goal.

- Set measurable staff development goals for each supervisor. Supervisors must be responsible for the timely review and development of their staffs. By setting development deadlines every six months, project deadlines may be less likely to interfere with attainment of development goals.

- Enable the use of work/family balance benefits. For example, if flextime or telecommuting is offered but employees are discouraged from using it, turnover can result.

- At all levels, treat people in a special way—like customers—and tell them why!

Culture Tactics

An organization's culture is made up of spoken and unspoken rules, policies, dress code, work styles, schedules, management style, and the physical environment, all of which impact the employees' ability and willingness to do their jobs. When employees were competing for positions, they downplayed the importance of work environment or culture in their survey responses. Today, the trend is changing as employees grasp their value to their employers and are presented with more choice in job opportunities.

By 1998, both Gen X (born 1960–1980) and Gen Y employees (born after 1980) were demanding more control over their work environment, work content, schedules, performance, and rewards. Three concerns ranked at the top of their list, according to a survey by Davis & Neush:

- Intellectual challenge

- Competitive base pay and benefits

- Job atmosphere

A variety of culture strategies are working for IT EOCs:

1. RELAXED DRESS CODE. In some cases, *very* relaxed dress codes prevail, especially if the employee has no external-client contact.

2. FLEXIBLE SCHEDULES. By 1999, two out of every three companies surveyed offered flexible hours, according to a Mercer study presented at the Human Resources Association of Central Indiana. If your staff produces more between 9:00 P.M. and 2:00 A.M., why not let them?

3. TELECOMMUTING OPTIONS. Today, if your organization does not offer this option, you are losing candidates and employees of all types.

4. FUN! Monthly on-site and off-site events strengthen relationships and build esprit de corps.

5. OFF-SITE THINK TANKS FOR TECHIES. Many organizations are sequestering IT staff to encourage internal and external speed-to-

market and to minimize the dress-code and other differences that may exist between technical and other staff.

6. TEAM APPROACH. No one can judge the ability of a techie better than another techie—and no one can match the impact of peers. Peer-group pressure within teams keeps quality up and management problems down.

7. REGULAR FEEDBACK. Compliments and recognition for each problem solved encourage ongoing efforts. Deliver positive feedback one-on-one, in front of peers, and in e-mail communications.

8. DIVERSITY TRAINING FOR ALL. Assimilate all IT employees—and consider age differences to be as significant as differences in race, ethnicity, religion, or country of origin.

9. PARTNER WITH SUPPLEMENTAL STAFFING ORGANIZATIONS. Avoid employee burnout and solve temporary skill shortages by teaming with a staffing organization that can provide the level of skills and the number of consultants needed to complete projects or even run projects from beginning to end!

10. REGULAR COMMUNICATION. Just do more! Weekly one-on-one meetings, department meetings, suggestion boxes, anonymous e-mail suggestion mechanisms, employee opinion surveys, and focus groups are all needed to keep information and ideas flowing up and down the organization.

11. RECOGNITION. Just do more! Formal or informal, whatever it takes to spotlight the hours, efforts, and achievements of your IT staff.

Once a term of derision, "techie" is now a badge of honor. Your IT staff is changing the viability of your organization. To ensure that your organization will continue to be viable, treat your IT employees as the strategic asset that they are. Recruit the strongest IT staff possible, and then develop and retain them.

REFERENCES

BOOKS

Booz, Allen & Hamilton. *Strategy & Business Noteworthy Quotes.* New York: Booz, Allen & Hamilton, 1995.

Collins, James C., and Jerry I. Porras. *Built to Last.* New York: HarperCollins, 1994.

Fitz-Enz, Jac. *The 8 Practices of Exceptional Companies.* New York: AMACOM, 1997.

Hagerup, William. "The Fast Track Approach to Changing Organizational Culture," Leadership Reprint excerpted from Harold E. Glass (ed.), *The Handbook of Business Strategy.* Ridgefield, Conn.: N. Dean Meyer and Associates (NDMA), 1999.

Herman, Roger E. *Keeping Good People.* Winchester, Va.: Oakhill Press, 1997.

James, Robert M. "Basic Compensation," in *The AMA Handbook for Employee Recruitment and Retention.* New York: AMACOM, 1992.

Judy, Richard W., and Carol D'Amico. *Work Force 2020.* Indianapolis, Ind.: Hudson Institute, 1997.

Levering, Robert, and Milton Moskowitz. *The 100 Best Companies to Work for in America.* Rev. ed. New York: Plume, 1994.

Marlin, Alice T. *Students Shopping for a Better World.* New York: Council on Economic Priorities and Ballantine Books, June 1993.

Nelson, Bob. *1001 Ways to Reward Employees.* New York: Workman, 1994.

Pfeffer, Jeffrey. *The Human Equation: Building Profits by Putting People First.* Boston: Harvard Business School Press, 1998.

Stack, Jack. *The Great Game of Business: Unlocking the Power and Profitability of Open-Book Management.* New York: Doubleday, 1994.

Stoner, Jim, and R. Edward Freeman. *Management.* Englewood Cliffs, N.J.: Prentice-Hall, 1992.

RESEARCH REPORTS

"America @ Work: The 1999 Workforce Commitment Index," Executive Summary. Aon Consulting, Inc.

"America's New Deficit: The Shortage of Information Technology Workers." A report by the U.S. Department of Commerce, Office of Technology Policy, Washington, D.C.

"Attracting and Retaining Employees: Mercer Viewpoints on a Study by the Conference Board," 1998. William M. Mercer Companies LLC, New York.

"Attracting and Retaining High-Technology Talent." A 1997 survey featured in "Attracting and Retaining Employees: Mercer Viewpoints on a Study by the Conference Board," 1998. William M. Mercer Companies LLC, New York.

"Cause-Related Trends Report," 1999. Cone/Roper.

"Competing as an Employer of Choice," 1996. HR Executive Review, Volume 3, Number 4. Conference Board, New York.

"Corporate Character." Highlights of a national survey measuring the impact of corporate social responsibility, 1994. Walker Information, Indianapolis, Ind.

"Hot Technologies Survey," 1998. Davis & Neusch (now merged with Hewitt & Associates), Minneapolis, Minn.

ICEX Survey, Spring 1998. CIO Communications, Framingham, Mass.

IT Salary Survey, April 26, 1999. *Information Week.*

"National Employee Relationship Report," 1999. A nationwide survey co-sponsored by Walker Information and the Hudson Institute (**www.walkerinfo.com**).

"Nursing Watch," February 1999. An analysis of recruiting and retention issues. Advisory Board, Washington, D.C.

"Strengthen Your Nucleus: Manage the Careers of High-Performing Employees," March 1998.

"Turnover—How Does It Affect Your Business?" 1999. A Fax Facts short survey. William M. Mercer Companies LLC, New York.

"The War for Talent," 1998. McKinsey & Co., New York.

"Workforce Turnover and Firm Performance," 1998. Corporate Leadership Council.

BRIEFINGS/SPEECHES/WORKSHOPS

"Branding the Employment Relationship to Increase Employee Retention and Attract New Employees," presentation by Melanie J. Arsenault, L. L. Bean, Inc., and Mitchell C. Potter, William M. Mercer, Inc., at the 1999 Conference Board Seminar on Attracting and Retaining Employees, in Chicago, Ill., June 1999.

"The Crisis in Hot Technologies . . . It IS the Pay, But Not JUST the Pay," presented by John H. Davis, Ph.D., CCP, Hewitt & Associates, at the SHRM 51st Annual Conference.

"Employee Retention: 25 Keys to Keeping the Right People," breakfast briefing by Rick Cartor, Ph.D., Vice President, PeopleTech, in Indianapolis, Ind., May 1999.

"Flexibility and Adapting to the Needs of Your Future Employees," presentation by Major Rick E. Ayer, Chief of the Marketing Research and Plans Division, Program Analysis and Evaluation Directorate, for the U.S. Army, at the Workforce Solutions '99 Conference sponsored by the Mid-America Plastics Partners, Inc. (MAPP), January 28, 1999, in Indianapolis, Ind.

"Generation X and Workforce Strategies," presentation by Mary Walk, VP Labor Relations, At&T Worldwide, at the Workforce Solutions '99 Conference sponsored by Mid-America Plastics Partners, Inc. (MAPP), January 28, 1999, in Indianapolis, Ind.

"'HiRRRe'—A New Approach to Recruitment," presentation by Bob D'Orso, Human Resources Manager, Fazoli's Restaurants, at the Workforce Solutions '99 Conference sponsored by Mid-America

Plastics Partners, Inc. (MAPP), January 28, 1999, in Indianapolis, Ind.

"Issues for the New Millennium: Demographics-Technology-Economics-Workforce," presentation by Richard W. Judy, Hudson Institute, at the 1999 Indiana State SHRM Conference, August 1999.

"National Employee Relationship Report—Benchmark Study Results," presentation by Marc Drisin, Vice President, Business Alliances, Walker Information, Indianapolis, Ind., at the Indiana Executive Forum, December 1, 1999 (**www.walkerinfo.com**).

"1999 Workforce Study," presentation by Tom Mahan, Vice President, Saratoga Institute, at the Human Resources Association of Central Indiana meeting, November 18, 1999 (**www.saratoga-institute.com**).

"1998 Compensation Planning Briefing," presentation by Robert Roeder and William M. Mercer, for the Human Resources Association of Central Indiana, September 1998.

"1999 Compensation Planning Briefing," presentation by Steve Jones and William M. Mercer, Cincinnati, at the Human Resources Association of Central Indiana, September 16, 1999.

"Recruiting and Retention: Tools for Success," presentation by Susan Burleigh, SPHR, Senior Associate, Flexible Staffing, Eli Lilly and Company, and the Indiana Personnel Association conference, October 29, 1999, in Indianapolis, Ind.

ARTICLES

"Blue-Chip Execs Wooed by Web Start-Ups." *USA Today*. October 12, 1999, Section B, p. 1.

Burke, Robyn A., SPHR. "Strengthen Your Nucleus: Manage the Careers of High-Performing Employees." SHRM White Paper. March 1998, p. 1.

Dym, Barry. "Retire? No Way!" *Boston Globe*. September 20, 1998, p. 1.

"Firms' Actions Leave Workers with Little Loyalty, Survey Says." *Indianapolis Star*. October 26, 1999, p. 1.

Fishman, Charles. "Sanity, Inc." *Fast Company*. January 1999, p. 93.

"Ford Learns from Others in Handling Harassment." *Indianapolis Business Journal*. September 20, 1999, p. 51.

Friedman, Drew. "The Dynamic Dozen." *POV Magazine*. September 1999, p. 62.

Glube, Nancy. "Retention Tools for Turbulent Times." SHRM White Paper. 1998, p. 2.

Goins, Liesa. "Small Is Beautiful." *POV Magazine*. September 1999, p. 68.

"High-Tech Firms Urge More Worker Visas." *Chicago Tribune*. November 1, 1999, Section 4, p. 1.

Holton, Lisa. "Keeping It Current." *Chicago Tribune* (Jobs Section). November 15, 1998, p. 1.

"How to Manage Geeks." *Fast Company*. June 1999, p. 176.

Keifer, Francine. "What $100,000 Provides at New Halo Center." *Christian Science Monitor*. September 10, 1984.

Kirsner, Scott. "Designed Innovation." *Fast Company*, November 1998, p. 5.

Kleiner, Adam. "The Best Little Workplace in Texas (and America)." *POV Magazine*. September 1999, p. 65.

"Make Yourself a Leader." *Fast Company*. June 1999, p. 129.

Murray-Garrigan, Liz. "Work Hard. You Might Win a Prize." *New York Times*. August 8, 1999.

Reich, Robert B. "The Company of the Future." *Fast Company*. November 1998, p. 132.

Thompson, Robert W. "Recruiting for High-Tech Jobs May Mean Nontraditional Benefits." *HR News*. August 1999, p. 46.

"Tough Talk, Fast Action." *Fast Company*. April 1999, p. 38.

"We're for Hire, Just Click." *Time*. August 16, 1999, p. 47.

"What to Do When a Valued Employee Quits." *Fast Company.* August 1998, p. 142.

INTERNET ARTICLE

William T. Archey, President and CEO of the American Electronics Association, testifying before the Senate Judiciary Committee, October 21, 1999. PR Newswire.

INDEX

advertising: billboard, 137; direct mail, 138; newspaper, 136–137, 219; radio, 137, 219; television, 137–138
apprenticeships, 138–139
assessment of candidates: description of, 94; generic, 95–96; legal considerations, 96; personality, 95; purpose, 94–95; reliance on, 96; results tracking, 97

Baby Boomer expectations, 167, 234
behavior patterns, 179
benefits: communicating value of, to candidate, 217; employee expectations regarding, 205, 225–226; employee-friendly, 214–215; family-friendly, 214–215; generational differences, 213; for IT employees, 236–237; low-cost, 215–216; no-cost, 215–216; policy statement regarding, 212–213; resource agencies, 216–217; survey sources for evaluating, 216–217; types of, 212–213. *See also* compensation
billboard advertising, 137
birth rate: new hires and, 220; recruiting and, 3; in United States, 3
bonuses: hiring, 135–136, 141; referral, 128; tuition reimbursement, 194–195
branding: benefits of, 62; public relations firm for, 62–64
business awards, 61

candidates: assessments of, 94–97; automated screening of, 120–122; commitment of, 102; competencies for evaluating, 88–91; competition for, 101–102, 219–220; contact with, 103–104, 146; enticement of, 99–101; hiring bonuses offered to, 135–136; job offer. *See* offer; job simulations for, 91–94; loss of, 101–102; re-

recruiting of, 125–126; welfare-to-work, 144–145; "wowing" of, 99–101. *See also* job seekers
career development: certification programs and, 196–197; consultants as trainers, 192–193; corporate library, 198–199; description of, 86, 225; elements of, 187; experiences, 193; General Education Development programs and, 197–198; importance of, 183–184; in-house training and, 191–192; internal promotion and, 200–201; of IT employees, 235–236; for non-management-track employees, 199–200; ongoing nature of, 185–186; paid memberships, 195–196; performance reviews and, 46, 189–190, 235; plan, 190–191; retention and, 186–187; succession planning, 87–88, 187–189, 225, 235; training as part of, 184–186; tuition reimbursement, 194; turnover reduction and, 186–187
certification programs, 196–197
chat rooms: employee retention and, 158–159; intranet, 158–159; recruiting through, 117, 119
Collins, James C., 176
commission compensation, 208
communication: in Employers of Choice, 172; mechanisms for improving, 178–179; for negative headlines, 67–68
compensation: changes in, 210–211; commission, 208; communicating value of, to candidate, 217; elements of, 208; employee expectations regarding, 205, 225–226; incentive, 208; for IT employees, 236–237; for key employees, 207–208; marketplace assessments, 207; motivational nature

added to, 135–136; repeating of, 102–104; second, 153
older workers, 141–142
100 Best Companies to Work for in America, 25–26, 178
online recruiting. *See* e-cruit methods; Internet; Web site
open house, 139
opinion surveys, 158
organization: assessments of, 1; financial information sharing by, 171–173; leadership in, 173–175; qualities of, 25–26; reputation of. *See* reputation; "us vs. them" mentality of, 168–169, 179; Web site. *See* Web site
orientation of new hires: checklist, 107–108; description of, 105–106; methods of enhancing, 155; turnover and, 154–155
overtime, 13

paid memberships, 195–196
peer pressure, 170
performance: recognition programs for, 50; reviews for assessing, 46, 189–190, 235; tracking of, 191
Pfeffer, Jeffrey, 169, 178, 185, 227–228
Porras, Jerry I., 176
positive reputation: candidate selection and, 223; methods of creating, 58–61; payoffs for, 57–58, 222–223
productivity: employment security and, 178; turnover effects, 8–9
professional employment organizations, 214
professional organizations, 119–120
public relations firm, 62–64

quitting. *See* turnover

radio advertising, 137
recruiters: internal. *See* hiring managers; from recruiting firm, 135
recruiting: advertising methods, 136–138; alternatives, 85–86; apprenticeships, 138–139; candidates who declined offer, 125–126; college, 140; competencies, 88–91; customer participation in, 132; description of,

71–72, 123, 222; disabled workers, 144; entry-level employee reductions and, 3; ex-employees, 124–125; family members, 130; foreign workers, 143; friends, 130; improvements in, 44–45; individual-specific approaches for, 41; internal, 86–88; internships, 138–139; at job fairs, 139; military personnel, 140–141; minimizing need for, 85–86; networks, 131; older workers, 141–142; online methods, 84–85; open house, 139; opportunities for, 5; optimization methods, 77; persistence in, 146–147; reputation and, 56–57, 223; retirees, 126; sources, 31; strategic partnerships, 131–132; technology for improving, 84; tuition reimbursement offer and, 194–195. *See also* e-cruit methods
recruiting firms, 133–135
referral program: compensation, 127–128, 141; motivating employees to participate in, 129–130; new hires participation in, 130–131; problems associated with, 129; publicizing of, 129
reputation: building of, 46–47, 238–239; commitment to maintaining, 68; communication of, 46–47; crisis plan for restoring, 64–68; description of, 53; IT employees and, 238–239; negative headlines' effect on, 54–56, 64–65; positive. *See* positive reputation; recruiting and, 56–57, 223
résumé: keeping of by organization, 127; networking with other employers, 132–133; online registration and submission of, 82, 109–111, 115–116; reviewing of, 83; tracking of, 81
résumé banks, 116
retention: career development and, 186–187; departments involved in, 72; description of, 4, 222; employer's response, 6–7; EOC effects, 73; factors that influence, 29–31, 151; Generation X employees, 5–6; improvements in, 44–46; individual-specific approaches for, 41; of IT employees, 234; methods of enhanc-